D1720278

Wolfram Eberhard
Krzysztof Gawlikowski
Carl-Albrecht Seyschab
•EDITORS•

East Asian Civilizations
New Attempts at Understanding Traditions

2 NATION and MYTHOLOGY

Simon&Magiera

Publishers
FEDERAL REPUBLIC OF GERMANY

Title illustration:
Huangdi, the Yellow Emperor
(Stone engraving of the Han period from Wuliang Temple at Wuzhaishan,
in Jiaxiang county, Shandong province)

ISBN 3-88676-041-3

To our Readers

●

EAST ASIAN CIVILIZATIONS
New Attempts at Understanding Traditions
is an international, privately sustained book publication series
to be issued twice a year. Its subjects are: traditional, i.e.
pre-colonial cultures in East, Central and Southeast Asia, their
interrelations and historical development, and their cultural significance in modern times. It hopes to contribute to a deeper
comprehension of Asia as a whole.

EAC will focus on the following fields of research: sociology, social structures and social thought, social and cultural anthropology, history of culture, philosophy and sociolinguistics. Articles
on political topics will be excluded, as well as contributions
likely to offend individual nations.

The editors' intention is to improve the hitherto insufficient cooperation and discussion among scholars of various countries.
Though we do address (in the first place) to scholars already
working in the field of Asian research we are also committed to
giving scholars in these fields a chance for world-wide publication. Interest, participation and cooperation are especially expected from Asian countries.

In the editors' opinion the basic criteria and methods of ethnological and sociological research mainly derive from Western experience and have been formulated from the European point of
view at a time, when European-centered traditions of thinking
still predominated. Consequently, the structures of Asiatic societies and their cultures were only partially considered in the
search for general, synoptical theories. Some criteria still in
use nowadays are therefore limited to the range of their cultural spectrum and hardly applicable to Asia.

Therefore *EAC* – besides its special concern for Asian research –
wants to address all those who work in the field of ethnology
and sociology. Availability of information particularly interesting to the specialists and at the same time comprehensively formulated will, it is hoped, make a more exact knowledge of
Asia possible – and also lead to rethinking of methods and criteria. The editors hope to contribute eventually to the formula-
tion of criteria which correspond to the diversely structured cultures and societies of East and West and lead to better mutual
understanding.

Set–Up of EAC
EAC is divided into three parts:

1.Studies: For their orientation and subjects see above.

2.Hypotheses and discussion: Sometimes scholars develop new ideas, but neither have the time nor necessary conditions to elaborate these ideas or concepts (into voluminous books or articles). They might nevertheless wish to present these ideas to their colleagues as suggestions for further research without going too far into details. This part should present discussions on important and so far unsolved questions, polemics about books, different opinions on given topics (etc.) in the form of comparatively short papers (possibly not more than 10 pages).

3.Sources, field reports and information: Here the editors intend to present rare manuscripts or part of them (in the original language with translation and notes), interesting archive material, data collected in the course of field studies, information about libraries, institutions and research projects, etc.

As a rule, every issue will focus on one specific topic – which does not exclude continuing discussions stretched over several issues; therefore, commentaries on published materials will be gratefully welcomed.

While the editors accept responsibility for the selection of materials to be published, the individual author is responsible for statements of facts and opinions contained therein as well as the accuracy of all quotations and references.

We invite all our colleagues throughout the world to support our initiative and to submit their papers or contributions to discussion. New ideas, theories, methods, as well as critiques and polemics will especially be appreciated.

Wolfram Eberhard
Krzysztof Gawlikowski
Carl-Albrecht Seyschab

●

Wei Tuo
Protector of Books

EAC 2
Contents

STUDIES and ESSAYS

Krzysztof Gawlikowski
Nation: A Mythological Being
10
*

Armin Sievers
Mythography versus History:
The Wuji Case
38
*

Mitarai Masaru
On the Legends of the Yellow Sovereign
67
*

Srisurang Poolthupya
Thai Customs and Social Values in the Ramakien
97

DISCUSSION

Ulrich Neininger
Burying the Scholars Alive:
On the Origin of a Confucian Martyrs' Legend
121

FIELD REPORTS • SOURCES • INFORMATION

Chien Chiao
Cognitive Play:
Some Minor Rituals among Hong Kong Cantonese
138
*

Gu Jiegang
How I Came to Doubt Antiquity
145
*

Nguyen Tien-huu
The Village State in Traditional Vietnam
160
*

7

Petra Kolonko
The Challenged National Identity:
When Chinese Wanted to Become Westerners
168
***
Authors
175

EAC 3
Focus
PEASANTRY AND PATTERNS OF BEHAVIOUR

Studies
and
Essays

NATION: A MYTHOLOGICAL BEING
●
BY KRZYSZTOF GAWLIKOWSKI

In order to consider the relationship between a nation and its mythology, the author presents in this essay his theoretical concept of a nation. Various nations are discussed as examples: the Chinese, the Vietnamese, the Poles and the Jews. In the author's opinion, each human being has to identify itself with a certain group, and each group is - to a lesser or greater degree - mythicized. Larger and more stable communities, such as a nation, have to be highly mythicized due to their means of unity: "centres and systems of integration", both of which have a mythological core. These elements of unification are based on a "national mythological complex" which creates an ideological framework of national unity. Each individual usually identifies himself with several communities simultaneously, and all of these ties are interrelated. Therefore, for analytical purposes, "national identity" may be separated artificially, but it cannot be understood in isolation. Moreover, various identities may be considered "national"; they fluctuate and compete with each other. Many of them are predominantly related to a certain social ideology, religion or state, and are "anational" as far as their content is concerned, although they serve a national unity. Only in some cases does a nation have an idea of "being a nation." The author analyses a community development process and points out some particular features of the nation-building process, especially its mythological components. He considers mythology the basis of national unity and the creation of mythology (in the broad sense) as the mechanism of this process of unification which parallels the objectification processes and is interrelated to them. The creation of genealogical myths indicates, in his opinion, the birth of a nation.

The interrelationship of mythology and nationhood may be better comprehended by an introduction of the concept "nation". Hundreds of definitions and explanations have been offered and considered, but have been based mainly on European experiences in nationhood and on the European understanding of what a nation should be.

1. A NATION AS A POLY-INTEGRATED MYTHICIZED COMMUNITY

We should start with the statement that man is a social being. An individual's human nature is formed within a society by absorbing a given culture as handed down by past generations. An individual as a human being is incomplete in himself. One needs others with whom to relate directly and indirectly, through art, for example. Every individual identifies himself with a given social group. It may be a small or a large unit. It may be real, i.e. actually existing, and one with which an individual is in daily contact. The group may be potentially tangible; that is, real, yet distant in space and time. Or it may be an intangible group, such as gods, saints, spirits, or epic or fictional personalities, etc.

One often identifies oneself with several groups simultaneously – with a small family, with a generation within a clan, and with the clan itself; with a generation within a village community, and with the whole community; with a province and a country; with one's religious community or civilization; or – in modern times – with the propagators and adherents of a given ideology.

These identifications are not based on intellectual considerations, but on emotions, attitudes, wills, on the need to "belong to" and the need of acceptance, etc. When we speak of nation, we artificially separate a given spectrum of these identities operating on a scale analogous to that of a country. They are all, however, tied together, and are interdependent, with various links complementing each other. When, for example, there are large families, or if clan and village community ties are strong, there is no need for a strong country-scale sense of identification. In such cases, national, religious and civilization identities will be weak. When a society is atomized, isolated individuals and weak nuclear families seek broader identities: national, religious or political. A regional sense of identity (a smaller state or a province), may compete with the sense of identity with a larger political unit, just as two contradicting kinds of nationalism may compete with each other. The patriotism of Taiwan, or the ancient Shu state within China, and of Tamil Nandu within India, are examples. These social, cultural, and political identities may compete with religious ones (the Turkish versus Pan-islamic identity, the Bengali versus Islamic Pakistani identity).

11

Whereas identities on the low level (e.g. familial, local) are created spontaneously, at the upper level they are in a given sense artificial, created to serve a purpose. They are propagated and taught (1). Only some of them are "national" in a strict sense, that is, based on an idea of a "nation", however the ethnos may be defined. Other forms of social integration are based on the state, religion, common civilization, race, or a utopian political theory. Here these identifications, subnational, quasi-national, supra-national, are all regarded as "national" in a broad sense if a majority of the population within one state (or a territory considered by the people as a "country") can be made to feel that they belong together. And this is so even if the people consider themselves only a community of believers, citizens, "civilized human beings", etc., and not a nation.(2)

In empirical research surveys, the separation of "national" forms of identity (in a strict sense) is a rather difficult task, if not a meaningless play on words. Ethnic identity is usually multi-layered (3). Moreover, various identities may co-exist, compete with each other, or undergo a transformation. For example, during the Warring States period in China (475-221 B.C.) the individual states were "national", that is, there existed more or less integrated Jin, Lu, Qin, Chu, Wu nations (4). At this time, the concept of the cultural "Chinese" (Zhu Xia (I)) community as propagated by Confucianists was supra--national (5). It was similar to the ancient Hellenic community of city-states which considered themselves separate from "barbarians", and similar to the modern Indian community as envisioned by Gandhi, or to the Burmese community as propagated by Aung San. In China, Greece, India (despite the separation of Pakistan) and Burma, these originally supra-national identities became national. Similar pan-Arabic and pan-African ideas have failed; the fate of Western Europe, undergoing an economic and cultural unification, has yet to be determined.

If we analyse these processes in greater detail, we shall find that the Italians, French, and Germans also base their concepts of national unity on ideas which might have been regarded as "supra-national" two hundred years ago. As it happenend, not only non-national, but also religious, social and political ideologies in many cases successfully united previously separated groups into a nation or a nation-like community. The USA, Revolutionary France and the USSR were united by political and social ideologies. The best example of a new community based on religion is Pakistan. Centered on religion, supra-ethnic integration is gradually creating a Pakistani nation. After the separation of Bangladesh it is much more homogeneous culturally. Bangladesh, on the other hand, is changing from a "sub-national" community of Bengal muslims into a national community of

(I) 諸夏

12

Bengalis.

Whereas families, clans, and village communities remain basically stable, the unity of cultural regions and countries fluctuates, becoming stronger and then weaker. A nation is not something material, a "thing", existing after its creation "for ever", but rather a given state of society (6). A state of integration is brought about by a particular society under given circumstances, and changes according to circumstances. A nation may be compared with a magnetic field which influences all the small pieces of iron within it. However, in a society, the power of the centre (the "magnet") is created by the masses; their concepts, emotions, devotions, and readiness to act are related to the centres of integration.

The category, "centre of social integration", seems to be a basic one for ethnic studies. It may be defined as a tangible or intangible cultural object around which various institutions are built, an object being of great importance for group cohesion. This kind of centre simultaneously serves several purposes:
1) **normative integration** (because it encompasses cultural values, standards of behaviour and norms);
2) **functional integration** (because it encompasses, or is related to, headquarters of various organizations, a local leader's residence, a meeting place);
3) **communicative integration** (related to means of communication, a place in which information is preserved and distributed, where the young are educated);
4) **symbolic integration** (because it symbolizes group identity).
Therefore, such centres unite the group physically and spiritually (7).

A centre may be a communal house in a village where important decisions are made or religious celebrations held, where tutelary spirits reside and where various mythological, ritual, or historical objects are preserved. It may be a holy mountain, like Fujiyama in Japan, or Taishan in China; a holy or very special book such as the Torah for the Jews, the Ramakien for the Thais, the Confucian Canon for the Chinese, or, in another dimension, the Tale of Three Kingdoms.

Each centre is usually a very complicated structure because there is a strong tendency to ascribe new functions and meanings to old centres; each group tends to locate in one place as many institutions, or in one object, as many functions and meanings, as possible.

One of the peculiar characteristics of centres is a necessity of "equal social distance". There should be not one social group which dominates the centre. There should be common ground for all (8). The royal palace, for example, with the throne and other symbols of the state is more likely to become a centre of

Centres of integration:

Shwe Dagon Stupa, Rangoon

*Pavilion of Preservation of Harmony,
in the Winter Palace, Beijing*

*Central Well in Co Loa (near Hanoi),
old capital of the Kingdom of Au Lac*

the nation, if there is no dynastic family or if there are no pretenders to such status. If there are social groups using the centre as a vehicle for achieving a special privileged position within the group, then the centre will lose its attraction for the people (9).

Social (and ethnic) groups develop through several stages.

Stage 1: Various institutions are created; relations within a group and social roles become stable and constant. The group becomes an **institutionalized community** (10).

Stage 2: An organization evolves with a leader, differentiated functions, etc., to protect and promote group interests. The group becomes an **organized community** (11).

Stage 3: A group culture (or sub-culture) develops with commonly accepted values, norms, standards of behaviours and accompanying myths. In such a case there is a **culturalized community** (12). Only in this way can inter-generational stability be achieved.

Stage 4: A centre of integration evolves, encompassing cultural characteristics of the group and carrying some of its myths. In such a case there is a **mono-centric community.** But if there is only one centre of integration, it usually becomes overburdened with practical functions and cannot be mythicized enough. Then cultural and symbolic functions may play only a minor role and a group unity will not be very stable.

Stage 5: Several inter-related centres evolve. Some of them serve more practical functions; others serve cultural and symbolic functions. It is a **poly-integrated community** (13). And it is much more dynamic, as the power and functions of the individual centre may easily change. The whole structure of integration becomes separate from any particular group interest within the community.

Stage 6: Centres of integration combined with integrative systems (such as language and other forms of communication, administration, etc.) may be based on a national mythological complex, i.e. several highly mythicized items more or less tied together. In such a case there is a **poly-integrated mythicized community.** This mythological framework promotes creation of given centres and systems, their high evaluation and development. It establishes deep cultural inter--relationship among them, due to this second level of mythology, which is not related to any particular centre, but to all of them. The whole structure of integration becomes much more independent from any concrete structure of centres or systems. Various centres may easily change their meanings and functions within a system; the system may be modified, therefore it is quite mobile. On the other hand, it is a much more rigid and unchangeable form of

16

group organization. In general the system as a whole may be destroyed only through the destruction of its social substratum, the group itself. A nation is just a poly-integrated mythicized community.

2. A MYTHOLOGICAL ASPECT OF NATIONHOOD

Mythicization of the group itself, elements of its culture and organization is a quite common phenomenon. As many sociologists and psychologists assume, each group has common norms, beliefs and values (Proshansky, Seidenberg, p.377). Therefore, it has always at least rudiments of a certain mythology related to this group. According to Balandier, constitutional principles and values of the group are mythicized for their protection (pp.94-95). Each centre of social integration is surrounded by a mythological halo which endows it with necessary power.

Mythicization is understood here in a very broad sense, as the creation of special cultural meanings as ascribed to physical and cultural objects, which transforms them into values, or things highly esteemed (14). In the case of a negative evaluation, the thing is disdained. These values and evaluations, however, are believed to be facts. Mythicized objects are considered "good", or "bad", just as the rose is red, or snow is white. The Yellow Sovereign, for the Chinese, is a great ruler-ancestor, not a ruler **supposed** to be a great one. Actually, according to scholarly opinion, he is merely a fictional personage.

In ethnic groups the mythicization process is especially advanced, and their centres of integration bear many mythological meanings. These mythological elements create the possibility of group action, readiness to act even against the interests of the individual, without instruction from leaders. Each real object surrounded by a mythological halo arouses emotions among the population and a common wish to protect it.

Therefore, **the power of a centre of social integration is proportional to the degree of its having been mythicized.**

The way of thinking about an ethnic community, common among members of a nation, is also basically mythological, not rational; or, at least, the presuppositions are mythological. Only plans of action, the ways to achieve these mythological aims can be rational.

These "national meanings" of various objects were described quite well by Zhang Qiyun at the outbreak of Japanese aggression against China:

"Most people would look with sheer indifference at a large piece of stone lying in their presence. But, if the stone be the monument in honour of a great personage in

17

past history, they would be instantly struck by its sight, lingering around it for quite a while, and being unable to tear themselves away from the scene. The relationship between the natural environment and the cultural environment of a nation is just that between a large piece of stone and a monument. When we say, as we often do, that we cannot yield one single inch of our territory to some alien aggressor, what we have uppermost in our mind is not just the natural beauty of that slight piece of territory, nor just its rich natural resources, but the immeasurable amount of blood, sweat and tears that had been spilt by our ancestors upon that snip of soil. Every spot on the vast expanse of China's territory has left behind its trail a memorable history of the hard struggle of our forefathers. Every historic vestige and every ancient remains of China is a monument of the long, splendid life of the Chinese people. Whilst passing by such a spot, will her citizens not be stirred in feelings, and moved to tears?" (Chang Chi-yun, pp.XXIII-XXIV. Quoted from the original translation - K.G.)

From this passage it is clear that a mythological halo around a subject is not equivalent to knowledge of the subject. One does not **know**, but one simply **believes** in given information, and is ready to reject all contradicting opinions. People react from emotion, and their ideas about worshipped objects are shaped according to specific mythological patterns as described by Mircea Eliade. A "positive hero" is idealized, a "negative hero" is shown to be "bad" on all accounts. Idealization is done according to a given set of values and cultural images accepted by a particular society. In a description of past events categories of mythical actions are used instead of the remembrance of individual events; archetypes are used instead of real personages. (Eliade, pp.34-47; see also Campbell)

Emotional reactions of the people protect the mythology and the centres of social integration from destruction from within. If destroyed from without, a centre is reconstructed by the population. Cultural meanings and mythicization are usually much more stable than material artefacts. As long as the mythology is alive and the group exists, the corresponding structure of centres can easily be reconstructed. In some cases a mythology is still alive even after the dispersal of the group which created it, if there has been another group able to inherit this mythology.

As many scholars have pointed out, each ethnic group seeking to build a sense of community creates at some point a genealogical myth of its origin, explaining why all members are similar and should be similar. A myth of its destiny is usually created as well, to instil pride among members of the group, and to create confidence in their ability to mould their own future.(Brass 1974, pp.28-29; Emerson, pp.206-7; Ossowski, II, pp.110-127).

Myths develop not only to define an ethnos, but to isolate the outside world as well, and to separate "enemies", or simply "foreigners". For ethnic and social cohesion a myth of oppression is very useful (cf. Brass 1974, p.29).

An example of mythicization:
Buddha Gautama bathed after his birth by nagas-dragons
(According to "A Record of Buddhist Kingdoms Being an Account by the Chinese Monk
Fa-hien", tr. by J. Legge, Oxford 1886, from an unspecified Chinese original)

National myths express the twofold nature of a nation considered, on the one hand, as a closed community, distinguished from "outsiders", and on the other hand, as a group holding certain universal values common to mankind. An ethnic group is therefore likely to use genealogical myths to justify its superiority over other ethnic communities. It is commonly a main function of ethnic myths to establish a given inter-ethnic hierarchy and justify privileges for specific ethnic groups. Consequently, myths accepted by one ethnic community may be, and usually are, rejected by other communities, if not modified to serve their own purposes.

The Chinese myth of the Central State, its Heavenly Mandate, and the Zhu Xia people endowed with civilization and perfect moral virtues, is an example (15). In the pre-imperial era, various myths were used by particular kingdoms to justify their independence or suzerain-vassal relations (cf. Gu Jiegang 1981, pp.40-41). After creation of the empire new myths justified Chinese suzerainty over all neighbouring nations. The myth of the Yellow Sovereign was particularly important. He was considered a major creator of civilization, and the ruler of the Four Quarters of the World. His sons became the ruler-ancestors of many nations which, therefore, had filial obligations to the Central State and its rulers. (Cf. Chang Chi-yun, pp.117-140)

The Vietnamese, however, took as their ancestor the Holy Ploughman (Shen Nong), the ruler preceding the Yellow Sovereign. Therefore, Chi You, his offspring, the ruler of the South, and a principal enemy of the Yellow Sovereign, a "monster" for the Chinese, was a "legal ruler", and an unfortunate but respectable ancestor for the Vietnamese. They also included in their genealogy Gong Gong, another negative personage for the Chinese, a rebel hero, banished by Shun (cf. Linh-nam..., p.1). Thus, common myths, with the same personages, justified opposing political positions: For the Chinese they justified attempts to conquer Vietnam and include it in their empire; for the Vietnamese they justified centuries of opposition to China and the defense of their separate state.

As E. M. Janšina has pointed out, the popularity of mythological national genealogies in China coincided with the intensive processes of ethnic consolidation in the 3rd-1st centuries B.C. (p.16). According to Janšina, the formation of the new ethnic unity (narodnost') presupposed an idea of its centuries old existence which was expressed in a new pantheon of ruler-ancestors (16). It is worthwhile noting that Han myths were accepted until the 20th century. They have since been re-interpreted but not entirely rejected (17). A nation is rarely able to discard the mythological tradition which created it.

The creation of ethnic or national myths may be regarded as an important step towards the formation of a nation, as a symp-

tom of its birth. It may seem paradoxical, but the myth formation process may be easier to date than such "objective criteria" of the nation-building process as, for example, the "national economy", the "national communication systems" (language), or a "national culture" (cf. discussion on the Chinese
nation, Han minzu xingcheng wenti...).

Genealogical myths, of course, cannot be considered the only criterion for the evolution of a nation; they are merely a useful
indicator. A nation also requires certain material structures:
centres of social integration, territorial organization, meaning
carriers, national institutions, etc. The spread of myths must
be accompanied by an objectification process, by the growth of
a concrete supporting "skeleton". Only then can ephemeral and
small ethnic groups be integrated into large and stable units,
into nations.

If the Jews had only had an idea of God, perhaps only historians would know of them. But a holy book and a religious organization have given them the framework within which they
have survived across the centuries and even have reconquered
their lost "fatherland". Countless ethnic groups have cherished
a myth of the Central Place; but only the Chinese created an organization suitable for the support of this myth, the Central
State, with its peculiar ideology and related social systems.

**Myths determine the objectification process; determine which
centres should be erected. Yet existing centres need accompanying myths. Therefore, the character of centres is determined by
a national mythology. Once in existence, however, the centres
influence further development of this mythology.** These national
mythologies may evolve in several aspects simultaneously according to the nature of the nation. Moreover, various myths may
compete within one mythological system. This competition is
usually related to opposing group interests and competition between two or more centres (18).

3. THE THREE DIMENSIONS OF A NATION AND THE MYTH-BUILDING PROCESS

The complex nature of national communities may be better comprehended by distinguishing their three dimensions. First, every
nation is a community of a living population. Secondly, it is a
community of generations, those which existed centuries or even
millennia before, and those to come in the future. Consequently,
the generations of today adjust their actions not only to the
needs and expectations of their contemporaries, but also to the
supposed needs and expectations of their ancestors and of future generations. Contemporary interests may be sacrificed for
the benefit of future generations, or out of respect for a heritage established by ancestors.

The third dimension is transcendency. In varying degrees, every nation claims to be expressing and supporting a set of shared ideals: eternal values, the benefit of mankind, the will of God, "historical progress", etc. The Chinese empire, for example, purported to defend and promote "civilization" and universal values such as humanity and justice. Its mission was carried out in the name of Heaven. The Guomindang in the 1920s claimed to defend social justice within China and international justice throughout the world. In the 1960s the People's Republic of China similarly professed to be a defender of coloured and oppressed peoples, propagating Maoist ideas of a utopian and authoritarian order.

The "Marseillaise", in addition to expressing French nationalism, also propagated universal ideas of liberty, equality and brotherhood as embodied by the Revolution. The Vietnamese in the 1960s, fought not only for the unification of their mother country, but also against "world imperialism". They were also fighting for the "spread of the Revolution", and for a new "socialist progressive order". Their U.S. adversaries, for their part, defended not simply their imperial interests but "freedom and democracy". Burmese nationalism is said to integrate Buddhist values and ideas. Japanese nationalism purported to raise arms against the oppression of Asia by the "white race", and manipulated the idea of "uniting the world under one roof".

All three of these dimensions are mythicized. Only through mythology can a nation be perceived as a contemporary, historic and, in a certain sense, transcendental unit.

Because of the third dimension, nationalism can easily merge with religious or social ideologies into one inseparable unit.

Whereas nation in its first dimension (as a community of a living population) is based mainly on rational thought, in its second and third mainly on mythological beliefs; because "historical" and "eternal" aims are beyond real experience and are not identical to calculable profits to generations existing at the present time. Consequently, political charlatans can easily manipulate popular ideals and traditions, evoke a nationalistic zeal, especially among young people. A mythology of the "perfect social order" can be particularly useful. As mythological beliefs counteract rational thinking, the people deceived by mythology are unable to comprehend how self-interested a manipulating minority can be, or how absurd their ideas are. The power of myths can be enormous; they may mesmerize a whole population, including even the ruling elite.

Nations in their ideologies emphasize these three dimensions differently. They create various centres of integration according to their cultural heritage, political and social conditions, and the abilities of creative groups such as politicians, philosophers, writers, and artists. Therefore, mythology and given organizational structures are created by various societies around different objects. Moreover, the same objects are mythicized in varying degrees and in different ways.

There are close relationships between these "national objects" and a national mythology. Sometimes the object accumulates and provokes emotions; sometimes emotions exalt an object which afterwards serves as a focal point for their manifestation. **A national or ethnic identity, being an emotional group feeling, needs always certain objects for its manifestation, growth and popularization. There should be something which can be revered or hated.** Moreover, in a traditional society there is a tendency to evaluate everything, to combine neutral objects with the ones previously evaluated and thus ascribe to the secondary objects mythological meanings. This tendency is a little weaker in an industrial society but still exists.

The physical world is composed of objective things, actions, characteristics, personages – x, y, z. If these positive or negative social attitudes were to be represented by "$+\varphi$" and "$-\varphi$", the social and cultural world would consist of $+\varphi x$, $+\varphi y$, $-\varphi z$, etc. (19). An effective popularization of given symbols, customs and heroes requires a certain predisposition among the population, a readiness to react emotionally to these objects. Cultural tradition, historical experience and social conditions are essential for the selection of objects; however, there is also room for conscious manipulation by the elite.

Several peculiarities in the development of a national identity should be noted. First, **negative feelings toward "alien groups", and respective negative mythology about them usually precede evolution of a positive, mythologized "self-image".** It is much easier to separate "others", and make negative distinctions, than it is to feel a common identity, to perceive "us" as integrated and being "alike". Whereas myths concerning alien groups are mainly negative, those related to one's own group are predominantly positive. If, however, something outside one's own group is disdained, it must be disdained within the group as well. If something is disdained within, it is easily projected onto an alien group (20).

Secondly, **at the beginning of the identity-formation process, the group usually identifies itself with an outside object: a religion, a social ideology, a state or territory.** Consequently, early myths concern the occupied territory, the state, or religion. The community does not pretend to be an ethnic one, but the people perceive themselves merely as "fellow-believers", "comrades in supporting justice", "compatriots", etc. They feel unity due to their common attitude to this outside object. Only later on does a direct unity evolve; intermediate objects become less important. These changes can be represented in a schematic way:

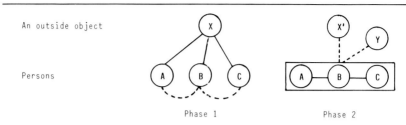

An outside object

Persons

Phase 1   Phase 2

Instead of personal contact with the outside object (phase 1), there is, later on, a group relation to this object (phase 2); an individual becomes related to it due to his membership in the group. Instead of direct relation to the outside object and indirect ties within the group (phase 1), there evolve indirect relations to the outside objects and direct ties within the group (phase 2). Therefore, the group as a whole becomes much more flexible in relation to its "objects of identification".

This process causes inevitable changes in the nature of a national unity and also causes decline in religious (or ideological) zeal among the population. Instead of objects requiring a personalized relation (such as God, moral or ideological principles to believe in), there arise new objects (Y), more suitable for a group identity, such as a state, territory, or canonical culture; worship and personal beliefs are substituted by public celebrations and public respect for certain objects without any necessity for personal practice, worship, or belief. Therefore, even the same objects (such as gods) change their function (the X becomes X'), and the nature of the religion is transformed.

The Chinese, for example, instead of having an everyday national culture and customs separating them from "barbarians" (customs accepted by everybody who wanted to be considered Chinese), as it was in the 5th-3rd centuries B.C., had accepted an idea of a historical state tradition and a canonical culture. One's being Chinese was therefore related to this historical political tradition and to the Canons but he may actually have lived in any place, in any state, and may have respected the Canons without reading them, he may also have ate and dressed in various ways, etc. But, it seems this evolutionary process has never been completed. Chinese national unity remains in an intermediate stage between phase 1 and 2. Outside objects (such as certain customs, beliefs, and ways of dressing) are still quite important for one's identity. It is related to weakness of the national cohesion. **When a national community becomes coherent and well-integrated, the people's strong identity with outside objects is lost.**

Thirdly, old identities often dissipate, and a common frustration prevails during the long time before new identities crystallize. During that time of "general confusion", several competing identities may arise simultaneously. Eventually, some are eliminated, others harmonize with each other. The process is very complicated, as group identity evolves by the formation of a new group arising from the "ruins and ashes" of an old social order. This explains why common frustration and negative emotional attitudes prevail at the beginning, and why group solidarity and common positive purposes are lacking (21).

Thus centres of integration often evolve for purposes other than national unity. They unite the population for a common purpose, and provide a common organizational framework. Later on, they acquire cultural meanings and are transformed into symbols of group unity, functioning as integrating systems.

In addition to centres of integration as presented above, there are other categories of cultural objects emotionally evaluated, i.e. mythologized by a national community.

A. Distinctive and Unitary Symbols

Distinctive symbols serve primarily to separate symbolically one's own from "alien" groups. As Paul R. Brass has pointed out, groups in conflict have a tendency to multiply these symbols, and seek to make these symbols congruent (1979, p.51). Unitary symbols serve mainly to evoke feelings of unity, and are used for various group rituals. A national anthem, for example, is a unitary symbol. The custom of Muslims that forbids them to eat pork, and the custom forbidding cow slaughter which distinguishes Indian Hindus from Muslims, are also distinctive symbols.

B. Integrating Cultural Systems

Each national group has to reside on a certain territory, produce or procure necessary material goods, protect its existence and interests, have possibilities to communicate among its members, normalize and control their behaviour and has to provide its members with a sense of collective life. For these basic social requirements special cultural systems have to be created: the system of settlements, housing and communication, and a mythology of a "fatherland", a certain system of economy, a political system (a state), a linguistic communication system, social norms and values, a system of punishments and a religion or social ideology.

The same basic social requirements can be satisfied in various ways by different cultural systems. One ethnic group, in order to obtain its means of existence, may hunt or fish, whereas another group may develop agriculture or animal husbandry. For normative purposes, the Arabs created the religious **Sharia**, the Chinese the civic **li** (ritual and customary norms), and the Romans the **state law**.

Some social requirements may be over-satisfied by multiple systems, centres and institutions; others may be satisfied only partially. Some of the aspects or elements of these systems and institutions are endowed with cultural and symbolic meanings while others remain nearly forgotten and are culturally under--evaluated. From the broad spectrum of the means of communication, for example, one community will standardize and develop the spoken language, another the literary written language, while still another, the Chinese for instance, may elaborate and revere a complicated script. Some of these systems can be regarded as "national", substantial for the ethnic identity, and may be transformed into distinctive or unitary symbols; others are neglected by a national community, they serve its unity but without being revered.

These integrating cultural systems usually are combined with certain centres of integration. The systems constitute a wider framework for the centres. The systems are also related to the national mythological complex which determines their development, inter-relations and a cultural value.

4. "NATIONAL MYTHOLOGICAL COMPLEX" - A BASIS OF UNITY

The character of a national unity, the "substance of a nation", may be described in various ways; one may describe the national centres and integrating cultural systems, their functions and cultural meanings, including the myths built around them. In a society differentiated into classes, political groups and interest groups, there are usually also cultural differences. Therefore, this kind of description, if precise, should present the ideas of a single thinker, a single political group, or the concepts propagated by a government during a certain period. One may also show competing concepts and structures.

If one intends to describe hypothetically the main national centres and integrating systems accepted by the majority over a long period of time, then one should analyse the social mythology and institutions, looking for the main topics around which they are built. Various written materials – as well as mass movements and celebrations – should be considered. Thus, behind the centres of integration and integrating systems, which are changeable and perceived within the same time in various ways, one may find in addition something which is much more stable: the **national mythological complex**. This complex constitutes the basis of the centres of integration and cultural integrating systems.

For example, national unity in Imperial China may be hypothetically presented in the following way:

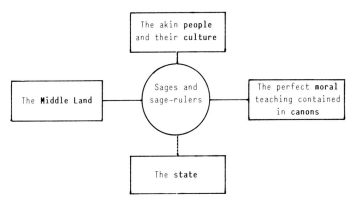

The Land and the Moral Teaching elements seem to be consist-
ent, strong, and persist for a long period. The importance of
the People along with their Culture, and the State, has fluctu-
ated and there have been various interpretations of these elements. Generally speaking, in late antiquity, the State was
the most important element, but at the end of the 19th century
and in the 20th century, the people came to be regarded as the
much more important element at the expense of the State. The
Cultural Revolution may be interpreted as an attempt to favour
the State at the expense of the People and their traditional Culture. Moreover, interpretation of the "People" has changed many
times. Mencius (372-289 B.C.?), for example, considered the
people as having perfect moral standards by their nature, and
therefore, they expressed the "will of Heaven". For Mencius, the
ruler was not very important; his duty was merely to create
and preserve a proper administrative system in which the natural morality of the people would flourish. Dong Zhongshu (179?-
104? B.C.), at the beginning of the Empire, held the opposite
opinion. According to him, it is the ruler who creates human,
i.e. moral nature within each individual. Therefore, the emperor
was the most important, he transmitted the will of Heaven and
the teachings of the sages to the people. Gu Yanwu (1613-1682)
considered the people the most important element in the state,
but according to him, they should be enlightened and guided
by the scholars.

In the People's Republic period one may find all three concepts
echoed and competing with each other: a mystical-democratic
one in which the people were considered as expressing naturally "true and right opinions" and "historical progress"; a
state-absolutistic one in which the sage ruler Mao Zedong was
considered as possessing the truth and enlightening the people

27

through the party and state apparatus, and guiding mankind according to the "path of progress"; and a bureaucratic one in which the "cadres" – new mandarins – were considered as guiding and teaching the masses. Moreover, these neo-traditional concepts competed with truly democratic modern ideas.

All elements given in the above scheme are closely related to each other. The **Middle Land** was considered to have been adjusted to the people's needs by a sage-ruler Yu the Great. He created its rivers, lakes and mountains thus eliminating floods and a natural "disorder". On the other hand, due to its central position in the cosmic order, the Central Land, in a natural way, "produced" sages and civilization. At the centre of the world, the moral order had to be highest.

The sages and sage-rulers constitute a corner-stone of this system. The sage-rulers of antiquity were considered ancestors of the people and creators of the moral teachings. They were, therefore, the founders of the people's moral nature, and they were also considered the inventors of the script and the authors of many canonical books, as well as founders of the state and culture.

It is worth noting that the Guomindang and the Chinese Communist Party have tried to change this system, to re-interpret it, and to introduce their own "sages", who complement the traditional ones, such as Sun Zhongshan (Sun Yat-sen), or who supplement them, such as Mao Zedong (Mao Tse-tong). **The national world-order as such, could not be rejected without basic changes in the national unity.**

A structure of traditional Vietnamese unity may be presented hypothetically in the following way:

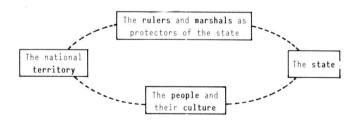

The **rulers**, it seems, were predominantly considered the protectors and creators of the state and its tutelary spirit, after their death, who – in a religious way – continued to fulfil their protective functions. Therefore, they were accompanied by the military leaders, marshals and generals in defending the country, also its tutelary spirits. Rulers' functions as "sages" and preservers of culture were less significant.

According to popular legends, they introduced various local customs and ceremonies, but not moral standards, or "culture" in its ethical Confucian interpretation. Therefore, their mythological image substantially differs from the Chinese image of sage--rulers. These rulers, worshipped by the people as tutelary spirits, were, it seems, only one element of the Vietnamese mythological complex, not its corner-stone. Other elements were not as closely related to the rulers as they were in China.

The **national territory** was also interpreted in a different way. It encompasses rivers, lakes and the sea. The waters constituted its vital part, therefore, it was not considered merely as the land. The territory, due to political and social changes, the presence of numerous alien ethnic groups and wide frontier areas, was important but not well delineated. The capital was its mythicized centre.

It should be noted that the spoken Vietnamese language became very important in modern times (in the past Chinese was used for various official, literary and religious purposes). Now the spoken language seems to be the main criterion for the national identification of an individual person. Therefore, the language should be included in "the people and their culture" element. One may note generally that the national culture is understood in Vietnam much more as an everyday culture than as canonical and normative. The state, previously interpreted according to Confucian ideology (with some inevitable modifications), is now interpreted in a Marxist-revolutionary way which does not actually contradict basic Confucian ideas.

The presence of a corner-stone element is not a Chinese peculiarity. One may find a similar structure in the traditional Jewish culture in Europe. The Jewish national mythological complex may be represented as follows:

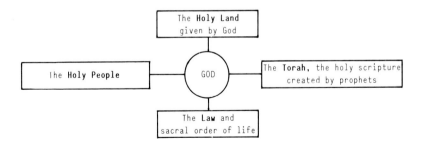

As may be seen, here the God constitutes the corner-stone of the whole system. He is the primary element, all others are secondary, and were created or established by him. It should be noted that the Holy Land mentioned here, was, perhaps, insignificant until the 19th century. It was simply an "ideological fatherland", a place of "holy history". It became a very important factor, however, at the end of the 19th century, when the modern nationalist movements spread through Europe. During this time the people became much more closely related to their land, and the religious factor in Jewish identity became less significant.

The Polish national pattern seems to be closer to the Vietnamese type; a corner-stone element is lacking.

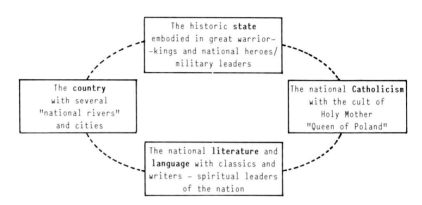

These four elements actually are independent. There is no close relationship between the religion and the literary classics; indeed, many of the classics lack religious spirit, or include critical opinions about the clergy and Church. The warrior-kings and national heroes are generally not related to the religion, there are only a few links. They are related, of course, to the country, but each element has its value by itself; many heroes have no corresponding territorial mythology, and many important places have no links to kings or heroes. In the national literature there are not many descriptions of kings and heroes, and large parts of the national territory are omitted. The "national cities" and "national rivers" in some cases only base their position in national mythology on literary classics. Even the country is not identical with the state, due to frequent boundary changes.

"National complexes", it may be noted, are relatively stable, although dynamic, structures. Their elements constitute certain "crystallization points" for a national mythology which is then built around them. Therefore, the centres of national integration and the systems of national integration combine with these crystallization points due to the centres' own mythological dimensions. Thus the mythological structure and the material-organizational structures of one nation may merge together.

● ● ●

●

Each nation – to conclude this essay – is united by its systems
and centres of integration, and by distinctive and unitary symbols. These are all surrounded by myths. A nation, due to its
inter-generational dimension, must be a historical entity but its
history is inseparable from its mythology. Myths develop parallel to history, constitute a sense of history and a foundation of
the common knowledge of history, all of which are parts of national consciousness. When a national unity is necessary, a
mythology has to be created; it may arise gradually and spontaneously, or it may be produced consciously for a purpose.

Social myths related to social institutions and organizations
serve their own purposes. Institutions, for their part, often
support myths, even defending them against their real interests
and the interests of the nation. Myths, once created, become a
powerful part of reality. The social psyche may be objectified
in mythology, but mythology may even subdue social consciousness, the consciousness of the people as well as the consciousness of the ruling elite.

Nations do exist, of course. They are based, however, on myths,
and their substance is constituted by myths built around their
centres of integration. Therefore, nations are real entities, and
simultaneously mythological entities, created by mythologies
which are mythicized again. Mythology determines the nature of
a national community and the behaviour of its members: It determines whether the people would be ready to die in defence of
the state border or capital, the religion or national spoken language, or some other elements considered vital to the nation according to its mythological structure.   ●

NOTES:

1. A nation is considered by some sociologists a natural group, which does not, however, seem justifiable. See, for example, the analysis of the classification advocated by I. Mandieta, and critical comments on it, by Pitrim Sorokin (Sorokin 1966,
pp.558-565).
Paul R. Brass accepted a compromise solution. He considers an ethnic group as a group
of individuals who have some objective characteristics in common beyond their mere
place in social division of labour. For him, an **ethnic group** is objectively distinct;
but its members do not necessarily attach subjective importance or political significance to that fact. He uses the term, **community**, to refer to ethnic groups whose members have developed an awareness of a common identity, and who have attempted to define the boundaries of their respective groups. A community becomes, for him, a
nation, when it mobilizes its members for political actions and becomes politically
significant, making political demands and achieving political results through group
action. One of the possible demands is political sovereignty (see Brass 1974, pp.
8-9). He also shows quite well the process of artificial, purposeful creation of the
nation with the accompanying destruction of many traditional loyalties and elements

of culture.

In my opinion, an ethnic group larger than a village community or tribe, is artificial. Its distinct characteristics are purposefully accepted by the group as its group characteristics; they are supported and taught, and deviations from them are punished. In my opinion the range of artificialness is increasing, but ethnic unity is artificial from the beginning.

2. Therefore, a nation is strictly related to a state, which actually exists, or has existed in the past, or whose existence is demanded. It is a twofold community; cultural and political. It expresses and protects ethnic interests and clan interests as well (cf. Malinowski, pp.252-275; Taylor, pp.256-257; Akzin; Wiatr). I agree, however, with Brass that the nation-state is a particular case, and that a nation need not necessarily aim to create such a state. A national political organization may function within a framework of a multi-national state (Brass 1974, pp.9-15; cf. also Geertz, pp.117-118).

The relationship between a political identity and the state identity is rather complicated; various social groups, such as classes, religious communities, etc., may develop a political identity. But not all citizens identify themselves with the state, and sometimes a majority of the people even rejected the state. On the other hand, as David Taylor has pointed out, a political identity constitutes only a part of the broader cultural identity. A historical consciousness of the community can even be formulated outside a political framework of the state, as in India (ibid.). In addition, the nature of states can be different and the "state identity" may contain various meanings. One state may be merely an administrative organization, another may be predominantly ideological, and still another religious. The Chinese empire, for instance, emphasized its moral-ideological and cultural functions, whereas Tibet in the 18th and 19th centuries predominantly the religious aspect.

Many scholars have proposed the term, **nationality,** for ethnic communities without political structures and which are predominantly united by culture (by a "mechanical solidarity" according to Durkheim's categories). (Cf. Wiatr, pp.212-213, 223) The term **nation** I would reserve for communities with political aims and organization and which have differentiation of functions (Durkheim's "organic solidarity" in a political sense may be used here). The nature of national identity may be multifarious, based on ethnicity, religion, common territory, state, ideology, or culture. A nation, in the broad sense, is a community which does not necessarily regard its members as "one people", but which has, besides a political organization, some cultural characteristics in common: a system of values, customs, and way of life. Within this framework of nationhood may exist some more or less distinct ethnic groups. Communities of this kind can be named **complex nations.**

3. The concept of a hierarchical nature of ethnic identities was elaborated by the Soviet ethnological school (cf. Broley, pp.125-153). The Don Cossacks, for example, constitute a part of the Russians and the Russians belong to the Eastern Slavs who are a part of the Slavs in general. Bruk and Cheboksarov have proposed a new term: **meta-ethnic community,** defined as a community with elements of an ethnic consciousness, based on ethno-genetic affinity, or on long-lasting cultural and economic relations (p.17).

It should be noted, however, that micro-ethnic, macro-ethnic, and meta-ethnic communities may be based on different ties and affinities. The composite nature of a nation or of ethnic groups has been noticed and analysed many times (cf. Brass 1974, p. 12; Cushman, I, pp.74-147).

These concepts differ from the well-known theory of a **plural society** which emphasizes an institutional differentiation among the sections of this kind of society, and accepts a racial, ethnic or cultural basis of cleavage; these sections are often regarded as sub-systems. The "plural society" concept is applicable to empires, colonies and certain industrial societies. It explains how various ethnic groups may co-operate within a common state and one economic system. (For details see Furnivall, Smith, Edelstein)

4. See Walker (esp. pp.35-37); Seyschab. Sinologists have usually concentrated their studies on the development of the "Chinese" unity, identity and culture. The pluralistic nature of ancient and early medieval China seems to have been underestimated.

5. Wolfram Eberhard has pointed out that "Chinese culture" evolved by the integration of several primitive cultures (proto-Mongolian, Turkish, proto-Tungusic, Tibetan, Thai, Viet, etc.) and crystallized as a high culture of the ruling Zhou class. Only afterwards did this culture become widespread and accepted by the people (Eberhard, pp.16-29). The Chinese identity (Zhu Xia) developed, it seems, during the Chunqiu period (8th through 5th century B.C.). Cf. Krjukov et al, pp.267-291.

6. In a similar way any social group may be understood in 1) a material way, as a "thing", as a given number of related individuals, or 2) as an attribute, a system of relations among individuals, a "social system" in Parsons' interpretation (Parsons, Shils, p.26). See also Hiller.

7. I use here, in a modified way, the concept of the centre of group unity (cf. Szczepanski, p.264). The concept, "centre of social integration", is also close to a "central ideological-behavioural-material cultural set" as elaborated by Pitrim Sorokin (1947, ch.4, 8, 9; 1966, pp.28, 215). In his opinion, each social group is built around a system of meaning-value-norms which may be rooted in behaviour and in material objects. I accept many elements of his analysis of the relation between culture and society, but his orientation is mainly theoretical. Therefore, his categories are very abstract and cannot be directly used in describing a certain culture. I have also used Stanislaw Ossowski's studies on nationhood in the elaboration of the concept **centre of integration** (cf. vol.II, pp.65-67, III, pp.216-217).

The term, **normative integration,** is used here in a way similar to Parsons (1951, 1960); the second term, **communicative integration,** should not need additional explanation either. Detailed analysis was given by Karl W. Deutsch in his classic work on nation-building processes. **Functional integration** has been much discussed in sociological literature (see, for example, Merton 1949, pp.21-81; Gouldner). Here **functional integration** is used in a very simple way as integration related to actions of individuals and organizations, and as integration achieved through these actions (cf. Landecker).

8. Central place theory, however elaborated for other purposes, seems to be useful and applicable (in a modified way) to the "centre of integration" (cf. Berry/Pred). Theories of communication also contain concepts of **centrality** and **distance** (cf. Bavelas). The most central position is defined as the position closest to all other positions (see Leavitt, p.38; Lindzey and Aronson, IV, pp.138-139).

9. For example, as Paul R. Brass has mentioned, the presence of the maharaja in Maithili, who pretended to be a hereditary prince, and who advocated the creation of a separate state, was more of an obstacle than a help to the development of Maithili identity. That Shivaji, the hero of defensive wars against the Muslims, had no descendants in Maharashtra, on the other hand, did not hinder development of national myths related to him and Maharashtran identity (Brass 1974, p.58). In my opinion, the presence of a group (or of an individual) who would achieve substantial social privileges should a certain myth be accepted, would usually become an obstacle. Therefore, dead heroes, equally distant from all sections of the society, are best for the creation of an ethnic or national identity.

10. This process of institutionalization was well described by Znaniecki (p.809).

11. It seems to be easiest for classification purposes to accept, as R. M. Stogdill

33

proposed, the emergence of leaders within a group as a turning point in its transformation into an organization (p.3).

12. Culture is defined in various ways (cf. Kroeber and Kluckhohn). I assume, as do many other scholars, that culture is a balanced system, more or less coherent, based on certain fundamental values, norms and assumptions (cf. Kluckhohn). According to many sociologists and psychologists, each group tends to establish norms, and standards of behaviour, etc. (Sherif), and to become balanced.

13. This differentiation of a mono-integrated community from a poly-integrated community was established following Pitrim Sorokin's distinction of uni-bonded and multi--bonded groups (cf. Sorokin 1947, ch.9-20; 1966, pp.31-32).

14. See R. Barthes, esp. pp.114-129. Consequently, an ideology may be considered a mythology, and classical Marxist concepts related to an ideology may be used for the analysis of mythology (cf. Huaco, p.436). As Eliseo Verón has pointed out, through the social communication processes, a certain image is usually transmitted: It is an image of the society, of the social reality and the concept of social organization. This transmission of the image is possible, however, only through meta-communication, that is, at an implicite level of meaning. In this way it is presented as obvious, and any potential discussion concerning that particular ideological vision may be avoided. Therefore, quite apart from denotative meanings, "ideological meta-messages" are transmitted (cf. Verón, pp.65, 68). It should be added that these ideological or mythological meanings are transmitted by communication of real facts, information partially deformed, or of a pure fiction. Consequently, an ideological function cannot decide that a message is false in its basic denotative level.

15. The Central State and Central Place concepts elaborated by various cultures and the Chinese organizational patterns are well presented by Paul Wheatley. Cf. also Gawlikowski, 1980. These sinocentric concepts in medieval times are described by Ch'en Yüan.

16. E. M. Janšina emphasizes the process of integration of various local traditions and gods, or mythological ancestors, into one all-Chinese pantheon. This concept has been commonly accepted since Gu Jiegang's early publications (Gu Jiegang 1926, 1927, 1936; cf. K. C. Chang, pp.166-170). Janšina, however, has also pointed out another aspect: the justification of imperial centralistic tendencies by these state-genealogies (p.16). Therefore, a "national genealogy" was related not only to the new Chinese, Han ethnos, but also to the state, the Chinese empire.

17. See, for example, these well-known general histories of China published in the Peuple's Republic, Lü Zhenyu, I, pp.36-74; Fan Wenlan, I, pp.88-98. Chang Chi-yun's book, published in Taiwan, supports completely the traditional vision of Chinese history, and presents all myths as the real past of the Chinese people. This is rather surprising if one considers the political and social position of this celebrated scholar.

18. Therefore, contradictions within ideology of a certain period should not be considered only as an expression of class interests and socio-economic contradictions, as many Marxist scholars assume. The ideology and mythology of a certain period also express the interests of various institutions and organizations: the state and the Church, the various ministries of the central government, the administrative apparatus and the army, etc.

19. Here I follow the method of description proposed by Stanislaw Ossowski (vol.II, p.67). As he has pointed out, within a population there is a whole range of attitudes towards a revered object; "+x" is merely a simplification.

20. Attitudes toward alien groups were studied predominantly as "national stereotypes" (a valuable description of research was prepared by John S. Harding et al). This category, however, does not seem to be the most fortunate one. It should be noted that an ethnic group may occasionally produce a negative stereotype of its own characteristics (cf. Bayton and Byoune; Rath and Sircar). Moreover, as Roger Brown has stated, if a group consists of people playing a specific social role, there is a strong tendency to behave according to stereotypes. What is prescribed for this social category is ordinarily performed by the members of the group, and it is expected not only by others but by themselves as well (p.172). The Jews and the Gipsies in traditional European societies are good examples, but similar cases may be found in Asia. For the origins of "we-feeling" see Sherif and Sherif, ch. 6, 9.

21. Lucian W. Pye described this state of great confusion and hatred for foreign powers among the Chinese very well, pointing also various objective changes related to the modernization process, such as changes of economy, etc. (pp.67-84). The transformation of structures of integration is usually provoked by these economic, technological and political changes (cf. R. Bendix). The description of the identity-formation process, given above, is based mainly on Chinese data, but it seems applicable – more or less – to other nations as well.

QUOTED LITERATURE:

● B. Akzin: State and Nation, London 1964, Hutchinson University Library
● G. Balandier: Anthropologie politique, Paris 1969, Presses Universitaires de France
● R. Barthes: Mythologies, New York 1972, Hill and Wang (trans. Anette Lavers)
● A. Bavelas: A Mathematical Model for Group Structures, APPLIED ANTHROPOLOGY, 7 (1948), 16-30
● J. A. Bayton, E. Ryoune: Racio-national Stereotypes Held by Negroes, JOURNAL OF NEGRO EDUCATION, 16 (1947), pp. 49-56
● R. Bendix: Nation-building and Citizenship; Studies in Our Changing Social Order, Berkeley 1977, University of California Press
● B. J. L. Berry, A. Pred: Central Place Studies; A Bibliography of Theory and Applications, Philadephia 1961, BIBLIOGRAPHY SERIES No.1, Regional Science Research Institute
● P. R. Brass: Language, Religion and Politics in North India, London 1974, Cambridge University Press
● M. V. Bromlej: Etnos i etnografia (:Ethnos and Ethnography), Moskva 1973, Nauka
● R. W. Brown: Social Psychology, New York 1965, The Free Press
● S. I. Bruk, N. N. Cheboksarov: Metaetnicheskije obshchnosti (:Meta-ethnic Communities), RASY I NARODY, vol.6, Moskva 1976, pp.15-40
● J. Campbell: The Hero with a Thousand Faces, New York 1956, Meridian Books
● Chang Chi-yun: Chinese History of Fifty Centuries, vol.I, Ancient Times, Taipei 1962, Institute for Advanced Chinese Studies
● K. C. Chang: Early Chinese Civilization; Anthropological Perspective, Cambridge, Mass., 1976
● Ch'en Yüan: Western and Central Asians in China under the Mongols, translated and annotated by Ch'ien Hsing-hai and L. Carrington Goodrich, Los Angeles 1966, MONUMENTA SERICA MONOGRAPH XV
● R.D. Cushman: Rebel Haunts and Lotus Huts; Problems in the Ethnohistory of the Yao, vol.1-2, Ph.D.Thesis, Cornell University 1970
● K.W. Deutsch: Nationalism and Social Communication; An Inquiry into the Foundations of the Nationality, Cambridge Mass. 1953, MIT Press
● W. Eberhard: The Local Cultures of South and East China, Leiden 1968, E.J. Brill
● J.C. Edelstein: Pluralistic and Marxist Perspectives on Ethnicity and Nation-build-

ing, in W. Bell, W.E. Freeman: Ethnicity and Nation-building; Comparative, International and Historical Perspective, Beverly Hills,London 1974, Sage Publications, pp. 45-57
- M. Eliade: The Myth of Eternal Return, New York 1954
- R. Emerson: From Empire to Nation; The Rise to Self-assertion of Asian and African Peoples, Boston 1962, Beacon Press
- Fan Wenlan 范文瀾 : Zhongguo tongshi jianbian 中国通史簡編 (: An Outline of General History of China), Beijing 1964, rev. ed., vol.I
- J.S. Furnivall: Colonial Policy and Practice, London 1948, Cambridge University Press
- K. Gawlikowski: The Origins of the Name "Middle State", CZASOPISMO-PRAWNO-HISTORYCZNE, vol.XXXII, no.1 (1980), pp.35-76
- C. Geertz: The Integrative Revolution: Primordial Sentiments and Civil Politics in the New States, in C. Geertz (Ed.): Old Society and New States; The Quest for Modernity in Asia and Africa, New York 1967, The Free Press
- A.W. Gouldner: Reciprocity and Autonomy in Functional Theory, in L. Gross (Ed.): Symposium on Sociological Theory, Evanston Ill. 1959, Row, Peterson, pp.241-270
- Gu Jiegang 顧頡剛 (Ed.) 1 : Gushibian 古史辨 (: Discourses on Ancient History), Beijing 1926, vol.I; 1927, vol.II; 1936, vol.VII,part 2
- ... 2 : Lun Ba Shu yu Zhongyuan de guanxi 論巴蜀與中原的关系 (: On Ba and Shu Kingdoms' Relations with the Central Plain), Chengdu 1981
- Han minzu xingcheng wenti taolun ji 漢民族形成問題討論集 (: Collected Essays on the Problem of the Formation of the Han Nation), Beijing 1957, Sanlian Shuju
- J. Harding, H. Proshansky et al : Prejudice and Ethnic Relations, in G. Lindzey, E. Aronson (Eds.): The Handbook of Social Psychology, Reading Mass.,Manlo Park Cal. 1968 (2nd ed.), vol.V, pp.1-76
- E.T. Hiller: Social Relations and Structures, New York,London 1947, Harper & Brothers
- G.A. Huaco: Ideology and Literature, NEW LITERATURE HISTORY (Ideology and Literature), vol.IV (1973), p.3
- E.M. Janšina: Katalog gor i morej (:The Canon of the Mountains and Seas), Moskva 1977, Nauka
- H.H. Kelly: The Two Functions of Reference Groups, in G.E. Swanson, T.M. Newcomb, E.L. Hartley (Eds.): Readings in Social Psychology, New York 1952, Holt
- C. Kluckhohn: The Study of Culture, in D. Lerner, H.D. Lasswell (Eds.): The Policy Sciences; Recent Development in Scope of Methods, Stanford 1959, Stanford University Press
- A.L. Kroeber, C. Kluckhohn: Culture; A Critical Review of Concepts and Definitions, PAPERS PEABODY MUSEUM, vol.47 (1952), no.1
- M.V. Krjukov, M.V. Sofronov, N.N. Čeboksarov: Drevnie Kitajcy; Problem etnogeneza (:The Ancient Chinese; The Problem of their Ethnogenesis), Moskva 1978, Nauka
- W.S. Landecker: Types of Integration and their Measurement, AMERICAN JOURNAL OF SOCIOLOGY, vol.56 (1951), pp.332-340
- H.J. Leavitt: Some Effects of Certain Communication Patterns on Group Performance, JOURNAL OF ABNORMAL AND SOCIAL PSYCHOLOGY, vol.46 (1951), pp.38-50
- G. Lindzay, E. Aronson: The Handbook of Social Psychology, vols.1-5, Reading Mass. - Menlo Park Cal. 1968, Addison - Wesley Publishing Co., 2nd. ed.

- Lĩnh-nam Chích Quài 嶺南摭怪傳 (:Marvelous Stories from Linnam), Lê Hũu Mục ed., Saigon 1960, Khai Tri
- Lü Zhenyu 呂振羽 : Jianming Zhongguo tongshi 簡明中国通史 (:A Short General History of China), Beijing 1964 (1st. ed. Chongqing 1941), vol.I
- B. Malinowski: Freedom and Civilization, New York 1944, Roy Publishers
- R.K. Merton: Social Theory and Social Structure, Glencoe Ill. 1957, The Free Press (rev. and enlarged ed.)
- S. Ossowski: Dzieła (:Works), vols.II-IV, Warszawa 1966-67, PWN
- T. Parsons, A. Shils: Toward a General Theory of Action, Cambridge Mass. 1951, Harvard University Press
- T. Parsons: Durkheim's Contribution to the Theory of Integration of Social Systems, in K. Wolf (Ed.): Emile Durkheim, 1858-1917, A Collection of Essays, Columbus 1960, Ohio State University Press, pp.118-153
- H. Proshansky, B. Seidenberg: Basic Studies in Social Psychology, New York 1965, Holt, Reinhard and Winston
- L.W. Pye: The Spirit of Chinese Politics; A Psychocultural Study of the Authority Crisis in Political Development, Cambridge Mass. 1965, MIT Press
- Rounag Jahan: Pakistan; Failure in National Integration, New York 1972
- R. Rath, N.C. Sircar: The Mental Pictures of Six Hindu Caste Groups about Each Other as Reflected in Verbal Stereotypes, JOURNAL OF SOCIAL PSYCHOLOGY, vol.5 (1960), pp.277-293
- C.A. Seyschab: The Origin of National Identity in China, EAST ASIAN CIVILIZATIONS, no.1 (1982), pp.152-174
- M. Sherif, C.W. Sherif: An Outline of Social Psychology, New York 1956, Harper, (rev. ed.)
- M. Sherif: The Psychology of Social Norms, New York 1966, Octagon
- M.G. Smith: Institutional and Political Conditions of Pluralism and Some Developments in the Analytic Framework of Pluralism, in L. Kuper, M.G. Smith (Eds.): Pluralism in Africa, Berkeley-Los Angeles 1969, University of California Press, pp. 27-65
- P. Sorokin 1: Society, Culture and Personality; Their Structure and Dynamics; A System of General Sociology, New York-London 1947, Harper and Brothers
- ...2: Sociological Theories of Today, New York-Tokyo 1966, Harper & Row
- J. Szczepanski: Elementarne pojęcia socjologii (:Basic Categories in Sociology), Warszawa 1970
- D. Taylor: Political Identity in South Asia, in D. Taylor, M. Yapp (Eds.): Political Identity in South Asia, London-Dublin 1979
- E. Verón: Ideology and Social Sciences; A Communicational Approach, SEMIOTICA, vol. 3 (1971), p.1
- R.L. Walker: The Multi-state System of Ancient China, Connecticut 1953, Shoe String Press
- P. Wheatley: The Pivot of Four Quarters; A Preliminary Enquiry into the Origins and Character of the Ancient Chinese City, Chicago 1971, Aldine Publishing Comp.
- J.J. Wiatr: Naród i państwo (:Nation and State), Warszawa 1973, PWN, 2nd. ed.
- F. Znaniecki: Social Groups as Product of Participating Individuals, AMERICAN JOURNAL OF SOCIOLOGY, vol.44 (1939), pp.799-811

MYTHOGRAPHY versus HISTORY:
The Wuji Case

●

BY ARMIN SIEVERS

*Chinese mythology knows many legendary races who live on the edge of or entirely beyond the known world (China). Some take half-man, half-animal form; some are covered with curious body markings. (Cf., for example, the snake-people in the Land of Xuanyuan from the essay by M. Mitarai.) One of these legendary peoples is the **Wuqi**. Known as "men without bellies or abdomens", "men without calves" or even "men without descendants" (propagating by means of re-animation), they have fired the fantasy of Chinese authors from the time they were first mentioned in the Shanhaijing (:Classic of the Mountains and Rivers, compiled from the 4th century B.C. to the 3rd century A.D.) right through the middle of the last century. The author of the present study shows that the nation originally depicted in the Shanhaijing is identical with the historically identified nation of the **Wuji**, earliest mention of which occurs more than five hundred years later in the historical annals of China in the 6th century A.D. The Wuji lived in Northern China in the wooded areas of Manchuria and hitherto existing research had failed until now to uncover their history and provenance before the 6th century A.D. Not only does this study clarify the early history of the Wuji tribes, the existence of which must now be dated five hundred years earlier than previously, but it also reveals the myth of the legendary people of the Wuqi as a myth*

based on an oral misunderstanding made possible by the dual-
ity of Chinese characters. They can be understood both phonetically as well as graphically. It was, then, as the historical-
-linguistic analysis of the author shows, a pure misunderstanding that the fully phonetic transcription in Chinese of the
foreign tribal name Wuji led to the myth of the Wuqi as the
"people without calves", "bellies", "descendants", etc. Further,
the fantasy of Chinese commentators who adhered to graphic interpretations and embellishments of the name Wuqi contributed
in large portion to the growth of this myth. Methodologically
this study is interesting for the possibilities set forth as to
how the genuine historical nucleus of a myth can be exposed
through a contrastive study of mythological sources and substan-
tiating historical evidence on the linguistic basis of comparative phonetics. In this manner mythological sources can be
made to surrender dates and information of a historical nature
which hitherto had been treated as pure mythological invention;
thus, traces of historical life become visible behind the myths
themselves. With specific regard to the field explored here,
namely tribes outside of China, ways are also indicated as to
how to render intelligible the historical development of the border tribes of China who for so long have been considered to be
without history due to their lack of a writing system.

***

Sketch Map of the Dongbei Region

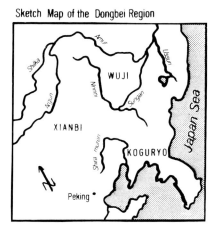

A HISTORICAL INCONSISTENCY

Although Chinese and Korean historical sources agree on most particulars about the supposed ancestors of the **Jurčed** and **Manchus**, viz. the **Wuji** (I) people, as well as on their ethnic identity with the **Mohe** (II) they nevertheless differ considerably in dating the first appearance of those peoples. Modern historians of East Asia, whether from the East or from the West, tend to take the Chinese dating which makes at least the Mohe a few hundred years younger than Korean sources would do as the correct one. No effort to explain this gap has yet been made.

On the Chinese side there are no official dynastic histories older than the **Weishu (WS)** (:History of the Wei Dynasty), compiled in A.D. 573, and the **Beishi (BS)** (:History of the Northern Dynasties), compiled about fifty years later, which mention the Wuji/Mohe; thus the above time gap leads to the question whether there might be any other Chinese sources before WS and BS in which to find evidence for an earlier existence of the Wuji/Mohe. This question would be reasonable even should the traditional identification of the two prove untenable: but that is another problem and no subject of the present paper.

There is archaeological as well as literary evidence to indicate at least indirect early contacts between China proper and the regions northeast of it comprising the present Manchurian realm and the Amur-Ussuri region. Both Han dynasties (206 B.C.-A.D. 220), e.g., had a considerable demand for sable furs from the northeastern realm of Fuyu/Puyŏ which was renowned for the quality of its furs (1). In the Amur region Chinese coins from the time of the Warring States (475-221 B.C.) and later have been discovered and are now kept in a museum at Chabarovsk (2). Such coin finds do not prove that there was direct contact between northeastern tribes and China for they could have been merely part of booty acquired occasionally during one of the incessant raids of those tribes into territory where Chinese coins were common currency. Nevertheless, the Chinese demand for sable furs is a definite hint that some form of trade existed between China and e.g. Fuyu in Manchuria (3). But if there did exist trade relationships in Han times we might confidently expect some references to the Wuji/Mohe in early Chinese sources, as well as the Korean ones.

●

THE DATINGS

The Korean Samguksa chŏryo (:Essentials of the History of the

(I)勿吉   (II)靺鞨

40

Three States) mentions the Mohe, or **Malgal** in Korean pronunciation, first in the year 37 B.C., then again in the year 17 B.C. (4). Thereafter references to them continue till to the 8th century A.D. (5). The Wuji name occurs in the same source only in A.D. 504 (6) which roughly corresponds to the Chinese dates for them. The WS speaks of a tributary mission of the Wuji to the Toba-Wei court in the Yanxing period (A.D. 471-476), led by a certain Yilizhi (I), whose itinerary is preserved in the same source, and of another such mission in the second year of the Taihe period (A.D. 478) (WS, j.100, p.2220). However, in its chapter on the "line of descent" (Xu Ji (II)) of the Wei emperors the WS states that the later Wei territory in the times of Emperor Pingwen (III) comprised all land west of the Wuji, this emperor of Toba origin was a contemporary of Emperor Min (IV) of Jin (V) (r. A.D. 313-316). Accordingly the Wuji would have been known to the Toba at latest at the beginning of the 4th century A.D. (7).

One might object that the Xu Ji reference to the Wuji is no definite proof of their real existence at the beginning of the 4th century, the Chinese frequently made some anachronistic use of ethnonyma. The statement could have meant that all land west of the region inhabited by the Wuji at the time of compilation of the WS had formerly been occupied by the Toba. This, however, would be a mistake, as we shall see that e.g. the well--known commentator of the **Shanhaijing (SHJ)** (:Classic of the Mountains and Rivers), **Guo Pu** (VI), who lived at the turn of the 3rd to the 4th century A.D., must have had some informations about the Wuji. He partly misunderstood this information which he used for a comment on a SHJ reference. This comment is the one we shall have to trace. The internal problems and seeming inconsistencies of the Korean sources concerning the supposed identity of Wuji and Mohe must not bother us any further while we are looking for earlier Chinese references.

•

THE SOURCES

Sources most likely to yield an answer to our question are those that contain geographical and ethnographical informations, viz. SHJ and **Huainanzi (HNZ)** (:Book of the Prince of Huainan). In the case of the SHJ we immediately have to weigh its historical value, since in the course of being transmitted it fell into such a deplorable state of corruption and confusion, that it is sometimes impossible to distinguish the original text from later commentaries on it or to give an accurate date of

---

(I)乙 力支　　　(II)序紀　　　(III)平文

(IV)愍　　　(V)晋　　　(VI)郭璞

single passages. Needham, e.g., is of the opinion that it is "a Former Han book built around material from Warring States times" and that "the later chapters may be of Later Han or even Jin date" (Needham, p.448 note, mod.) (8), whereas Maenchen-Helfen and Janšina tend to see in it a pre-Han work (Maenchen-Helfen, 550 ff; Janšina, 12 f) (9). For our purposes it will do if we take the present SHJ text as of Han times at latest.

Of the descriptions of peoples living outside China in both SHJ and HNZ most interesting are those passages concerning the northern realm, i.e. in the chapters 8 and 17 of SHJ, occasionally recurring to chapters reporting on the peoples of the north-east and the north-west, respectively; in HNZ it is mainly chapter 4 on geography that will concern us.

SHJ as well as HNZ mention a people called **Wuqi** (I) and **Wuji** (II), respectively, in the order of those inhabiting the northern regions comparison of both lists shows that - with the exception of two names being mutually exchanged - they are indeed identical though inverted (10): The first name of the SHJ list is the last in HNZ and vice versa; nonetheless both works introduce their lists of the northern peoples with an identical remark about the direction of counting, i.e. from north-east to north--west. How then can the inverted series of names be explained?

A second conspicuous fact is that HNZ mentions the direction of enumeration only in its introductory remark, whereas SHJ gives additional directional hints for every single people by relating its geographical position to the preceding people as follows: "B east of A, C east of B ..." etc., even though by doing so it contradicts the general counting direction from north-east to north-west given in its own introduction.

If we proceed in the SHJ text from these relative directional positions (B east of A), without regard to its introductory statement, but only to the position of neighbouring peoples of other regions, we shall find the same sequence for SHJ and HNZ, as shown by the following schematic representation:

---

*FIG. A: **Northern Realm - HNZ***

◗ *north-west*   *north-east* ◀

Changgu...Wuji...Yimu... ... ... Qizhong
⋮
Sushen
⋮
Baimin

(I) 無 臂   (II) 無 継

42

▷ *north-west*   *north-east* ◁

Changgu...Wuqi...Yimu... ... ... Qizhong
⋮
Sushen
⋮
Baimin

This leads us to conclude that the introductory remark of SHJ about the counting direction north-east to north-west is not to be taken literally, but as a general statement on the region where the peoples in question dwell (11). It does not give the order of sequence of these peoples so we do not have to consider this seeming contradiction within SHJ but can rely on its relative directional indications, i.e. on its identity with HNZ (12).

If we were to take the directional hints of both SHJ and HNZ at face value we would be obliged to locate the Wuqi (I) and Wuji (II) somewhere in the north-west of China. This, however, would lead to another confusion, since in both texts the Wuqi/Wuji are mentioned as mediate neighbours of the **Sushen** (III) who are located in the northwestern realm according to both sources, but are historically traceable as a northeastern people, as all reliable Chinese and Korean sources confirm. Thus the SHJ and HNZ lists of the northern peoples obviously do not give their real geographic position but an inverted sequence. How can this be explained? The localization of the Sushen in the north-west might simply be taken as a copyist's error (13), but this seems no good explanation since it would mean a simultaneous occurrence of the same mistake in two separately compiled texts.

We can merely speculate about the reasons for the inversion in HNZ. The "author" of this work, Prince **Liu An**, may have intently inverted the sequence in order to express his political ambitions for the throne, by placing himself in the south-facing position of the emperor (which is the normal orientation for maps, too), for whom the cardinal points are the reverse of the view of ordinary men, because he has the east to his left and the west to his right. In connection with a rebellion planned by him the prince was accused of having studied geographical maps (so he must have had a considerable knowledge in this field). The **Shiji** (:Records of the Historian) has him stating his ambitions as follows: "How can I bear to face north and serve a bastard!" (Shiji, j.118, p.3085) (14). However this explanation of the inverted sequence remains "unproved" to a certain degree, even though it corresponds well to what Granet termed

---

(I) 無啓   (II) 無継   (III) 肅慎

the "emblematic thinking" of the Chinese (15).

The textual assignment of the Wuqi to the neighbourhood of the Sushen as well as the specific use of the terms "east" and "west" induce us to rearrange the inverted sequences of HNZ and SHJ. We have to place the Wuqi in the north-east, whereas the people "standing on tiptoe" (Qizhong) have to be placed somewhere north-west of China proper (16).

Having sketched the geographic difficulties raised by both sources we can interpret what they say about the Wuqi people.

HNZ mentions the Wuji (I) people as one of those inhabiting the northern realm. It gives no information beyond pure enumeration (HNZ, j.4, 5r-5v). In the SHJ, however, we find three passages that mention the Wuqi/Wuji people and follow with some information about them (brackets indicate the commentary by Guo Pu):

●*Reference A:*

無啓之國（言啓或作繁）在長股東為人無啓
（啓肥腸也其人穴居食土無男女死即薶之其
心不朽死百廿歲乃復更生）。

"The land of the **Wuqi** *(sounds qi (II), also written qi (III)) lies 'east' of the* **Changgu** *(IV) (:'Longlegs'). They are people having no qi (V) (qi means* **feichang** *(VI), 'calves of the legs'; those people live in earthholes and eat earth; without discriminating between man and woman they bury their dead immediately; their hearts do not putrefy, after having been dead for 120 years they again begin to live)." (SHJ, 8:1r)*

●*Reference B:*

又有無腸之國（為人長也）是任姓無繼子食魚
（繼亦當作啓謂膞腸也）。

"Further there is the land of the **Wuchang** *(VII) (:'Without--bellies') (they are tall people (?)); they bear the clan name* **Ren** *(VIII) and are the sons of the* **Wuji** *(IX); they live on fish (ji (X) should be written qi (XI) which means 'calves of the legs')." (SHJ, 17:4r)*

(I)無継　(II)啓　(III)繁　(IV)長股　(V)啓
(VI)肥腸　(VII)無腸　(VIII)任　(IX)無継子(X)継(XI)啓

有継無民継無民任姓無骨子（言有無骨人也尸子
曰徐偃王有筋無骨）食氣魚。

*"There is the **Jiwu** (I) people. The Jiwu people bear the clan name Ren and are the sons of the **Wugu** (II) (:'Boneless') (that means people without bones. Master Shi says: King Yan of Xu had sinews but no bones); they live on stinking (?) fish."(SHJ, 17:6v)*

Of these three references we shall deal mainly with A, taking B and C merely as additional material that confirms some points of our hypothesis. The latter are difficult to date, though they are presumably of Han times, the reason for this assumption being mainly their conformity to the efforts at rationalization and systematization of all kinds of phenomena by the Han literati. Thus the ascribed clan names of the Wuji/Jiwu reveal typical traits of rationalization and cannot really be taken as of non--Chinese origin. Besides, Yao Weiyuan in his useful study on the barbarian surnames of the northern dynasties does not list the name Ren among those he investigated (17).

Before discussing the contents of the above three references our hypothesis about the identity of the Wuqi/Wuji of SHJ and HNZ with the **Wuji** (III) of the historical sources has to be corroborated linguistically: The striking similarity in pronunciation in the modern Beijing dialect of all variant forms will have to be shown to have existed in the old pronunciations too. According to Karlgren's Grammata Serica Recensa (GSR) we get the following pronunciations:

Wuji 勿吉		$*m\underset{\smile}{i}wat\text{-}k\underset{\smile}{i}et/miu$ə$t\text{-}kiet$,	Korean mul-kil 물 길	
Wuqi 無啓		$*m\underset{\smile}{i}wo\text{-}k'i$ə$r/m\underset{\smile}{i}u\text{-}k'iei$,	Korean mu-ki 무 기	
Wuqi 無綮		" " / " "	Korean mu-kye 무 겨	
Wuqi 無啟	(18)	" " / " "	Korean " " 무 겨	
Wuji 無継		(old form / $m\underset{\smile}{i}u\text{-}kiei$, not given)	Korean " "	(19)

We find that the old pronunciations for each of the names are so close to each other that we may indeed speak of written variants of one and the same name. In other words, our hypothesis has been confirmed phonetically - in Chinese as well as in the

---

(I) 継無   (II) 無骨   (III) 勿吉

45

modern Korean forms.

What else do the references tell us? In reference A there are
statements about the geographic location where the Wuqi were to
be found, about their name, their dwellings and their food,
their burial customs, and their religious beliefs. We have already discussed their location. As neighbours of the Sushen
they must be taken as inhabitants of the north-east, their near-
ness to the Changgu does not concern us here, because it is
not at all clear whether the Changgu should be taken as mythical Longlegs or as another historical people whose name has
been transcribed into Chinese as Changgu.

In his commentary on the Wuqi name Guo Pu clearly shows that
it has not at all to be taken literally, but as a phonetic transcription of a foreign name, otherwise it would not make sense
to write it in the variant form **Wuqi** (I), this qi meaning a
sheath for spearheads, but not "calf of the leg", as **qi** (II) is
supposed to. The third qi (III) in Guo's commentary is only
given as phonetic equivalent, but it is the variant of the Wuqi
name that we find in the **Youyang zazu** (:Miscellany of Youyang
Mountain; j.4, p.44) (20). If, however, the Wuqi variants are
merely phonetic transcriptions then the sentence "weiren wuqi"
(IV) (:"they are people without calves of the legs") is a mysti-
fication and clearly a later addition to the text which logically
does not belong to it. The original SHJ text must have ended
after "zai Changgu dong" (V) (:"they live east of the Changgu"). By the way, "weiren wuqi" would be a tautology, if it is
taken as belonging to the original SHJ text.(21)

●

THE BEGINNINGS OF MYTHIFICATION

This phrase "they are people without calves of the legs" contributed to the mythification of the Wuqi. It is, by the way, un-
clear whether **qi** (VI), explained as **feichang** (VII), really
means "calves", which might be expressed as **feichang** (VIII);
but the only modern lexical reference to feichang (IX) in that
sense is to just this SHJ passage. **Fei** (X) alone means "fat"
etc., **chang** is "belly, intestines". The **Shuowen** (:Analytical Dictionary of Characters) defines qi (XI) as feichang (XII), fei
(XIII) is defined as "much meat/flesh" (XIV), chang as "great

(I)無繁　　(II)腓　　(III)啟　　(IV)為人無腓

(V)在長股東　　(VI)腓　　(VII)肥腸

(VIII)腓腸　　(IX)肥腸　　(X)肥　　(XI)腓

(XII)肥腸　　(XIII)肥　　(XIV)多肉

and small intestines"; it is not clear, why a combination of the words "fat" and "intestines" should yield the new meaning "calf of the leg" (Shuowen jiezi, pp.87 and 90).

De Mély took the Wuqi as people without intestines, basing his judgement on the **Sancai tuhui** (:Universal Encyclopaedia) (De Mély, p.366). He was not the only one who did so; obviously Guo Pu himself must have had something else in mind than "calves", because in reference B he defined qi (I) as zhuan-chang (II), of which zhuan (III) means "sliced meat" (IV) according to the Shuowen (22). Furthermore, in a rather obscure prognostication text of unknown date, the **Wanbao quanshu** (WBQS) (:Complete Treasure Book) we read of a northeastern people called **Wubi** (V), "Without-arms", the same old story of the SHJ Wuqi. It is clear that Wubi is a copyist's mistake for Wuqi, since the graphs bi (VI) and qi (VII) are easily confounded. Besides, Janšina used for her SHJ translation an edition that has Wubi instead of Wuqi; accordingly she translates these people as "bezrukie", "armless people" (23).

The above mentioned prognostication text now states that the Wubi are not only without arms, as implied by their name if taken literally, but also without bellies, **wu duchang** (VIII).

It is not of primary importance to find out whether the proper original meaning of **qi** (IX) was calf of the leg or abdomen. What is important is that a misinterpretation of a foreign "ethnonym" once made – because some commentator was not aware of its mere phonetic representation in Chinese characters – resulted in the construction of explanatory theories that do anything but explain the ethnographic facts as a little further examination shows.

The Wuqi in SHJ (j.8) are said to be reproduced in a very peculiar way from non-decaying inner organs; a kind of reproduction differing strangely from that of ordinary mankind, which requires the existence of the abdomen (24). Supposedly there was no need for the Wuqi to be provided with such a thing. Simple calculation shows that the number of Wuqi can grow, since those dying are simply replaced through reanimation. Consequently there is no mathematical need for any posterity, which moreover would contradict the laws of logic: Every Wuqi has only one heart, liver, pair of lungs etc. to generate a successor, so only one new person comes from each dead one. Logically there is thus no necessity for the Wuqi to have children (which

---

(I) 啓   (II) 膞腸   (III) 膞   (IV) 切肉

(V) 無臂   (VI) 臂   (VII) 啓   (VIII) 無肚腸

(IX) 啓

無膂國在北海
人無膓腸含土
穴居男女死即
埋之其心不朽
百年化為人厀
不朽埋之百二
十年化為人肝
不朽埋之八年
化為人
三才圖會

人物十四卷

二十

The **Wuqi**
shown here as people "without intestines" in the Sancai tuhui

for the Chinese meant, of course, sons); accordingly the Wujizi
(I) of reference B must (for Chinese) be the people "without posterity", as in HNZ they correspond to the Wuqi.

No further thought that Wuqi and Wuji were variant phonetic
representations of a foreign name. Instead, they became first in
the manuscripts people without qi and without posterity and
later without bellies and arms. Further, is it not said in Guo's
comment to SHJ 8 that "without discriminating between man and
woman they (the Wuqi) bury their dead immediately"? Commonly
sinologists take this phrase as consisting of two sentences, viz.
"wu nan nü" (II) "they do not know of the difference of man
and woman" and "si ji mai zhi" (III) "when dead, they are
buried". Could they know the sexual difference between man
and woman? Would they need to since their manner of reproduction was similar to parthenogenesis? Well, we want to show that
this particular problem is neither an ethnographic nor a mythographic one, but one of correct punctuation of the text. If we
take the above phrase as one sentence, we translate it as follows:

*"Without making any discrimination between men and women,
they are buried immediately after death" (25).*

"Wu nan nü" (II) might of course be taken as a complete sentence and could indeed mean "there are neither men nor
women"; but in any ethnographic description we would not expect a simple statement of the fact that dead persons are
buried. What we would expect, is particular information about
the way this happens, and if we take the first clause, "wu nan
nü", as belonging to the second, we have such information.
Grammatically **wu** (IV) then is treated as a preposition, corresponding to colloquial Chinese **bu lun** (V), "regardless of"; the
prepositional formula "wu (IV) x x" is quite common (26).

Finally there is another argument for the translation here offered. In comparing it with what both WS and BS say about the
burying customs of the historically confirmed Wuji (VI) in the
Manchurian woodlands, we find that the latter tell us of two
different ways of burial, differing not according to sex but according to the seasons of the year: If father or mother dies in
spring or summer, the story goes, they are buried upright, a
hut being erected over them in order to protect them from rain
and wetness. If they die in autumn or winter, however, their
corpses are used for attracting sables, which eat of their flesh,
and by this means the Wuji catch many of those animals (WS
100, p.2220; BS 94, p.3124). There was indeed no distinction

(I) 無継子   (II) 無男女   (III) 死卽薶之

(IV) 無   (V) 不論   (VI) 勿吉

49

made because of the sex of the dead and the information contained in both dynastic histories thus confirms in a more elaborate way what Guo's comment on the SHJ tells laconically about the Wuqi.

We have seen thus how the mythification of the Wuqi people began in a misinterpretation of their foreign name, how this misinterpretation seemed to find support in the very particular reanimation theory (27), and how it all ended up in mythological fancy and late Chinese fiction (28). We shall now have to examine whether the rest of the informations of the SHJ comment on the Wuqi is comparable to and compatible with what the dynastic records tell us about the Wuji.

●

ETHNO-HISTORICAL INFORMATIONS

We have already noted that Guo's comment on the Wuqi deals with a couple of supposed ethnographic traits and have discussed certain problems of geography and name, created by them. A few words have still to be said however about the latter, as well as about the statements on dwellings, food, and religious beliefs.

A. Dwellings

The SHJ assertions about the Wuqi living in earth-holes correspond to that of WS and BS (WS 100, p.2220; BS 94, p.3124). In all cases the term xueju (I) is used, which is common in Chinese descriptions of north-eastern peoples, denoting their dug--out dwellings. The description of these sunken houses in WS and BS is more detailed though. It explains that the entrance into such lodgings was on the upper part and that a ladder consisting of a notched trunk (ti (II)) had to be used to climb down.

B. Food

Concerning the food of the Wuqi there is some uncertainty about the meaning of the statement **shi tu** (III), "they eat earth". It seems to be a clear statement which would imply the practice of geophagy by the Wuqi, but it may also be linked to ideas we find in HNZ (HNZ, j.4, p.84). Here characteristics of soil, climate, growth, human character etc. are combined speculatively, and we find mankind differentiated according to what they "eat": whether water, earth, trees, herbs, leaves, meat, ether, grain or nothing at all; those who eat earth are intelligent without consciousness (lit. without a heart).

(I) 穴居　　(II) 梯　　(III) 食土

Finally one could take the phrase "shi tu" as elliptical for **"shi tu zhi mao"** (I), "to eat the plants (lit. the hairs) that grow on local soil". We prefer this possibility to others since it fits with what WS and BS say about nutrition. In them the Wuji are said to live from growing cereals and vegetables and breeding pigs and other animals and by hunting. Again the dynastic records are more detailed, but there is no definite argument why we should **not** interpret the phrase "shi tu" in an economic sense; so we can take mere coincidence between SHJ and WS in this respect as plausible. References B and C speak also of the consumption of fish, about which WS and BS are silent. Fish, however, was a common food of north-eastern tribes in all periods of history, a fact affirmed by written sources and archaeological finds alike.

C. Burial

More needs to be said about the Wuqi burials. In historical sources we read that the Wuji (II) used corpses to attract sables in winter, and the special term for burial used in SHJ seems to imply it also. Both WS and BS use the term **mai** (III), whereas SHJ has **mai** (IV), which is interchangeable with the former, but at least in Zhou times connoted burying by covering the corpses simply with grass or rushes.(29)

Although it seems dangerously near to popular etymology of Chinese characters, we want to point to the fact that the SHJ burial term, mai (IV), is composed of the radical "grass" (V) and the phonetic li (VI), adopting the pronunciation mai as a synonym for mai (III) (:"burial, to bury"). Li itself means "a small animal of unknown species, probably a wild cat" (GSR, 978 h) (30), but earlier might have denoted a sable or some similar animal. Thus the use of this particular character for burial in SHJ might be justified by the burial customs of the Wuqi people, possibly analogous to those for the historical Wuji. Catching sables must have been a rather profitable activity for the tribes of the Manchurian forests, because of the relatively great need for the furs at the Chinese court. It is very probable also that through this bartering ethnographic information about those tribes was transmitted to China. During the last few years archaeological expeditions in Manchurian territory have unearthed burial sites in which male and female persons alike were found with the same sort of grave goods. These burials are ascribed to the Xianbi by Chinese archaeologists, but it was certainly not only a Xianbi custom (31). Finally the fact that the SHJ comment speaks of an immediate burial after death (32) is parallelled by comparatively recent customs in North-

---

(I) 食土之毛　　　(II) 勿吉　　　　(III) 埋

(IV) 蘱　　(V) 艹　　(VI) 貍

-East Asia (33). To sum, the SHJ information on Wuqi burials fits well into a meaningful frame of ethno-historical data.

D. Religious Beliefs

Apart from remarks on burial customs and on the veneration of mountains, WS and BS do not make any statements about the religious beliefs of the Wuji (I). Transmitted only in non-official records like the above mentioned Youyang zazu (YYZZ) etc. the reanimation theory contained in SHJ cannot be confirmed by the histories. The still extant **Bowuzhi** (BWZ) (:Comprehensive Records of Things) (34), if really a work of **Zhang Hua** of about A.D. 290 and not a later compilation by an anonymous author as some scholars suspect (35), was probably the first to record this peculiar theory. This text could have been the literary source for Guo Pu's comment on the SHJ Wuqi, since he was a younger contemporary of Zhang. Zhang, however, must have had an even earlier source for his information, since he cannot be supposed to have done ethnographic "field work" among the north-eastern tribes.(36)

According to Taiping guangji (TPGJ) (:Miscellany of the Taiping (A.D.976-983) Period) (j.480, p.3950) the Wuqi reference of the YYZZ is identical with that of BWZ. To facilitate comparison, we give the reanimation theories in tabular form (37):

Text	part of body involved	time span for reanimation	social specifications
SHJ BWZ YYZZ	heart 心、	100 years	none
BWZ YYZZ	joints, knees 膝	120 years	men of rank 錄 民
BWZ YYZZ	liver 肝	8 years	ordinary men 細民
WBQS		10 years (38)	none
WBQS	lungs 肺	20 years	none

The assertions about the non-decaying bodily parts as well as those about the time needed for reanimation that we find in the diverse sources are not uniform, and are thus unlikely to be of Chinese origin. Obviously they represent a genuine Wuqi concep-

---

(I) 勿 吉

52

tion of the cycle of life and death, appearing in a distorted form within the Chinese sources. Lopatin for example collected Nanai folk tales in which is recounted the reanimation of the whole body by means of only one part of it (39), a process taking only days, not years. Nonetheless, such ideas are not merely of recent origin. The older Chinese sources prove that similar concepts existed already around two thousand years ago.

The Tungus conception of the soul was, still recently, tripartite, one being called **chanjan** (var. **han'a, panja, fanja**) i.e. "mirror-soul, shade-soul"; a second was **omi** (:"a child's soul"); the third **bejen** (:"body, bodily soul"). The "shade-soul" (chanjan) continues after death to exist as **omi** in order to be reanimated after having spent a certain time in **omi-ruk**, the "land of the omi-souls". Bejen, however, continues to exist in the underworld (land of stream of the dead) (40).

Paulson assumes that the separation of the soul into the "bodily soul" and the "shade-soul", which alone is reborn from the heavenly world (omi as a child's soul is "insignificant" for adults, according to Paulson), is a "secondary shift" within the Tungus conceptions of the soul, and does not represent the "original" complex (Paulson, p.251). He may be right; however, our sources indicate that as early as in the 3rd century A.D. comparable ideas were ascribed to a group of people, i.e. the Wuqi, whose historical existence we must admit in spite of all mythographic masquerade that superficial and careless Chinese commentators draped around them (41).

The process of the mythification of a historical people caused by the simple **misinterpretation of a foreign name** not only made unintelligible the ethnographic information about them, it even created a totally new species of beings, the "Armless", because of a simple error in copying the original text. Myths thus do not consist only of some original tale (the origin of which can never be reconstructed), but of all concepts derived from them, even if the latter seem to be rationalizations. It is not the Wuqi/Wuji who are the mythological original, but the distortions of their historical and social reality by commentators who did not well understand, stubbornly insisted on their preconceived ideas about those strangers, and thus – consciously or not – affirmed the cultural values of their own society.

•

PERSPECTIVES

In footnote 28 we have already pointed out that we might be able to detect similar cases of mythification within the SHJ tradition. Even the Wuqi case has not been dealt with extensively. Their story in SHJ is embedded in mythological and geographical surroundings which we did not consider within the frame of this study; in their vicinity are found one-eyed beings that also today belong to the stock of Siberian and North-East Asian mythology. As to geography there are hints that the Wuqi were neighbours of the historical Fuyu/Puyǒ (I) and had some other myths in common with them; we did not pursue all these traces that form a sound basis for a critique of Maenchen-Helfen's theory of the Indo-Iranian origin of the later SHJ chapters (Asia Maior, I/1924).

Finally we have refrained from examining at etymology as it seems problematic to compare old Chinese representations of foreign sounds with comparatively recent linguistic materials of Tungusic languages. Menges tried to do so in his "Tungusen und Ljao", arguing that "das vorliegende Žürčen-Material läßt keinerlei Schlüsse auf bedeutende sprachgeschichtliche Entwicklungsphasen zu, so daß wir auf süd-tungusischem Gebiet bis ins XV./XVI. Jh. hinein mit keinerlei größeren Unterschiedlichkeiten zum Neu-Tungusischen zu rechnen haben" (Menges, p.3), a fact which according to him substantially facilitates the analysis of old Tungus forms in Chinese phonetic transcriptions. In the case of the Wuqi/Wuji a phonetic comparison of their name with Tungus ethnonyma or clan names would have been possible, whether it also would be plausible is another question. We have to remember that the Wuji might not have belonged to Tungusic speaking groups; the old pronunciations of their name are astonishingly close to a clan name which is documented since the beginning of the 6th century A.D., it is also said to have been a clan name of either **Xiongnu** or **Xianbi** origin, and it finally is not recognizable as close to the Wuji name at first glance. The name in question would nowadays commonly be spelt wansi (II), but old compilations on clan and family names indicate an old pronunciation equivalent to either moqi (III) or moqi (IV), yielding *mək-g'i̯ər/mək-g'i̯ei and *mək-ki̯əg/mək-kji, respectively, according to GSR (42). Thus we cannot exclude that the Wuji might have been of Xiongnu or Xianbi stock, whose languages both are not very well known. To treat, much less resolve, the problems remaining here would require a whole range of interdisciplinary studies. A lot of work has still to be done.

A final question has still to be discussed: Why was it that old texts like the SHJ and HNZ have known the Wuji name at least, which disappeared from the records during the following centuries, till it reappears in the WS? One of the main reasons could have been the fact that the existence of a semi-"barbarian" state in Liaodong under the **Gongsun** clan was inhibiting direct contacts between China and north-eastern tribes, resulting in the cut-off of tributary relations, which were resumed only after the execution of **Gongsun Yuan** (V) in the period Jingchu (A.D.237-239) (Sanguozhi, Weishu, j.30, p.840).

(I) 扶餘   (II) 万俟   (III) 墨祈   (IV) 墨其   (V) 公孫淵

Unless being a permanent military threat to China's imperial authorities the "barbarians" were of interest to them mainly as tribute bringers; were such tributary relations lacking then the Chinese used to take no notice of foreign peoples. With the establishment of the Toba-Wei dynasty, itself being of northern origin, the remote Manchurian realm gained new significance, and thus reports on its inhabitants were again of interest.

●

CONCLUSION:
SOME GENERAL REFLECTIONS ON CHINESE MYTHOGRAPHY

Ancient China has known a considerable amount of mythic tales which unfortunately have been handed down to us only in fragments. Therefore it is not easy to decide which fragments originally belonged together unless we have parallel variants of which either the one or the other contains episodes that do not appear in the respective counterparts. Moreover, many of those original myths have been rationalized already in very early times by philosophers and ideologists to fit their own purposes; thus we know them only in a distorted form. But it is not only the process of rationalization of those original tales, imparting to them a certain measure of pseudo-historicity, we have to cope with; it is also the reverse process of mythification of historical events, personalities etc. For example, it has been assumed that behind the culture heroes of the myths (who invented agriculture, cooking, writing and other useful things) historical personages or social groups are hidden which cannot be traced any more. Further we know of deified and mythified war heroes, ministers and high officials, but there is one phenomenon that has not been paid the attention it deserves, i.e. **the mythification of ethnic groups** that were not integrated into Chinese society for whatever reason.

Why is it that members of foreign peoples, even whole populations are transformed into mythical beings? Let us, for instance, take the Dingling people of Siberia who in Chinese dynastic records are treated as historical but at least in later pictorial representations are furnished with mythological elements. An illustration in the Sancai tuhui encyclopedia of Ming times shows them as human beings whose physical appearance and costumes point to some Central Asian or Siberian origin - were it not for a small detail betraying their mythification: In place of human feet they are represented with the claws of a bird of prey.(The Sancai tuhui is a rich source for representations of such kind).

An analysis of this problem should reveal some insight into Chinese self-perception in contrast to non-Chinese groups also in cultural and ethnic prejudices, stereotypes of behaviour, political and social attitudes etc. The foreigner who at first glance appears to be human but by a small detail is characterized as not belonging to humanity - this "tema con variationi" resounds in all periods of China's history (though not alone in China's; in one way or another it is a problem of every society).

Another striking example for the Chinese perception of foreigners can be found in a short report on the landing of a few members of the **"Hairy People"** (**Maoren** (I), perhaps **Ainu**) on the China coast. It is handed down in a commentary to SHJ (9:4r, SBBY edition). The only survivor of the group spoke in an unintelligible idiom until he gradually learnt to speak "the language of men", i.e. Chinese of course. Having achieved that the same man confirmed that he originally had belonged to the Hairy People which simply means that he not only had learnt the Chinese language but had accepted the Chinese classification of foreign ethnic groups and of strangers like himself.

As this example shows direct cultural contact need not necessarily lead to a differentiation of national and/or ethnic stereotypes, on the contrary it may result in their consolidation.

As it seems, myths play a very important part in the formation of national or ethnic self-perception, no doubt in a dual way: Myths of ethnic origin make for the glorification of one's own descent and thus strengthen the attitude (syndrome) of "We, the humans". This kind of myth might be termed positive. De-historicizing and mythifying of foreign ethnic groups ("the others - the barbarians, the monsters, the demons") result in the same kind of self-glorification, albeit at the cost of the barbarization of foreigners. This we might call a negative myth. In that way national identity might come into being, at least be promoted.

Any analysis of myths has to consider those two aspects of shape and function, the more so as the above mentioned rationalizations of ancient myths by political thinkers may be determined by them. However, before the positive and negative myths might become fruitful for a sociological analysis of cultural and other attitudes and stereotypes there is a bunch of quasi technical problems of investigation to be solved, some of them will be mentioned here.

The structure of mythographic sources like the SHJ can be seen analogous to stratigraphic sequences in archaeology. This allows in certain cases, i.e. in short texts to be investigated, the set--up of a relative textual chronology (as shown above in the Wu-qi case). The more relative chronological data there are, the greater the probability of arriving at an absolute dating of a given textual source. Wherever possible, we will take into account all other available historical data concerning a given period or epoch to check the correctness of our mythographical find-

---

(I) 毛 人

ings. The starting point of investigations of this kind are philological and linguistic methods. They are indispensable as the
materials to be analysed are contained in textual sources, but
they must be applied critically. The data gained by such
methods are then to be analysed according to the interest of
the investigator be it sociological, historical or of any other
kind. Again in the Wuqi case we have tried to compare the seem-
ingly ahistorical mythographic statements about them with ethnographic reports about the historically confirmed Wuji, the latter
representing an ethnographically significant pattern which could
be recognized within the SHJ mythography, too, though expressed
in different words. Therefore the apparently mythical Wuqi of
SHJ could be re-historicized, so to speak. It seems as if this
were not the only case that such a procedure might be applied
successfully (cf. note 28). Like archaeological findings in the
soil the ethnographically significant patterns are covered by
the textual layers of the sources; in both cases one has to uncover them by patient spade-work. Whether the uncovering of
mythographic layers will be successful or not depends on the
particularities of every single object of investigation; in every
case analytical procedures have to be determined anew. Principally, however, it is possible to convert mythographical statements into historical data. A certain frequency of similar attempts might perhaps lead to statistical regularities which
could form the basis for new methodological approaches. This
means that not only well-documented ethnography is supplying
significant patterns, but also mythical transformation of historical facts is subject to certain patterns which are discernible.
Certainly it is a reconstructed history we thus arrive at; but
all historiography is reconstruction unless it is chronology pure
and simple.   ●

APPENDIX

● ● ●

NOTE ON ROMANIZATIONS:

Chinese: Hanyu pinyin
Korean: McCune/Reischauer
Russian: German scientific transliteration
Exception has been made for citations from secondary works in which the original tran-
scriptions have been retained.

●

LIST OF ABBREVIATIONS:

AM = Asia Maior
BS = Beishi
BWZ = Bowuzhi
GSR = Grammata Serica Recensa

HNZ = Huainanzi
SBBY = Sibu beiyao
SCC = Needham: Science and Civilisation in China
SHJ = Shanhaijing
SSTMJa = Sravnitel'nyj slovar' tunguso-man'čžurskich jazykov
TPGJ = Taiping guangji
WBQS = Tianwen dili huitu zengbu wanbao quan shu
WS = Weishu
XSSM = Zhongguo wenyan xiaoshuo shumu
YYZZ = Youyang zazu
ZWDCD = Zhongwen da cidian
ZZHY = Zhuzi huiyao

•

NOTES:

1. Cf. Guangzhi, j. shang, 11r; jade and other precious things from Fuyu are repeatedly mentioned in the same text. Chinese preference of things barbarian, among them the
roast beef of another north-eastern origin, since the Taishi reign (96-92 B.C.) was
held responsible for the later barbarian invasions of China by another text of Jin
(*) times, the Soushenji (p.57). Even in pre-Han times Chinese knew of a famous product of the north-eastern regions, i.e. the special arrowheads of the Sushen (**)
people, cf. Guoyu, j.5, p.214 sq.; also Laufer: Jade, pp.57-59.

(*) 晉   (**) 肅慎

2. Lishi yanjiu, 1974/I, p.131; Wenwu, 1976/7, pp.33 and 35, ill.4; Sovetskaja Archeo-
logija, 1959/3; a distributive map for Chinese coins in the period from the 5th to
the 3rd centuries B.C. showing two types of coins being common in the South Manchurian mountains is found in Felber: Austauschverhältnisse, p.291.

3. No attempt has yet been made in the West to elucidate the history of Fuyu and similar "states" bordering China and Korea.

4. Samguksa chŏryo, p.16 sqq., given date: 2nd year of the Jianzhao period of Han =
37 B.C.; ib., p.201, given synchronism: 41st year of King Sijo (*) of Silla = 3rd
year of King Yuri (**) of Koguryŏ = 2nd year of King Sijo (***) of Paekje = 4th year
of the Hongjia period of Former Han = 17 B.C. In this last reference the king of
Paekje states that the "cunning" Malgal were roaming "our northern boundary"; Paekje
is said to have occupied the south-western part of the Korean peninsula, extending
not far north of the present Sŏul; do the king's words imply that the Malgal occupied
the northern parts of Korea, or were they on a raid deep into Korean territory, or
did the king think of the northern Koguryŏ border as of "our Korean boundary" that
had to be defended against foreign invaders? In the 9th month of the same year a
Malgal raid into northern Paekje (ib., p.21) is recorded; are we to reconsider the
geographic situation of Paekje? There seems to be want of clearness, at least, in
these statements, but this problem is of no concern for the present paper.

(*) 始祖   (**) 瑠璃   (***) 始祖

5. Samguksa chŏryo, p.231, given date: Tang dynasty, Kaiyuan period, 22nd year = A.D.
734

6. Samguksa chŏryo, p.112, given synchronism: 7th year of King Chijŭng (*) of Silla
= 15th year of King Munja (**) of Koguryŏ = 6th year of King Muyŏng (***) of Paekje
= 3rd year of the Tianjian period of Emperor Wu of the Chinese Liang dynasty; this
seems to be the first Wuji reference in Samguksa chŏryo, unless we failed to notice

an earlier one.

(*) 智證   (**) 文咨   (***) 武寧

7. WS, j.1, p.9, also BS, j.1, Weibenji, p.6, indicating the year 317 A.D.
8. SCC, vol.III, p.488 note; see also H. Maspero: La Chine antique, rev.ed., Paris 1965, p.507 sqq. for the textual history of this work.
9. Maenchen-Helfen in AM I/1924, 550-586; E. M. Janšina, Katalog. Janšina thinks that the latest possible date for the compilation of the SHJ is the 2nd to 1st century B.C., but it might well have been compiled in the 4th to 3rd century B.C. (pp.12 and 15). Maenchen-Helfen writes that "the passages of the book treating of the outer world cannot have been created earlier than in the 5th century B.C."; cf. XSSM, p.3, dating the mountain parts of SHJ to the beginning or middle period of the Warring States, and the sea parts to Qin or early Former Han.
10. SHJ, j.8:1r; HNZ, j.4:5v; cf. the text reproduced by Maenchen-Helfen in AM I/ 1924, p.558. Crosswise mixed up are the names of the Shenmu (*) (:"Deep-eyed") and the Wuchang (**) (:"Without-bellies").

(*) 深目   (**) 無腸

11. It might as easily be explained as a copyist's mistake.
12. A graphic comparison of both lists shows a greater consistency of HNZ, as shown in the following graph:

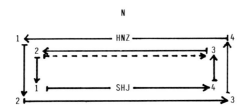

The outer arrows indicate the HNZ sequel, beginning with north-west to south-west, south-west to south-east, south-east to north-east, north-east to north-west; the inner arrows indicate the SHJ sequel: south-west to south-east, north-west to south-west, north-east to north-west (according to the introductory remark, but actually counting the opposite way, i.e. from north-west to north-east, as indicated by the dotted arrows), south-east to north-east. (The numbers 1 to 4 indicate the respective starting points of enumeration.) We might infer from this inconsistency of SHJ that its sequel as we have it today is dependent on the HNZ list especially if we consider the contradiction within the northern realm. This, however, does not necessarily mean that this part of the SHJ text is younger than HNZ. The problems of textual priority cannot be solved here, but obviously a copyist has tried to reconcile the SHJ list with that of HNZ; this will become clear in considering a directional contradiction contained in HNZ concerning the positions of "East" and "West", see the ensuing discussion.
13. Such mistakes occur frequently in SHJ, e.g. the "White People" (Baimin (*)) appear once in the West (SHJ 7:4), once in the East (SHJ 14:3); again, the Sushen themselves are placed among the peoples of the northern wilderness (SHJ 17:1), this time being localized in the north-east in the Buxian mountains (**) that are believed to be an old name for the Changbaishan (***).

(*) 白民   (**) 不咸山   (***) 長白山

14. Cf. Needham, SCC, vol.III, p.507

15. The relativity of cardinal points in ancient China has been studied by Granet: La droite..., p.269 sqq. In a bamboo slip fragment of the military classic "Sunzi" recently found in a Han tomb on the Yinque mountain we read: "In topography dong (:east) is left, xi (:west) is (right)..." (*), cf. Sunzi bingfa xinzhu, p.164; in the Zhoushu wanghuijie (**) it is said with regard to the Sushen: "Right in the north on the west side are the Jishen (another name for Sushen) with their big zhu-deer" (***), to which Kong Zhao adds a commentary: "The Jishen are the Sushen, who bring zhu-deer as tribute, which resembles a stag" (****). The mentioning of the zhu-deer is interesting, although its zoological identification is not quite clear; it is identified as either Alces machlis or A.alces, as Elaphurus davidianus or as Rangifer tarandus. The Manchu equivalent for the Chinese term is kandahan or uncehen golmin bugu, the latter denoting a stag-like animal with a long tail; cf. Cihai s.v. zhu; Cincius, SSTMJa, I, 372 s.v. kandaɣa; Han-Han-Ch'ŏng munǵam, kwŏn 14:4v, s.v. zhu; Cincius, SSTMJa, I, 325, s.v. (evenk.) irgi; in short, this animal belonging to an Alces, Rangifer, or Elaphurus species is unlikely to have existed in the desert north-west of China; but this clearly indicates that xi (:west) with regard to the Sushen is to mean "east". Relativity of cardinal points, esp. of east and west is met with Tungus peoples, observed by Širokogorov as related to the courses of rivers (reference taken from Jensen: Wettkampfparteien..., p.183 sq.); cf. Vasilevič, Èvenki, p.183; for Turkic examples cf. A. N. Kononov: Terminology of the Definition of Cardinal Points of the Turkish Peoples, ACTA ORIENT. HUNGAR., t.XXXI (1977), pp.61-76.

(*) 地刑東方為左西方為〔右〕...　(**) 周書王會解

(***) 西面者正北方稷慎大塵　(****) 稷慎肅慎也貢塵似麀

16. The contradictions in the use of geographical terms in SHJ (which might be interpreted as an unsuccessful attempt of reconciling the somewhat confused sequel of the northern realm with that of HNZ) are not definitely explained by our assumptions; an attempt to do so could form the subject of another study.

17. Beichao huxingkao; the name Ren is that of the posterity of the Yellow Emperor; ascribing it to non-Chinese peoples obviously stressed the Chinese claim of – at least – her suzerainty over all and everything under Heaven, even the barbarians in the remotest corners of the world since times immemorial.

18. This variant occurs in a passage of the YYZZ of Tang times on the Wuqi people to be discussed later.

19. The old final -t in both syllables of Wuji (*) in Chinese should not mar their compatibility with the final vowels, or the final -r respectively, of the other forms. As their corresponding Korean pronunciations show, change from Chinese final occlusiva dentalis to Korean final liquida vibrans or lateralis (r/l ㄹ) or Ø is frequent, and within Korean itself change from -t to -r/l is obligatory for the so-called t/r-bases. Thus mi̯uət-ki̯et/mul-kil is comparable to *mi̯wo-k'i̯ər/mi̯u-k'iei/mu-kye! The same change from final occlusiva dentalis to liquida is e.g. found in the case of the Mohe (**) ⁺mwât-g'ât/Kor. mal-kal (***).

(*) 勿吉　(**) 靺鞨　(***) 말갈

20. According to TPGJ j.480, p.3950, this latter variant is also that of the BWZ which is ascribed to the Jin (*) dynasty author Zhang Hua (end of 3rd. century A.D.).

(*) 晋

21. If in commenting upon the SHJ Guo Pu had found the phrase in question already incorporated into the text this would mean that the reference together with his own

60

comment consisted of three textual layers: 1. the original version, 2. the phrase in question taken as an earlier commentary confounded with the text, and 3. Guo's own comment.

22. Whereas Guo simply copies the Shuowen dictionary in defining "qi, feichang ye" (*), commentators of later centuries insisted on defining "feichang: fei dang wei fei" (**) (e.g. He Yixing in his Shanhaijing dingwei (***), p.11r, appended to the SBBY edition of the SHJ) in order to support the "calves of the legs" theory; however, it is impossible to "prove" a definite meaning of a word by declaring that its original definition is hidden behind a mistake of writing, if that is not at all the case, vide Shuowen. The same goes for the pretended equation zhuanchang (****) = zhuanchang (*****) = "calves etc.", cf. SHJ 17:4r, s.v. Wuji.

(*) 脼,肥腸也　(**) 肥腸:肥當為腓

(***) 山海經訂譌　(****) 膞腸　(*****) 腨腸

23. Janšina, p.99. Janšina's edition of the SHJ text must either have omitted the philological comment on "qi, feichang ye" (*), or she has suppressed the translation thereof, as this sentence makes absolutely no sense, if instead of the Wuqi the Wubi are talked of. She translates the rest of Guo's comment in her annotation to the reference (op.cit.p.188, note 2) correctly stating that the people in question, her "Armless", correspond to the Wujizi (**) of HNZ and SHJ 17. Nonetheless, she, too, takes the Wuji name literally and translates it as "people having no posterity" (:narod ne imejuščich potomstva); thus she is unaware of the fact that 1. the "Armless" and the people "without posterity" are not only identical because of their position within the geographical frames of both SHJ and HNZ, but because they are linguistically identical, and 2. that a mythification of ethno-historical traits and informations took place very early due to misinterpretations by Chinese commentators. We shall have to discuss this process a little later.

(*) 脼,肥腸也　(**) 無継子

24. For the moment it will not be necessary to discuss the probable origins of those reproduction theories.

25. In a special way which is expressed by the word mai (*) to be discussed later.

(*) 薶

26. As the following examples will show:

a) 無巧不巧,工皆以此五者為法.〔墨子,法義〕

"Whether skilled or unskilled, all craftsmen have to take these five (things) as a rule."

b) 百姓聞之,知与不知,無老壯,皆為垂涕.〔史記,李將軍傳〕

"When the people heard of that - whether wise or unwise - old or vigorous, they all shed tears."

c) 悉捕諸呂男女,無少長,皆斬之.〔漢書,高后傳〕

"They imprisoned all men and women of the Lü clan, regardless of their age, and killed them all."

d) 事無小大,因顯白決.〔漢書,石顯傳〕

"Regardless of how trifling or important the affairs, Xian decided all of them."
(Examples a-d are taken from Yang Shuda: Ciquan, p.403 sq.)

e) 勒兵捕諸宦者,無少長皆殺之.〔東漢會要〕

"They advanced troops to imprison all eunuchs; regardless of their age, they were all killed." (Donghan huiyao, j.24, p.266)

f) 鄉人無老少咸集奮鬭. 〔廣東新語〕

"The villagers, regardless of their age, all gathered together making strenuous efforts." (Guangdong xinyu, j.9, p.301)

These examples may suffice to show that the phrase "wu nan nü" may reasonably be interpreted as preposition to the SHJ clause about the Wuqi burial customs, not as a separate complete sentence.

27. The fact that all Chinese sources reporting this theory are somewhat contradictory in what concerns the necessary agents for reanimation, implies with all probability the non-Chinese origin of it.

28. The land of the Wuqi is one of the many fabulous countries visited by the heroes of the Qing time novel Jinghuayuan (*) by Li Ruzhen (**). The author, who takes the lacking sexual difference of the Wuqi for granted, clearly states that due to the reanimation of non-decaying corpses the number of Wuqi individuals can neither grow nor lessen. They finally cause him to speculate about the change of society and of life in general.

The Wuqi case is by far not the only one that led to mythification through misinterpretation of just a simple name. Within the southern realm of the outer world of SHJ (6:3v) we find a people qishe (***), to which corresponds the fanshe (****) in HNZ and Lüshi chunqiu. Originally the appellation fanshe simply meant people whose language was not understandable for Chinese ears, as the comment by Gao You (*****) to HNZ says - very much like the Russian "nemec" = "German" < nemet' = "to become mute"; but what finally happened to those "people with an inverted tongue" was that a comment to the Lüshi chunqiu changed them into beings whose tongues are fixed in the front part of their mouths, the loose tips pointing backwards. Probably something similar happened to the shenmu (:"Deep-eyed") of SHJ and HNZ, who appear also in the above mentioned Jinghuayuan as people who have their eyes not in their faces, but in the palms of their hands; now there is one reference to them in Wang Chong's Lunheng (j.7, p. 313), telling us that a certain Lu Ao (******) once travelled to the northern regions where he met a man with deep eyes (:shenmu) on a mountain called Menggu (*******) (should this be an early reference to the Mongol name?); obviously here an alien looking man is meant who might have belonged to some Turkic people; in the period of the Six Dynasties there are quite a lot of references to Turkic and probably also Iranian peoples who amongst other characteristics are said to have shenmu, as Eberhard reveals in the lists which he published in two articles: "Kulturtypen im alten Turkestan" and "Die Kultur der alten zentral- und westasiatischen Völker nach chinesischen Quellen", both now in Eberhard: China und seine westlichen Nachbarn. Unfortunately those regrettable peoples all vanished completely from the realm of history into that of mythology; we might wonder what in 2000 years ahead will have happened to the Long--noses of our days.

(*) 鏡花緣　(**) 李汝珍　(***) 岐舌　(****) 反舌
(*****) 高誘　(******) 盧敖　(*******) 蒙谷

29. ZWDCD 33042; cf. Qianfulun, j.3, p.154; J. J. M. de Groot: Religious System, vol. I, p.311

30. GSR 978 h; modern dictionaries give it as Nyctereutes procyonoides, "raccoon-dog, a fox-like creature which is neither raccoon nor dog" (E. H. Schafer in K. C. Chang (ed.): Food in Chinese Culture, p.100); however, its ancient identity might have been different; a Chinese-Korean-Manchu dictionary of 1777, the Han-Han-Ch'ŏng mun'gam, p. 426, takes it for a kind of wild cat of black colour (li (*), Manč. ujirhi) or with a reddish fur (chili (**), Manč. fulgiyan ujirhi). According to SSTMJa II, 250, s.v. uǯirxi even a rabbit or hare could have been understood by the Manču word.

(*) 貍　(**) 赤貍

31. Cf. the article by Su Bai in WENWU 5/1977, 42-54; sexually undifferentiated burials were common already in the neolithic Serovo culture on the Angara river; cf. L. Vajda: Untersuchungen, p.255.

32. Si ji mai zhi (*), ji (**) as an adverb can be translated as "immediately, as soon as, forthwith".

(*) 死即薶之　(**) 即

33. See the works of Lopatin, Preuß, Findeisen
34. For the time being inaccessible to the author of the present paper
35. XSSM, p.15
36. A. V. Smoljak states, without indicating his source, that the tribal name Wuji appears in Chinese sources of the 3rd century A.D., cf. his article in SOVETSKAJA ÉTNO-GRAFIJA, 1959/1, p.33.
37. BWZ according to TPGJ 480; YYZZ j.4, p.44; WBQS j.4, p.11v
38. WBQS has "gan bu wu ren shi nian hua wei ren" (*), probably "ren shi nian" (**) is an error for "ba shi nian" (***) (:80 years), as the 8 years of BWZ and YYZZ might equally be an error for 80.

(*) 肝不朽人十年化為人　　(**) 人十年

(***) 八十年

39. I. A. Lopatin: Tales from the Amur Valley, p.248
40. Cf. Friedrich's article in Mühlmann/Müller (ed.): Kulturanthropologie, pp.186-195; this article is a summary of the studies of Anisimov.
41. We do not pretend Guo Pu and his fellow literati to have been ignoramuses; but Guo's interest lay certainly not in the ethnographic field, instead, at least partly, in speculative theories on life prolongation and similar subjects. It seems to be typical for him that he finds secrets where none are to be detected; as an example we cite one of his commentaries to another SHJ reference. In j.14:1r the text says: "Shaohao zhi guo Shaohao xu di Zhuanxu yu ci" (*) (:"The land of Shaohao; Shaohao reared Emperor Zhuanxu here"), to which Guo commented that the meaning of xu (**) was not known; Yang Shen (***) (1488-1559) who appended his Shanhaijing buzhu to his SHJ edition, comments on this comment: "Xu means 'to rear, to beget' (:zhangyu (****)) and has no other meaning. As Guo is hunting for the marvellous he misses (the truth) (*****)." (SHJ buzhu, p.25, ZZHY ed.)

(*) 少昊之國少昊孺帝顓頊于此　　(**) 孺

(***) 揚慎　(****) 長育　(*****) 郭蓋以奇求之反不得耳

42. Ad wansi (*) cf. Yao Weiyuan, op.cit., p.248 and p.249 note 1. This clan name is found in BS, Beiqishu (**) and other dynastic histories.

(*) 万俟　(**) 北齊書

63

LIST OF WORKS CONSULTED:

● Beishi 北史 (:History of the Northern Dynasties), Zhonghua Shuju 中华书局 edition, Beijing 1974

● K. C. Chang (ed.): Food in Chinese Culture, New Haven, London 1977
● V. I. Cincius: Sravnitel'nyj slovar' tunguso-man'čžurskich jazykov (:Comparative Dictionary of the Tunguso-Manchurian Languages), AN SSSR, Moskva 1975-77, 2 vols.
● Ciquan 詞詮 (:Explanations of Words), by Yang Shuda 楊樹達, Beijing 1979
● Donghan huiyao 東漢會要 (:Institutes of the Eastern Han), Shanghai 1977
● W. Eberhard: China und seine westlichen Nachbarn, Darmstadt 1978
● R. Felber: Die Entwicklung der Austauschverhältnisse im alten China (Ende 8.Jh. bis Anfang 5.Jh. v.u.Z.) = Schriften zu Geschichte und Kultur des alten Orients, 10, hgg. von der Akademie der Wissenschaften der DDR, Zentralinstitut für alte Geschichte und Archäologie, Berlin 1973
● H. Findeisen: Schamanentum, Stuttgart 1957
● A. Friedrich: Das Bewußtsein eines Naturvolks von Ursprung und Haushalt des Lebens, in W.E.Mühlmann/E.W.Müller (eds.): Kulturanthropologie, Köln, Berlin 1966
● M. Granet: La droite et la gauche en Chine, in id.: Etudes sociologiques sur la Chine, Paris 1953
● J. J. M. de Groot: The Religious System of China, repr. Taibei 1976
● Guangdong xinyu 廣東新語 (:New Discourses on Guangdong), by Qu Dajun 屈大均, Hong Kong 1975
● Guangzhi 廣志 (:Extensive Records), by Guo Yigong 郭義恭, reconstr. by Ma Guohan 馬國翰 in Yuhanshan fang jiyi shu, zajia lei 玉函山房輯佚書雜家類, Taibei 1970
● Guoyu 國語 (:Discourses on the States), Shanghai 1978, 2 vols.
● Han-Han-Ch'ŏng mun'gam 韓漢清文鑑 (:Korean-Chinese-Manchu Dictionary), repr. by the Yŏnhŭi University, s.l, s.d.
● Huainanzi 淮南子 (:Book of the Master from Huainan), Zhuzi huiyao 諸子薈要 edition, Taibei 1969
● E. M. Janšina: Katalog gor i morej (Šan' Chaj Czin) (:Catalogue of the Mountains and Seas), AN SSSR, Moskva 1977
● A. Jensen: Wettkampfparteien, Zweiklassen-Systeme und geographische Orientierung, in Mühlmann/Müller (eds.): Kulturanthropologie, Köln, Berlin 1966
● B. Karlgren: Grammata Serica Recensa, repr. Stockholm 1972
● A. N. Kononov: Terminology of the Definition of Cardinal Points among the Turkish Peoples, in ACTA ORIENTALIA HUNGARICA, t.XXXI, 1977, 61-76

- B. Laufer: Jade, a Study in Chinese Archaeology and Religion, repr. New York 1974
- I. A. Lopatin 1: The Cult of the Dead among the Natives of the Amur Basin, = Central Asiatic Studies, VI, The Hague 1960
- ...2: Tales from the Amur Valley, 1933
- Lunheng jiaoshi 論衡校釋 (:Discourses Weighed in the Balance), ed. by Huang Hui 黃暉, Taibei 1964, 4 vols.

- O. Maenchen-Helfen: The Later Books of the Shan Hai King, in AM I/1924, 550-586
- de Mély: Le 'De Monstris' chinois et les bestiaires occidentaux, in REVUE ARCHEOLOGIQUE, IIIe série, t.XXXI, 1897
- K. H. Menges: Tungusen und Ljao, Wiesbaden 1968
- J. Needham: Science and Civilisation in China, vol.III, Cambridge 1959
- I. Paulson: Seelenvorstellungen und Totenglaube bei nordeurasischen Völkern, in C. A. Schmitz (ed.): Religionsethnologie, Frankfurt/M. 1964
- K. Th. Preuß: Die Begräbnisarten der Amerikaner und Nordasiaten, Königsberg 1894
- Qianfulun 潛夫論 (:Discourses of a Hidden Man), by Wang Fu 王符 Shanghai 1978
- Samguksa chŏryo 三國史節要 (:Essentials from the History of the Three States), by No Sasin 盧思慎, repr. in the Hangukhak kojŏn series 韓國學古典씨리즈, Seoul 1973
- Sanguo zhi 三國志 (:Records of the Three Kingdoms), Zhonghua Shuju ed., Beijing 1974
- Shanhaijing jianshu 山海经箋疏 (:Commented Catalogue of the Mountains and Seas), by He Yixing 郝懿行, SBBY ed.

- Shiji 史記 (:Historical Records), Zhonghua Shuju ed., Beijing 1974
- Shuowen jiezi 說文解字 (:Explanation of Characters), Zhonghua Shuju ed., Beijing 1977
- A. V. Smoljak: Nekotorye voprosy drevnej istorii narodnostej priamur'ja i primor'ja (:Some Problems of the Ancient History of the Peoples in the Amur and Coastal Provinces), in SOVETSKAJA ÉTNOGRAFIJA, 1959/I, 29-37
- Su Bai 宿白 : Dongbei, Neimenggu diqu de Xianbi yiji 東北內蒙古地區的鮮卑遺迹 (:Xianbi Relics in the Northeastern and Inner Mongolian Territories), in WENWU 文物 5/1974, 42-54
- Sunzi bingfa xinzhu 孫子兵法新注 (:New Comments on Master Sun's Military Classic), ed. by the Military Academy of the People's Liberation Army, Beijing 1977
- Taiping guangji 太平廣記 (:Extensive Records of the Taiping Reign),

Zhonghua Shuju ed., Beijing 1981
- Tianwen dili huitu zengbu wanbao quanshu 天文地理绘图增補万宝全书 (:Astronomical, Geographical, Illustrated Enlarged Complete Book of Treasures), ed. by Lin Youlai 林有来 , Xinzhu 1965

- G. M. Vasilevič: Évenki, istoriko-étnografičeskie očerki (XVIII-načalo XX v.) (:The Evenks, Ethno-Historical Sketches from the 18th to the Beginning of the 20th Century), AN SSSR, Leningrad 1969
- L. Vajda: Untersuchungen zur Geschichte der Hirtenkulturen, (= Veröff. des Osteuropainstituts, München), Wiesbaden 1968
- Weishu 魏書 (:History of the Toba-Wei Dynasty), Zhonghua Shuju ed., Beijing 1974
- Xinjiao Soushenji 新校搜神記 (:Newly Edited Reports on Spiritual Manifestations), Shijie wenku 世界文庫 series, Taibei 1970
- Yao Weiyuan 姚薇元 : Beichao Huxing kao 北朝胡姓考 (:Analysis of the Clan Names of the Northern Barbarians of the Northern Dynasties), Beijing 1962
- Youyang zazu 酉陽雜俎 (:Youyang Miscellany), Zhonghua Shuju ed., Beijing 1981
- Zhongguo wenyan xiaoshuo shumu 中國文言小説書目 (:Catalogue of Classical Chinese Novels), ed. by Yuan Xingpei 袁行霈 , Beijing 1981

Another example of a people with curious body markings:
the people "with a hole in the chest"
(according to the Sancai tuhui)

ON THE LEGENDS
OF THE YELLOW SOVEREIGN
BY MITARAI MASARU

Translated from Japanese by Ilse Lenz and Derek Herforth

The Yellow Sovereign, known also as the Yellow Emperor, since the first century B.C. has been considered the founder of Chinese Empire and civilization. He was also identified with the god: the Sovereign of the Centre, i.e. the highest deity. Moreover, he was regarded as an ancestor of other sage-rulers, of the Chinese and of many other tribes. Even for modern nationalists he was the most revered person. Mitarai Masaru analyses in his study ancient materials related to this personage and modern scholarly discussions about him, particularly the concepts advocated by Gu Jiegang's school. The author accepts the basic assumptions of this school that mythological sage-rulers are historicized local or clan deities. He finds doubtful, however, the idea that this sovereign was merely a fictional personage added in the late antiquity to the evolving state-genealogy, a personage promoted predominantly by the Daoists. The author raises many particular doubts about the commonly accepted interpretations and shows how intricate was the creation of the Yellow Sovereign myth, and how many various corresponding elements were combined together in this process. In his opinion the Yellow Sovereign was not originally identified with the Celestial Emperor. Only during the late stage of the evolution of this myth does he become the Sovereign of the Centre. This late form has no direct connections with his original role as the tutelary deity of an eastern clan. The author accepts the hypothesis that the Yellow Sovereign was previously imagined as a dragon and he proves that it was the reason for his latter connections with Heaven (and clouds) and Earth. The author analyses also the origins and meanings of the various names of this sovereign, and his close relations with animals. The author concludes that this sovereign was originally a water deity, related to the Zhou clan, and worshipped in the Shandong-Jiangsu area. The second part of this study, containing these conclusions, will be published in the next issue of EAC.

1. A CRITIQUE OF YANG KUAN'S IDENTIFICATION OF THE YELLOW SOVEREIGN (Huangdi (I)) WITH THE CELESTIAL SOVEREIGN (huangdi (II))

Historiographical criticism of the ancient mythological traditions of China was begun in the modern era in a brilliant manner by the **sceptical school of historiography (Yigu xuepai (III))** centered around **Gu Jiegang. Yang Kuan** wrote his study **Zhongguo shanggushi daolun** (: Prolegomenon to the Ancient History of China) with the purpose of correcting some of the excessively sceptical views of this school. Calling his research "**The** Interpretation of Antiquity", Yang proposed the establishment of a "**school of interpreting antiquity**" and attempted to bring some measure of order to the chaotic picture presented by the legends of ancient China.

According to Yang Kuan, the Yellow Sovereign (**Huangdi** (I)), mentioned at the top of the list of the Five Sovereigns (Wudi (IV)), derives ultimately from the Celestial Sovereign (**huangdi** (II), identical with God in High, **Shangdi** (V), the highest god in China). This hypothesis appears to have become very influential over the years. In spite of the extreme confusion – absurdity, even – of the traditions concerning the Yellow Sovereign, his derivation from the Celestial Sovereign is, for Yang, founded on evidence from the textual corpus of early Chinese thought. But are Yang Kuan's evidence and arguments reliable enough to justify his conclusion?

The first evidence Yang presents for his conclusion is the fact that the characters at the beginning of the names of both sovereigns have the same pronunciation, "**huang**", and that they were used interchangeably. Yang quotes the following examples:

1. Whereas one finds the Yellow Sovereign (Huangdi) in the **Yijing**, chapter **Xi Ci Zhuan** (:Book of Changes, ch. Explanations of Prognoses), in the quotation of the Xi Ci Zhuan in the later **Fengsu tongyi**, ch. **Sheng Yin** (:Popular Traditions and Customs, ch. Tones) the expression **huangdi** (:Celestial Sovereign) is used.

2. In the chapter Sandai Gaizhi Zhiwen (:Description of the Changes in the Administrative Systems of the Three Dynasties) in the Chunqiu fanlu (:A String of Pearls on the Spring and Autumn Annals) one finds the phrase: "They changed the title of xuanyuan and made him huangdi"; thus "Yellow Sovereign" obviously occurs in texts as **huangdi**.

(I) 黃帝   (II) 皇帝   (III) 疑古學派
(IV) 五帝   (V) 上帝

3. The Yellow Sovereign in the chapter Gui Gong (:Honourable Princes) of the Lüshi chunqiu (:Master Lü's Spring and Autumn Annals) appears as **huangdi** in the Ming dynasty Long-ruchong (I) edition.

Such are Yang Kuan's illustrations of the interchangeable use of the two characters **Huang A** (II) and **huang B** (III). The quotation Yang mentioned from the Xi Ci Zhuan, however cannot be found in the Fengsu tongyi, ch. Sheng Yin. On the other hand, we find a statement there, that huangdi commanded **Ling Lun** (IV) to bring bamboo from Xie Valley. The same legend can be found in the chapter Gu Yue (:Ancient Music) of the Lüshi chunqiu and there it is the Yellow Sovereign who is mentioned as author of the command. In the chapter Shi Xing (:Clans) of the Fengsu tongyi one finds the statement: "**Leng Shi** was vassal of the Yellow Sovereign and descendant of **Shun**'s Music Codifier, Ling Lun (IV)." Thus one can clearly see that huangdi in this case is identical with the Yellow Sovereign. Consequently, Yang's statement about the citation from the Xi Ci Zhuan in the Fengsu tongyi, ch. Sheng Yin, can be explained as an inadvertent misquotation. Here, in place of Yang's first example, we will record the fact that the huangdi in the legend about Ling Lun appears as the Yellow Sovereign in some textual traditions.

As Yang wants to trace the origin of the Yellow Sovereign back to huangdi, his argumentation here is a natural first step in that direction; he certainly has established the fact that the terms Celestial Sovereign (huangdi) and Yellow Sovereign (Huang-di) were used interchangeably. But his examples do not amount to positive proof that the origin of the Yellow Sovereign lies, in fact, in huangdi. If one refers, for instance, to the Fengsu tongyi as in Yang's first example, among the 24 passages in which the Yellow Sovereign appears, we find only the one instance mentioned above of the use of "huangdi" in a context where one would expect the Yellow Sovereign. This by no means indicates that **Ying Shao** (V), author of the Fengsu tongyi, thought that these two legendary figures had a common origin.

Items of textual evidence **2** and **3** presented by Yang involve similar difficulties. Here I will refer only to instance **2**. The Yellow Sovereign appears three times in the chapter cited, the Sandai Gaizhi Zhiwen; Yang's example concerns the second occurrence. Now, on the very first reading of this chapter one should notice that the author depicts the Yellow Sovereign as a sovereign of men (**Rendi** (VI)) who formerly reigned over the earth in the same way as the latter-day emperors.

(I) 龍 如 寵　(II) 黃　(III) 皇　(IV) 伶 倫

(V) 應 劭　(VI) 人帝

The Yellow Sovereign is clearly not described here in terms reminiscent of God in High (Shangdi). Therefore, it seems most reasonable to conclude that the appearance of huangdi in this chapter is no more than an inadvertent "misspelling" of Huangdi, based on the homophonous pronunciations of huang and Huang. In short, one cannot say that people who have graphically or phonetically identical names will always have been originally the same persons; Yang's arguments show only that "huang B" and "Huang A" were used interchangeably, but they have no conclusive significance whatever concerning the ultimate origin of the Yellow Sovereign.

Yang next refers to the chapter **Lü Xing** (:Lü's Punishments) of the **Shangshu** (:Book of Documents):

"According to the teachings of ancient times **Chi You** was the first to produce disorder which spread among the common people, till all became robbers and murderers, owl-like in their conduct, traitors and villains, snatching and filching, dissemblers and oppressors. Among the people of **Miao**, they did not use the power of the good, but the restraint of punishments (...) They slaughtered the innocent (...) The mass of the people were gradually affected by this state of things and became dark and disorderly. Their hearts were no more set on good faith, but they violated their oaths and covenants. The multitudes who suffered from the oppressive terrors and were (in danger of) being murdered, declared their innocence to Heaven (or God). God (Shangdi) surveyed the people (...). The supreme Emperor (huangdi) compassioned the innocent people who were (in danger of being) murdered, and made the oppressors feel the terrors of his majesty. He restrained and finally extinguished the people of Miao, so that they should not continue to further generations." (tr. Legge, vol.3, pp.591-593, mod.)

Citing this legend in which huangdi plays a central role, Yang then assumes that it forms the source for the famous legend of the subjection of Chi You (1) by the Yellow Sovereign. He considers this evidence as clearly demonstrating the identity of the Yellow Sovereign with huangdi.

As Yang points out, the Yellow Sovereign's subjugation of Chi You is recorded in Zhuangzi, ch. Dao Zhi (:Zhuangzi, ch. Robber Zhi), Shanhaijing, ch. Dahuangdong Jing (:Canon of the Mountains and Seas, ch. Description of the Great Eastern Desert), **Zhanguo Ce**, ch. Qin Ce (:Intrigues of the Warring States, ch. Intrigues of Qin), **Dadaili** (:Norms Compiled by the Elder Dai) and Wudide (:Virtues of the Five Sovereigns). But I think that, on the basis of the close connection between the Yellow Sovereign and Chi You, one can propose an interpretation of the Lü Xing which differs from Yang's.

The subjugation of the Miao people which in the chapter **Shun Dian** (:Canon of Shun) of the Shangshu and in the chapter Chu

─────────

(1) 蚩尤

70

人文初祖殿

The Palace of the Yellow Emperor

M C 3　(3-2)

极限明信片

Maximum Card

轩辕柏

The Cypress Planted by the

Yellow Emperor

M C 3　(3-3)

极限明信片

Maximum Card

*Two examples from a series of postcards,
published by the People's Republic of China,
related to places connected with the Yellow Sovereign*

Yu (:Accounts of Chu) of the Guoyu (:Accounts of the States) is credited to **Yao** (I) and **Shun** (II) is attributed to the highest god huangdi, identical with "God in High" (Shangdi), in the Lü Xing. Likewise, in the Guoyu, ch. Chu Yu the actions of **Zhong Li** (III) who is said to have severed "the way between Heaven and Earth" are described as motivated by **Zhuan Xu's** (IV) commands. The Lü Xing, on the other hand, states clearly that not only was Zhong Li following orders from huangdi, but also that the actions on earth of the three princes (**Bo Yi** (V), **Yu** (VI), **Ji** (VII)) (1), who in the Shun Dian appear as faithful servants of Shun, are likewise prompted by huangdi's decrees. The Lü Xing can thus be seen as coordinating under the central theme of a pre-eminent deity, viz. huangdi, several earlier traditions concerning the motivation of the deeds of sage emperors and heroes. This interpretation then allows us to view the incident about huangdi's wrath toward Chi You in the Lü Xing as having supplanted the more original account of the antagonism between the Yellow Sovereign and Chi You.

If one follows this interpretation in considering the Lü Xing account of huangdi and Chi You, it appears that basic elements of the then-current legend about the Yellow Sovereign and Chi You were appropriated and woven into the text, huangdi appearing in place of the Yellow Sovereign. For this reason, it is anachronistic to attempt to trace the legend of the Yellow Sovereign and Chi You back to the legend of huangdi and Chi You in the Lü Xing; hence the account in the Lü Xing cannot be cited as conclusive evidence for the identity of huangdi and the Yellow Sovereign.

Yang's third argument for the identity of these two figures is that, according to the Shanhaijing, the Yellow Sovereign resides in the **Kun Lun** (VIII) mountain and that Kun Lun was "the lower capital of the Sovereign", viz. the castle town of the Celestial Sovereign (**Tiandi** (IX)). Therefore, according to Yang, the Yellow Sovereign is none other than the Celestial Sovereign. But in the chapter **Wuzangshan Jing** (:The Canon of Mountains of the Five Stores (i.e. the cardinal directions and the centre)) which is considered the earliest part of the Shanhaijing, it is clearly stated that Kun Lun, a holy mountain serving as "lower capital of the Celestial Sovereign", was administered by the god **Lu Wu** (X) and that Mountain **Mi** (XI) was the residence of the Yellow Sovereign. Consequently, while Kun Lun was literally the lower capital of the supreme Sovereign (Shangdi (XII)), it was not the residence of the Yellow Sovereign. On the contrary, the

---

(I) 堯　　(II) 舜　　(III) 重黎　(IV) 顓頊　　(V) 伯夷

(VI) 禹　　(VII) 稷　　(VIII) 崑崙　　(IX) 天帝

(X) 陸吾　　(XI) 峚山　　(XII) 上帝

Yellow Sovereign as described in the Shanhaijing should be understood as merely one of a host of sovereigns (**Zhongdi** (I)) under the rule of the Supreme Sovereign. In this sense one can say that the Yellow Sovereign in the Wuzangshan Jing is not essentially different from the Yellow Sovereign in the writings of **Zou Yan** (II) where he is depicted as under the cyclical control of the five virtues, i.e. the heavenly mandate. Furthermore, as the Yellow Sovereign, according to the Wuzangshan Jing, did not reside in Kun Lun, it is doubtful whither the introduction of Kunlun as "the lower capital of the (Celestial) Sovereign" is pertinent to a consideration of the original character of the Yellow Sovereign.

Furthermore, on the assumption that the nature of the Yellow Sovereign's residence is of help in understanding his character, one should probably attach more importance to **Zhuo Lu** (III) than to Kun Lun. The former is unambiguously identified as the Yellow Sovereign's capital, both in the genealogy of sovereigns preserved in the Dadaili and in the chapter **Wudi Benji** (:Basic Annals of the Five Sovereigns) in the **Shiji** (:Records of the Historian). To be sure, the chapters Zhi Le (:Perfect Happiness) and Tian Di (:Heaven and Earth) of Zhuangzi and the Mu tianzi zhuan (:Account of the Travels of Emperor Mu) etc., mention that the residence of the Yellow Sovereign was located on Kun Lun mountain, but in the period of the Warring States, Kun Lun was believed to be the place of communication between Heaven and Earth. Furthermore, it was during this period that the status of the Yellow Sovereign appears to have risen considerably and as there was even a tradition of the Yellow Sovereign's ascension to heaven (cf. **Shiji**, ch. **Feng Shan Shu** (:Records of the Historian, ch. Description of Sacrifices)), his residence may well have been "upgraded" to a place in the holy Kun Lun mountain, the highest point on earth, as related above (cf. the author's essay: The Kun Lun Legend and Myth of the Eternal Return, in appendix to: The Deities of Early China – Studies in Archaic Legends).

Lastly, Yang refers to the Lüshi chunqiu, ch. Shieryue Ji (:Master Lü's Spring and Autumn Annals, ch. Records of the Twelve Months), the **Liji**, ch. **Yue Ling** (:Record of Norms, ch. Monthly Dispositions), and Huainanzi, ch. Shi Ze Xun (:The Book of the Prince Huai Nan, ch. Precepts on Principles of Time). There, according to Yang, the Yellow Sovereign appears as the Sovereign of the Centre, with the Prince of the Earth (**Houtu** (IV)) as his auxiliary deity, and when both are listed together, there is a strong connotation of "the Supreme Heaven and the Prince of the Earth" (**Huangtian Houtu** (V)). Yang takes this as evidence that

(I) 眾帝　(II) 鄒衍　(III) 涿鹿　(IV) 后土

(V) 皇天后土

the Yellow Sovereign is "the Supreme Sovereign of Heaven and God in High" (**Huangtian Shangdi** (I)).

However, according to the Zuozhuan (:The Zuo Commentary), Duke Zhao, year 29, the deity Houtu is identified as **Gou Long** (II). The coupling, noted by Yang, of Houtu, an earth deity, together with the Yellow Emperor is not fortuitous. In the cosmology which arose after Zou Yan, the Yellow Sovereign was considered the ruler of the Earth Virtue. Consequently, one will not discover a pairing of Supreme Heaven with the Prince of the Earth in the text of the Yue Ling.

To be sure, Zheng Xuan (III) identifies Houtu, the Prince of the Earth, not with Gou Long, but with **Li** (IV) (cf. commentary to Liji, ch. Yue Ling). This is because **Zhong Li** (V), due to his original character as a sun god, had become the hero of the legend of the division of heaven from earth and moreover, he subsequently appears as two deities, namely **Zhong** (VI) and **Li** (IV). While Zhong came to be called "the Superintendent of Heaven" (**sitian** (VII)), Li in turn was known as "the Superintendent of the Earth" (**sidi** (VIII)) (cf. Guoyu, ch. Zheng Yu). Thus, even if we follow Zheng's identification of Houtu with Li, we see the shortcomings of Yang's reading of the Lüshi chunqiu passage in which he treats Huangdi and Houtu as antipodal deities, associating Huangdi with Heaven, i.e. identifying him as the Celestial Sovereign.

The fact that the Yellow Sovereign is described in some texts as the Sovereign of the Centre would seem to represent a later stage in the history of the traditions surrounding this figure, viz., when he came to be regarded as the highest deity among the Five Sovereigns. This development was influenced by the theory of the **Five Phases** (**wuxing** (IX)).

Furthermore, the later Yellow Sovereign as Sovereign of the Centre apparently has no connection with his original role as the tutelary deity of an eastern clan, to be discussed below.

2. THE DIVINE FORM OF THE YELLOW SOVEREIGN

In the foregoing section it was shown that Yang Kuan had noticed the apparant interchangeability in some texts of the names "Yellow Sovereign" and "huangdi" and attempted by isolating elements pointing to huangdi in the Yellow Sovereign's character to prove that the Yellow Sovereign derived from huangdi. His attempt to uncover conclusive evidence for his hypothesis,

(I) 皇天上帝　　(II) 句龍　　(III) 鄭玄　　(IV) 黎
(V) 重黎　(VI) 重　(VII) 司天　(VIII) 司地　(IX) 五行

however, failed. So, we are left with the question he attempted to answer: What was the original nature of Huangdi?

Sima Qian relates in his Shiji, ch. Wudi Benji (:Records of the Historian, ch. Basic Annals of the Five Sovereigns) that scholars have long maintained the Five Sovereigns existed in the past, but that the Shangshu accounts only go back as far as Yao and Shun. He states moreover that the passages concerning the Yellow Sovereign in the Philosophers of the Hundred Schools were vulgar and that scholars generally eschewed them. Thus he took the Wudide (:Virtues of the Five Sovereigns) and the Dixixing (:The Genealogy of the Sovereigns) as his sources for the Wudi Benji. Consequently it is only natural that the Yellow Sovereign appears in the Wudi Benji as a figure combining the character of a general with the virtues of a sage. But the Wudide which Sima Qian used contains imaginative passages not cited in the Wudi Benji, e.g. "The Yellow Sovereign, in his imperial embroidered robe with a great cincture and embroidered skirt, rode a dragon with the clouds like a screen at his back." Here one finds a "vulgar" tradition that the Yellow Sovereign travelled through the clouds on a dragon.

In the description of the fight between the Yellow Sovereign and Chi You in the Shanhaijing, ch. Dahuangbei Jing (:Canon of the Mountains and Seas, ch. Canon of the Northern Deserts) we find the passage:

"The Yellow Sovereign commanded the winged dragon to attack him (i.e. Chi You) in the plain of Jizhou. The winged dragon mustered the waters. Chi You requested (help from) the Senior of the wind and the Master of the rain who released a great tempest."

Thus we learn that a winged dragon was allied to the Yellow Sovereign. The **Huainanzi**, ch. **Tian Wen Xun** (:The Book of the Prince Huai Nan, ch. Precepts on Astronomy) states:

"(The phase of) the centre is earth. Its ruler is the Yellow Sovereign. His assistant is the Prince of the Earth (Houtu) (...) Its animal is the Yellow Dragon."

and in the Shiji, ch. Feng Shan Shu (:Records of the Historian, ch. Description of Sacrifices) we find:

"The Yellow Sovereign was the recipient of the earth virtue. A yellow dragon and earthworms (**diyin** (I)) appeared."

Obviously, there was a deep connection between the Yellow Sovereign and dragons. In the Lüshi chunqiu, ch. Ying Tong (:Master Lü's Spring and Autumn Annals, ch. Responding to Identities) the following passage appears:

(I) 地 螾

"Whenever a sovereign king is about to arise, Heaven shows omens to the people. At the time of the Yellow Sovereign, Heaven in advance (of his accesssion) made big earthworms (**dayin** (I) and **dalou** (II)) appear."

The yellow dragon does not appear in this account. On the other hand, in the dictionary **Shuowen jiezi** (:Explanations of Simplex Graphs and Analyses of Compound Characters) we find the word **chi** (III) defined as:

"similar to a dragon, but yellow. In the north it is called **dilou** (IV)."

The dalou (II) mentioned in the chapter Ying Tong may possibly stand for dilou (IV), a northern dialect word referring to a dragon-like creature.

Tang Lan reviewed the theories of several scholars on this point and hypothesized that the yin (second character of notes (I) of this page and preceding page) mentioned in the Feng Shan Shu and the Ying Tong refers not to the earthworm, but to a dragon-like creature. (Tang Lan, p. 41a) If we accept this explanation, the contradictions between the Feng Shan Shu and Ying Tong accounts are practically resolved.

Though Sima Qian, in compiling the Wudi Benji emphasized the importance of eschewing "vulgar" sources, we find in the Feng Shan Shu passages like the following in which he seems to have quoted popular traditions almost verbatim, perhaps with a view to pointing up their absurdity.

"The Yellow Sovereign gathered copper at Shou Mountain and cast a tripod at the foot of Jing Mountain. When the tripod was ready a dragon with dangling whiskers appeared and came down to where the Yellow Sovereign was. The Yellow Sovereign climbed up and mounted the dragon. More than seventy officials and inmates of the Sovereign's private apartments followed him. When the dragon started to fly away the remaining lower officials were unable to climb up, so they held on to the dragon's whiskers which came out, dumping them back onto the ground. The Yellow Sovereign's bow was dropped."

It is clear from this episode that the Yellow Sovereign was believed to have mounted a dragon and ridden up into the sky.

Further textual evidence for the close connection between the Yellow Sovereign and dragons can be cited, viz. "Long ago the Yellow Sovereign drove a chariot of ivory drawn by water--dragons." (Fengsu tongyi, ch. Sheng Yin). The "dragon-like" face of the Yellow Sovereign is mentioned both in the chapter Sheng Ren (:Sages) of the same work and in the Qianfulun, ch. Wu De Zhi (:Discourses of a Recluse, ch. Monograph on the Five Phases). In the course of her analysis of the images of Poseidon, Jane Ellen Harrison has stated: "The animal on which a

---

(I) 大 螾　　(II) 大 螻　　(III) 螭　　(IV) 地 螻

The "Snake People",
the inhabitants of
the Land of Xuanyuan

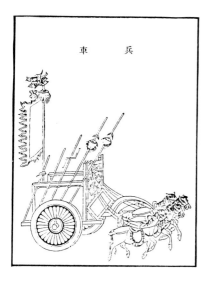

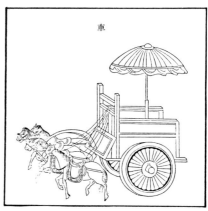

Two examples of an ancient Chinese chariot (cf. p.87)

god stands or rides or whose head he wears is, it is now accepted, the primitive animal form of the god." (Harrison, p.21) If this principle is valid, then an attempt to elucidate the nature of the Yellow Emperor through his connection with dragons may be well worthwile.

In many ancient sources the Yellow Emperor is described just like a human being. For example, in the Wudi Benji we find him depicted in the following way:

"The Yellow Sovereign was the son of **Shao Dian** (I). His surname (xing (II)) was **Gongsun** (III) and his name (ming (IV)) **Xuanyuan** (V). He was a person with superhuman inborn talents: Though still a small baby he was able to speak, as a youth he was robust and sharp, in his adolescence he grew to be both liberal and quick-witted and when he had grown up, he was perceptive and astute."

In some cases, however, the description differs. For example, in the Shanhaijing., ch. Haiwaixi Jing (:Canon of the Mountains and Seas, ch. The Canon of the Western Lands beyond the Sea) we read:

"Xuanyuan's state is located at the edge of Mt. Qiong. The shortest-lived inhabitants have life-spans of eight hundred years. The state is found to the north of the land of woman. Its inhabitants have human faces and serpentine bodies with their tails joined to the top of their heads."

Likewise, as if in correspondence to this tradition, the Shiji, ch. Tian Guan Shu (:Records of the Historian, ch. Description of the Celestial Stations) states:

"The stars **Quan** (VI) belong to the Xuanyuan-constellation, which has the shape of the Yellow Dragon's body."

Quan, that is to say the constellation **Xuanyuan**, is composed of 17 stars. They are located in the Southern Mansion (**nangong** (VII)). According to popular belief, the spirit of the Xuanyuan constellation governs thunder and rain (cf. Jinshu, ch. Tian Wen Zhi (:History of Jin, ch. Treatise on Astronomy)).

Putting aside temporarily for later consideration the question of why the word Xuanyuan is so often connected with snake-like creatures, the author can express his agreement with Wen Yiduo's conclusion, based on citations above, that the Yellow Sovereign was originally a dragon. However, in the Zuozhuan, Duke Zhao, year 17, there is a passage which seems to confound this theory:

(I) 少典　　(II)姓　　(III)公孫　　(IV)名

(V)軒轅　　(VI)權　　(VII)南宮

"When the Viscount of Tan came to the court, the Duke (of Lu) feasted with him and Zhaozi asked what was the reason that **Shao Hao** named his officials after birds. The Viscount replied: 'He was my ancestor and I know (all about) it. In antiquity the Yellow Emperor came to rule with (the omen of) a cloud and therefore he had cloud officers, naming them after clouds. **Yan Di** came to (the rule) with (the omen of) fire and therefore he had fire officers, naming them after fire. **Gong Gong** came to (the rule) with (the omen of) water and therefore he had water officers, naming them after water. **Tai Hao** came to (the rule) with (the omen of) a dragon and therefore he had dragon officers, naming them after dragons. When my ancestor **Shao Hao** succeeded to the throne, there appeared a phoenix and therefore he arranged his government under the nomenclature of birds, making bird officers and naming them after birds.'" (tr. Legge, p.667, mod.)

According to the explanation given by Tanzi, a descendant of Shao Hao (I) of Tancheng (in present province Shandong), a special association existed between the **Yellow Sovereign** and **clouds**, between **Yan Di (II)** and **fire**, **Gong Gong (III)** and **water**, **Tai Hao (IV)** and **dragons**, **Shao Hao** and **birds**. Tanzi expresses these associations in a traditional way by relating the individual ruler to the natural phenomenon which characterized the beginning of his reign. Let us consider these statements one by one in an analysis of the ancient images of these ancestor-gods.

To begin with, the reason that Gong Gong "came to the rule with water" was that as a deity he was conceived of as a snake. In both Gao You's commentary to the Huainanzi, ch. Zhui Xing Xun (:The Book of the Prince Huai Nan, ch. Precepts on Geomorphs) and in Guo Pu's commentary to Shanhaijing, ch. Dahuangxi Jing (:Canon of the Mountains and Seas, ch. Canon of the Western Deserts), Gong Gong is described as having "a human face and a snake-like body". In Zuozhuan, Duke Zhao, year 29, Gong Gong's child is called "Crooked Dragon" (Gou Long (V)). In the Shanhaijing, ch. Haiwaibei Jing (:Canon of the Mountains and Seas, ch. Canon of the Northern Territories beyond the Sea), it is noted that Gong Gong's official, Xiang Liu (VI), has "nine heads with human faces and a snake-like body". These descriptions seem strongly to suggest that Gong Gong was imagined as a snake-like being and it is hardly surprising to find this orphioform deity closely associated with water. However, on the basis of the single statement about Gong Gong in the passage from the Zuozhuan cited above, one could scarcely arrive at a conception of this figure as a snake deity. This is because in the account given by the Viscount of Tan the archaic myths already show a high degree of the rationalization. Consequently, one should not conclude that the divine form of the Yellow Sovereign who reportedly "came to the rule with a

(I) 少皞　(II) 炎帝　(III) 共工　(IV) 大皞
(V) 句龍　(VI) 相柳

79

cloud" was literally a cloud. This may be demonstrated by the analogous example of Shao Hao's relationship to birds.

Yang Kuan previously demonstrated that **Hao Yao** (I), **Xu You** (II) and **Bo Yi A** (III), are all derived from one god and the research of Katō Jōken confirmed that Bo Yi A (III), **Bo Yi B** (IV), **Bo Yi C** (V) and **Shao Hao** (VI) are one and the same deity (Yang Kuan, vol.7, pp.345-352; Katō Jōken, pp.488-549). Therefore, there is preserved a common tradition that Bo Yi B and Bo Yi C became ministers of the ecology (**yuguan** (VII)) to Sovereign **Shun** (see Shangshu, ch. Shun Dian; Guoyu, ch. Zheng Yu (:Accounts of the States, ch. Accounts of Zheng)). Likewise according to the Shiji, ch. Qin Benji (:Records of the Historian, ch. Basic Records of the Qin Dynasty), the deity of the **Ying** (VIII) clan, Bo Yi C, was "assisted Shun by training and domesticating the birds and beasts." His son **Da Lian** (IX) was also called **Niao Sushi** (X), i.e. the Lord Raiser of Birds. His grandchildren **Meng Xi** (XI) and **Zhong Yan** (XII) were reportedly freaks "with birds' bodies and men's speech."

As **Fu Sinian** has pointed out, these facts correspond to the passage from Zuozhuan quoted above, where Shao Hao, ancestral deity of the Ying clan, is said to have "named his officials after birds" (Fu Sinian, vol.4, p.77).

Moreover, as **Katō Jōken** showed for the first time, the reason Bo Yi C became Shun's minister of the ecology and had a very close affiliation to birds such that his divine form was that of a bird, is surely that Bo Yi C (i.e. Shao Hao) was together with Yun Ge (XIII) deity of the marshes of the Yun River where a multitude of birds and beasts lived.(2)

Thus, it would seem that Shao Hao was essentially a deity of the marshes, though he appears in later legends as the master of birds. Similarly, one may interpret the legend told by the Viscount of Tan that the Yellow Sovereign "came (to the rule) with a cloud", to mean that, though his nature or divine form may have had some connection with clouds, one need not assume that he himself was a cloud. Such analyses help us better to understand the divergent accounts contained in the ancient sources. At the same time, we must also attempt to answer the question why the Yellow Sovereign was so closely associated with clouds.

For example, in the Wenyanzhuan (:Explanations to the Scrip-

(I) 皋陶　(II) 許由　(III) 伯夷　(IV) 伯益
(V) 柏翳　(VI) 少皋　(VII) 虞官　(VIII) 嬴　(IX) 大廉
(X) 鳥俗氏　(XI) 孟戲　(XII) 仲衍　(XIII) 允格

tures) of the Yijing, Qian Gua 95 (:Book of Changes, Explanations of the Qian Hexagram, 95) it is noted that "clouds follow dragons". And Zhuangzi, ch. Tian Yun (:The Book of the Master Zhuang, ch. The Turning of Heaven) states: "The dragons ...riding on the pneuma of clouds (yunqi (I)) are nourished by Yin and Yang." Likewise one finds the following discussion in the Lunheng, ch. Long Xu (:Discourses Weighted in Balance, ch. Falsehoods about Dragons):

"Living in deep water dragons belong to the same category as fish and reptiles (...) The common belief that the dragon is a spirit, and rises to Heaven, is preposterous (...) As a matter of fact, the thunder and the dragon are of the same kind, and mutually attract one another when set in motion by the forces of nature. The Yijing says that the clouds follow the dragon, and the wind the tiger. It is further stated that, when the tiger howls, the wind passes through the valley, and that the variegated clouds rise, when the dragon gambols (Yijing, Qian Gua). There is a certain manner of sympathy between the dragon and the clouds, and a mutual attraction between the tiger and the wind. Therefore, when **Dong Zhongshu (II)** offered the rain sacrifice, he put up an earthen dragon with a view to attract the rain.(...) The sun is fire, clouds and rain being water. At the collision with water, fire explodes, and gives a sound, which is the thunder. Upon hearing the sound of thunder, the dragon rises, when it rises, the clouds appear, and when they are there, the dragon mounts them. The clouds and the rain are affected by the dragon, and the dragon also rides on the clouds to Heaven (...) Men seeing it riding on the clouds, believe it to ascend to Heaven, and beholding Heaven sending forth thunder and lightning, they imagine that Heaven fetches the dragon." (tr. Forke, I, pp. 352, 356-7, mod.)

In the chapter Luan Long (:A Last Word on Dragons) of the same book we find statements about the use of clay dragon figures to attract rain, based, no doubt, on the idea that clouds and dragons affect each other. The author, Wang Chong (1st century A.D.), gives credence to the efficacy of this practice, in spite of his scepticism concerning many traditional beliefs. The chapter contains the following interesting statement on the dragon:

"When a dragon suddenly emerges from the water, clouds and rain appear (...) The Yijing says that clouds follow the dragon, but not that the dragon follows the clouds. On the cloud goblet, thunder and clouds were carved, but did the dragon deign to come down?" (tr. Forke, II, p. 356)

Therefore, it seems that the ancient Chinese were of the opinion that clouds accompany the dragon but not the opposite. In the chapter Long Xu, an additional explanation of the dragon's affinity to rainclouds is given.

"Shenzi (the Taoist philosopher of the 5th cent. B.C.) informs us that the flying dragons mount the clouds, and that the soaring serpents ramble through the fog. When the clouds disperse, and the rain ceases, they are like earthworms and ants (...) The

---

(I) 雲氣   (II) 董仲舒

reason why the dragon is looked upon as a spirit is because it can expand and contract its body, and make itself visible or invisible. Yet the expansion and contraction of the body and visibility and invisibility do not constitute a spirit." (tr. Forke, I, pp. 357-358)

These records demonstrate the close affinity between clouds and dragons and the nature of their imaginative relationship. Therefore, the legend that the Yellow Emperor "came (to the rule) with a cloud" does not contradict the view that the divine form or the nature of the Yellow Emperor was the dragon; on the contrary, one could even say that it supports this view. (3)

3. ON THE MEANING OF THE NAME "XUANYUAN"

As mentioned before, Wen Yiduo considered the Yellow Sovereign identical to Xuanyuan and concluded that the dragon represents the original nature of the Yellow Sovereign and of the inhabitants of Xuanyuan's state. Why, then, does the Yellow Sovereign go by the name "Xuanyuan"?

Sima Qian, reiterating the account found in Wudide, notes in Wu-di Benji: "The Yellow Sovereign lived in the hills of Xuanyuan." It appears then that Sima Qian believed the Yellow Sovereign acquired his other name from the toponym "Xuanyuan". Be that as it may, the question remains - why did "the people of Xuanyuan" have the attributes "human face and snake-like body"?

Guo Moruo has attempted to explain the name **Xuanyuan** as a phonetic variant of **shan'e** (I) (a year when Jupiter appears in the eastern sky, the term later applied to the fourth of the twelve earthly branches, trans.), which is also found in the form **shan'an** (II). This word, Guo Moruo further believes, is related to the name **Šarru** used by the Babylonians to designate the star they regarded as "ruler of the Heavens, king of the Earth" (c.f. An Explication of the (Twelve Earthly) Branches and (Ten Heavenly) Stems, in Guo Moruo: Studies on Oracle Bone Graphs, pp.242, 254). In a later revision of this interpretation, in connection with his reading **tianyuan** (III) (i.e. **Sky Turtle**) for the emblematic character (F) often found at the end of Shang and Zhou bronze inscriptions, Guo speculates that Xuan-yuan/shan'e represent phonetic derivatives of this tianyuan. He stops short, however, of (F)
drawing a direct historical connection between the archaic use of Xuanyuan/shan'e in astronomy and the Yellow Sovereign:

"This clan name (viz. Xuanyuan) is probably of very ancient origin and seems to have

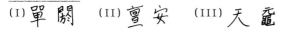

82

survived down to the early Zhou period before disappearing. Later the name became the subject of folk etymologizing and came to be associated with the figure of the Yellow Sovereign." (Studies on the Yin and Zhou Bronze Inscriptions, 1.7)

To reiterate, Guo believes that the terms Xuanyuan and shan'e are derived from tianyuan, the name of an early Zhou clan originally unconnected with the Yellow Sovereign.

In the Guoyu, ch. Zhou Yu 3, however, we find the following statement: "Long ago, when King Wu attacked the Yin, the Year Star (Jupiter) was in Quail Fire, ... and the Water Star (Mercury) was in the Sky Turtle (tianyuan)" (tr. by D. Nivison in: The Dates of Western Zhou, as quoted by Shaughnessy: 'New' Evidence on the Zhou Conquest, p.66, mod.). **Wei Zhao's** (I) commentary on this passage reads:

"The Sky Turtle is the name of one of the (twelve) stellar lodgings (**xingsu** (II)). It is also called **yuanxiao** (III) and lies between **ruxu** (IV) (Epsilon Aqr) and **wei** (V) (Alpha Aqr), eight degrees from the former and fifteen from the latter."

The asterism Xuanyuan, on the other hand, lies to the north of the three groups **liu** (VI) (Delta Hya), **xing** (VII) (Alpha Hya) and **zhang** (VIII) (Gamma Hya) and so, it cannot be identified with the Sky Turtle. As for the emblematic character Guo Moruo reads as Sky Turtle, **Sun Haibo** (IX) concurs (Phonetic System in Paleographs, author's preface) while **Wen Yiduo** (X), noting similarities of graphic structure, deciphers it as a single character, ancestral to **yan** (XI) (On the Interpretation of (F), in: New Explications of Ancient Canons, xia,p. 507). If we study closely the 49 specimens of this graph adduced by Wen Yiduo, it seems abundantly clear that the lower part of the emblem represents a frog rather than a turtle, and this argues strongly against Guo's reading of "Sky Turtle".

A rather different interpretation has been advanced by **Kaizuka Shigeki** (XII) who assembles a large number of examples of (F) along with other related emblematic characters. Kaizuka attempts to map a course of historical development for these graphs, proposing that what originally represented a marine deity mounted on the carapace of a sea turtle developed into an emblematic depiction of a composite creature incorporating both turtle and frog-like features. He further speculates that this graphic symbol should probably be understood as a clan token, perhaps that used by the **Xia** (XIII) (cf. Xia Clan Emblems Appearing on Bronze Vessels). Although Kaizuka, like Guo Moruo, seeks to ident-

---

(I) 韋昭　(II) 星宿　(III) 元枵　(IV) 如須

(V) 危　(VI) 柳　(VII) 星　(VIII) 張　(IX) 孫海波

(X) 聞一多　(XI) 黿　(XII) 貝塚茂樹　(XIII) 夏

ify the lower part of the emblem with a turtle, he clearly does
not adopt Guo's interpretation of the entire ensemble as standing for tianyuan, the Sky Turtle. Thus, in Kaizuka's understanding, there is no connection, phonetic or otherwise, between (F) and the Yellow Sovereign's name, Xuanyuan. To be
sure, Kaizuka proposed his identification of the emblem with the
Xia clan not on the basis of firm historical evidence but because of the important role played by turtles in the legends
concerning the control of the flood waters by **Kun** and **Yu** (I),
the founding ancestors of the Xia. In point of fact, however,
both Kun and Yu, on analysis, exhibit snake-like rather than
turtle-like features and this seems to militate against Kaizuka's
identification of (F) with the Xia clan.

Hayashi Minao (II), criticizing from an iconographic standpoint
Kaizuka's notion of a composite animal in the emblem, maintains that the image is devoid of turtle-like characteristics and
identifies it as a **frog** (cf. The Iconographic Emblems of the Yin
and Zhou Periods, p.28). Thus, the emblem in question has nothing to do with the bisyllabic tianyuan, "Sky Turtle". As for
the upper half of the character, understood as **tian** by Guo Moruo and **da** (III) by Wen Yiduo, Katō Jōken regards it as an
early pictographic form of the later **ao** (IV). Katō thus reads
(F) as **ao** (V) (:sea-turtle) and, on the basis of the similarity
with a turtle's humped carapace explicates it as "hunch-back"
which he takes as referring to a priest-like attendant to the
king. Guo's equation of (F) with tianyuan apparently failed to
satisfy Katō as well (cf. Studies in Ancient Chinese Culture,
pp.131, 975). We have seen how a number of scholars have proposed theories which differ fundamentally from Guo's. Furthermore, as Guo failed to provide sufficient evidence for his hypothesis of a phonetic connection between tianyuan and the
name Xuanyuan, we can hardly entertain his hypothesis without
voicing serious reservations.

As Guo's opinion on the meaning of the Yellow Sovereign's
name, Xuanyuan, seems for a number of reasons unsatisfactory,
we will attempt a re-examination of this question from a perspective rather different from that of Guo. As already mentioned
above, Xuanyuan's Knoll (VI) is mentioned in the "Virtues of
the Five Sovereigns" (Wudide) and the "Basic Annals of the
Five Sovereigns" (Wudi Benji). This elevation, according to the
Shanhaijing, ch. Wuzangshan Jing (Xicisan Jing (VII)), is located 480 li to the west of the mountain abode of **Xi Wang Mu**
(VIII). Guo Pu comments on this passage:

"The Yellow Sovereign lived at this knoll and (here) took to wife a daughter of the

(I) 鯀 , 禹　(II) 林巳奈夫　(III) 大　(IV) 傲
(V) 鼇　(VI) 軒轅之丘 (VII) 西次三經　(VIII) 西王母

Xiling clan. For this reason, he acquired the cognomen (**hao** (I)) 'Xuanyuan's Knoll'."

The original text of the Shanhaijing, however, reads:

"The place 180 li further west is called 'Xuanyuan's Knoll'. It is without vegetation; the Xun River flows forth from it southward to empty into the Black (Hei (II)) River."

This passage then, by itself, yields no information about the relationship between the Knoll and the Yellow Sovereign. In the Beicisan Jing (III) section of the same text, we again find mention of Xuanyuan's Knoll, but this passage does not help to elucidate our problem either:

"The place 200 li to the northeast is called 'Xuanyuan's Knoll'. Its summit abounds in copper while bamboo flourishes at its foot. There is a bird there in shape like an owl but with white head-feathers. It is known as the 'yellow bird', it cries its own name and those who eat its meat are not subject to envy."

Even in the passages on "the land of Xuanyuan" contained in the Haiwaixi Jing section of the Shanhaijing, we find no mention of Huangdi actually residing in these areas which bear his cognomen. For this reason, we cannot assume a direct connection between the figure of Huangdi and "the land of Xuanyuan" or "Xuanyuan's Knoll". Still, the fact that the inhabitants of "the land of Xuanyuan" are described as having human faces and snake-like bodies may provide a clue to the etymological meaning of the syllables xuan yuan. This is because snakes and dragons are similar types of creatures and we know from the previous discussion that the figure of Huangdi has an unmistakable and close affinity with dragons.

Let us next consider the syllables **xuan yuan** themselves to see whether they might yield a clue as to why the residents of the area with that name were described as orphiform with human faces. In the **Shuowen**, **xuan** is defined as "chariot with a curved thill and side-guards" and analysed as a semanto-phonetic graph with "vehicle" as signific and gan (IV) as phonetic (V). As for **yuan**, Shuowen states, "thill; the signific is 'vehicle', yuan the phonetic" (VI). **Duan Yucai (VII)** provides the following commentary on the Shuowen's entry for **xuan** (Va):

"(Xuan means) a chariot with curved thill and protective shield around the cart. According to my mentor **Dai** (Zhen's (VIII)) explanation of the term 'curved thill' (**qu-zhou** (IX)), zhou (X) is used to refer to this part of a light chariot while **yuan** (VI)

(I) 號   (II) 黑   (III) 北次三經   (IV) 干   (V) 軒,曲輈藩
車,从車干聲   (VI) 轅,輈也. 从車袁聲
(VII) 段玉裁   (VIII) 戴震   (IX) 曲輈   (X) 輈

is used for the same part on a larger chariot. Stability is a desideratum in vehicles which carry people; consequently, light chariots (have) extended hubs and bow-shaped thills. The larger chariots are merely for transporting loads, so their hubs are short and thills straight. The reason **Xu** (**Shen** (I), author of the Shuowen) makes a point in his definition of specifying 'a curved thill' before mentioning the side--guards is, I believe, that the term xuan is used only of chariots with thills which arch upward. The use of **xuan** (II) to mean 'rise up, arise' is an extension of this (basic sense 'bow-shaped'). 'Curved thill' (III) is itself a gloss on the expression 'Xuanyuan'. In his commentary on the Zuozhuan, **Du Yu** (IV) invariably glosses xuan as 'the chariot of a magnate' (dafu (V)); thus, in the commentary to Duke Ding, year 9, he says 'a rhinoceros-hide chariot (xuan) is the vehicle of a powerful minister' (qing (VI)). **Zhu Junsheng**'s (VII) commentary to the Shuowen entry for xuan reads as follows: ''A vehicle with a curved thill and protective guard' means a light chariot which carries people. It has an extended hub and its thill stretches upward, arclike; this is what is meant by Xuanyuan.'"

Wu Lingyun (VIII) has remarked on the semantic associations of the syllable **yuan**:

"It is my opinion that a zhou is a single, crooked thill with the emphasis on 'crooked' while a yuan is a double, straight thill, emphasis on 'double'. In our research into this word, we turn to 'The Rites of Zhou: Spring Offices, Senior (Officer) of the Great Ancestral Cult' (Zhouli: Chun Guan, Dazongbo (IX)) where we find 'The Duke holds the stud-shaped (**huan** (X)) jade token.' The commentary to this passage reads: 'The term huan is used of objects which stand double.' Shuowen defines huan as 'the guidepost of a courier station'. **Xu Kai** (XI) comments: 'The post erected at a courier station is a biao (XII); a pair of biao is called huan.' He also cites as evidence the Zhouli passage together with Zheng (Xuan)'s (XIII) commentary...In the **Erya**: Glosses on (Vocabulary Relating to) Mountains (XIV), we find huan (XV) defined as 'small mountains reaching (the height of) larger mountains'..., therefore the word huan refers to mountains which, though small, can be considered on a par with larger peaks. Thus, huan (XV) is simply huan ((XVI), to stand double). In the chapter Tan Gong of the Record of Norms (Liji, ch. Tan Gong (XVII)), the commentary to the passage 'The three great families (of Lu (XVIII)) modelled the **huanying** ((XIX) pillars) (with pulleys attached to lower the coffin into the burial chamber on those of the feudal lords)' reads: 'For feudal lords, four coffin-straps and two carved pulley-stakes (are used).' My own opinion on this matter is that, as the **ying** ((XIX) pillars) of the hall were originally erected in pairs (facing each other), moreover, as the commentary mentions 'two pulley-stakes', huanying must doubtless refer to a pair of posts. Furthermore, the first graph in the name **Yuan Taotu** (XX) (Zuozhuan, Duke Xi, year 4) is found as **yuan 1** (XXI) in the Guliang and Gongyang Commen —

(I)許慎　(II)軒　(III)曲輈　(IV)杜預

(V)大夫　(VI)卿　(VII)朱駿聲　(VIII)吳凌雲

(IX)周禮春官大宗伯　(X)桓　(XI)徐鍇　(XII)表

(XIII)鄭玄　(XIV)爾雅釋山　(XV)峘　(XVI)桓

(XVII)禮記檀弓 (XVIII)魯　(XIX)楹　(XX)轅濤塗 (XXI)袁

taries, while the 'yuan' of **Yuan Lou** ((I), a place name of Duke Cheng, year 2) is written **yuan 2** (II) in the Guliang Commentary. In the Guangyuan (III) 'yuan' is some-times written as yuan 2, while the Shuowen notes s.v. yuan 2 (II) that in the seal script, this graph was used for what later came to be written **yuan 3** (IV). On this basis we can affirm that yuan 1,2 and 3 are all used for the same syllable and sense. Again, according to Shuowen, yuantian (V) is reflected in the Zuozhuan as yuan-2-tian and in the Guoyu as yuan-3-tian. Thus, yuan 3 ought properly to be written **huan** (VI). Huan refers to wooden posts erected in pairs. The yuan 3 of a large chariot refers likewise to straight, parallel wooden shafts. Thus, in ancient times yuan 3 (IV) was also referred to as huan (VI). At the time of Shi Zhou ((VII), fl. 790 B.C., reputed deviser of the so-called large seal script), this word came to be written with the graph for the homophonous yuan 2 (II). From this time on yuan 2 and yuan 1 were used interchangeably resulting in the addition of radical 159 (VIII) to the loan character yuan 1 to create the new graph yuan 3 (IV)."(Wu Lingyun: Wushi yizhu,4,s.v. yuan (IV))

Accordingly, a **xuan** (IX) was etymologically **a light passenger-chariot** with a long single thill while a **yuan** (IV) was the long twin thill of **a heavier freight vehicle.** The rhyming binom composed of these two syllables, **Xuanyuan,** is not to be under-stood as a coordinate construction, i.e. a xuan and a yuan, but rather **the long curved chariot shaft** itself, also called **zhou** (X). Noting in his commentary: "The sixteen (sic) stars of the asterism Xuanyuan lie above the astral lodges Xing (XI) and Zhang (XII); Xuanyuan is crooked and twisted like a curved chariot-thill" (4), **Zhu Junsheng** seems clearly to concur with Wu Lingyun's interpretation of these terms, quoted at length above.

A passage in the chapter Tian Guan Shu (XIII) (:Monograph on the Celestial Stations) in the Records of the Historian equating the **Quan 1** (XIV) (Star) with Xuanyuan affords another line of inquiry. It seems that Xuanyuan was another name for the Quan Star; thus, it is scarcely surprising to find that the syllable quan also has the meaning "curved, rolled". In the Shuowen the graph **quan 2** (XV) is defined as "...walk with stooped back", while a homophonous graph (viz. (XVI)) with the same phonetic component is explained as "the curvature of a bow". It seems clear that the phonetic element (XVII) was used to write deriva-tives of the syllable **juan/quan 3** (XVIII), which means "rolled, curved". The fact that these two phonetics could be used to write cognate syllables is borne out by the polyphonic reading in Old Chinese of the graph now pronounced **quan 4** (XIX), pho-netic quan 3 (XVIII) which Shuowen defines as "...crooked teeth"

(I) 袁婁   (II) 爰   (III) 廣韻   (IV) 轅   (V) 趚田

(VI) 桓   (VII) 史籀   (VIII) 車   (IX) 軒   (X) 輈

(XI) 星   (XII) 張   (XIII) 天官書   (XIV) 權

(XV) 趯   (XVI) 弮   (XVII) 雚   (XVIII) 卷   (XIX) 齤

and for which it notes an alternate reading homophonous with
quan 1. (N.B. quan 1 and quan 3 were homophones even in Old
Chinese, though they belong to different phonetic series in
terms of graphic composition). It is hardly cause for surprise
then to realize that the early Chinese saw the shape of a
dragon in the asterism to which they gave the names Xuanyuan
(lit. "long, curved chariot-thill") and Quan (lit. "curved").
This is why the Shiji, ch. Tian Guan Shu describes Xuanyuan as
having the bodily form of a yellow dragon while Zhang Heng
(I) writes: "Gazing at the stellar mansion (II) Xuanyuan, it
looks exactly like the body of a 'rampant serpent'" ((III), a de-
scriptive name for a kind of dragon, according to the scholiasts;
citation from: Rhapsody on the Great Icons of Spherical Heaven,
Zhoutian daxiangfu (IV)). Returning then to the inhabitants
of the **Land of Xuanyuan** as described in the Shanhaijing, ch.
Hainei Jing, it is not at all difficult to understand why they
were described as having humanoid faces and serpentine
bodies.

Let us next consider one of the surviving legends about the Yellow Sovereign, a tradition which would seem to have arisen in
connection with the Sovereign's cognomen, Xuanyuan, whose original denotation we have been attempting to clarify. In the History of the Han, ch. Treatise on Musical Pitches and the Calen-
dar (Hanshu, ch. Luli Zhi) we find Huangdi's personal name
explained as follows: "He bequeathed (to later generations the
practice of wearing both) upper and lower garments and also
instituted the **xuan** and the **mian** (the xuan-type of chariot and
the official mian-garments); therefore, the populace nicknamed
him '**Sir Xuanyuan**'".

Thus, it appears that the institution of "xuanmian" was attributed to the Yellow Sovereign on the basis of his cognomen.
The tradition that the Yellow Sovereign instituted "xuanmian" is
also found in the even earlier **Shiben**, as quoted in the commentary and epexegesis to the Ceremonial Rites, ch. Rites for a
Knight's Capping (Liji, ch. Shi Guan Li zhushu (V)), and in the
Zuozhuan, Duke Heng, year 2. In this connection we should note
that yuan 3 was not unrelated to the pronunciation of the "mian"
of "xuanmian" as attested by the word written with the same
phonetic element as that of yuan 3, but pronounced bian (viz.
(VI)). In addition, Zheng Xuan notes in his commentary to Liji,
ch. Tan Gong, that huan (VII) is to be pronounced bian (VIII).

Mian is defined in the Shuowen as the official headgear worn
by those of magnate status or above. So, whether we understand
the name "Xuanyuan" literally as referring to a chariot with

(I) 張衡 (II) 宮 (III) 騰蛇 (IV) 周天大象賦
(V) 禮記士冠禮注疏 (VI) 曘 (VII) 還 (VIII) 便

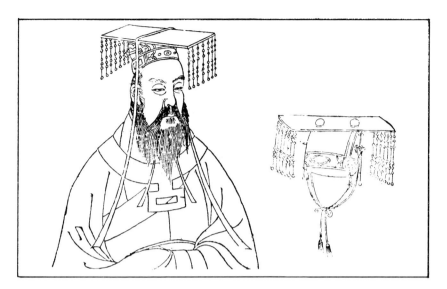

The ancient Chinese
"crown" - the "mian"
(headgear worn by
feudal rulers of
various ranks)

The Yellow Emperor's
basic affinity to
serpentine creatures
in legend:
the dragon

high sides and a curved thill, or as referring to both the chariot and the headgear of high status, it seems clear that the Yellow Sovereign was a figure of illustrious lineage. Thus it is only natural that we find the Shiji, ch. Wudi Benji, recording the Yellow Sovereign's surname as **Gongsun** (I), since this name means literally "scion of feudal lord".

*

Let us now summarize the conclusions reached on the basis of the evidence examined above.

1. The bisyllabic Xuanyuan seems to have referred to things with a dragon- or snake-like appearance and this supposition provides insight into the Yellow Sovereign's original nature and divine form.

2. Though the identification of Xuanyuan with the Yellow Sovereign is not made in the Shanhaijing, Zuozhuan or Guoyu, we do find these two names linked to the same figure in both the Shiben and the Dixixing. This second conclusion suggests that Xuanyuan became identified with the Yellow Sovereign at only a relatively late period and that originally the two were quite unrelated. If the textual evidence makes this seem the most likely possibility, we must ask why these originally distinct figures came to be identified.

As shown above, the name Xuanyuan has a fundamental, archaic connection with the Dragon Constellation and also with the name of an imaginary land whose inhabitants have serpentine bodies. Therefore, on the basis of the Yellow Emperor's basic affinity to serpentine creatures in legend, to which must be added the semantic connections of his cognomen Xuanyuan, we can state with confidence that he was most likely a deity of snakes and dragons.

The next problem to be considered will be the original meaning of the graph **huang**, "yellow". Does it afford insight into the original association we know to have existed between snakes, dragons and the Yellow Sovereign? ●

NOTES:

1. As examples of worthy men whom Heaven stimulated into activity, the author of **Mozi: Shang Xian** (*) (:Esteeming the Worthy) mentions Yu, Ji and Gao Tao (**) and adduces the chapter Lü Xing of the Shangshu as authority for his statements. In the transmitted text of the Lü Xing, however, the figures mentioned are Bo Yi (***), Yu and Ji. This alternation between Gao Tao and Bo Yi can be seen as evidence for the

(I) 公 孫

original identity of these two figures.

(*) 尚賢 (**) 禹,稷皋陶 (***) 伯夷

2. Katō Jōken has convincingly demonstrated that the three Bo Yi are identical and
that they were all originally water deities, in this sense resembling the figure
Zhuan Xu (*). Furthermore, Katō showed how the names of these four figures can be phonetically derived from the inverted form of the name of the **Yan** River (**) marsh deity, Yun Ge (***) (cf. A Study on Shao Gao, Gao Tao and the clan name Ying). As the
phonetic proximity between the "ge" of Yun Ge and the "bo" of Bo Yi can be readily in-
ferred from examples given in the body of this study, here we will focus on the affinity of "yun" and "yi". (*) 顓頊 (**) 流水 (***) 允格

Katō regards "yun" as a semanto-phonetic graph composed of the phonetic ((*), = later
(**)) and semantic (***) element. The earliest form of this graph was simply the semantic alone, i.e. it was a pictograph (****) which Katō believes originally meant
"hunchback" or, as the graph is found defined in the Shuowen, "kind person" (*****).

(*) 厶 (**) 耘 (***) 儿 (****) 兀 (*****) 仁人

According to Katō, in ancient Chinese society hunchbacks were regarded as sacred, a
sort of shaman who served and assisted the ruler. Among them were both fulsome, obsequious characters and talented men of high principles. Thus, in the Shuowen analysis of the graph "ning" (*) (:glib, obsequious), we find "ren" (**) given as phonetic
and the sense defined as both "skillful flatterer" and "highly talented". This is no
doubt the reason why the graph "yun" (***) (:sincere, loyal) is sometimes equated
with "ning" (i.e. in its second sense of "highly talented", cf. Erya, Shi Gu (****).
The above explanation of "yun" is based on Katō Jōken: Kanji no kigen, p.157 and Chūgoku kodai bunka no kenkyū, pp.133-164.)

(*) 佞 (**) 仁 (***) 允 (****) 爾雅,釋詁

This analysis of Katō's is no doubt correct, however, even if we cannot demonstrate
conclusively that (*) and (**) are variant graphs for the same syllable, there is
further paleographic evidence which would seem to bear out Katō's explanation. The
Shuowen's paranomastic gloss for "yun" is "xin" (***) (:sincere, trustworthy) and the
meaning of this "yun" can be regarded as "loaned" from "xin" (cf. Zhang Jianbo: Shuowen shengxun kao, p.439). Or again, in ancient seals we find an alternate graphic
form for "xin" which, like early forms of "ren" (****), shows "qian" ((*****), i.e.
the abbreviated form of "shen" (******)) as its phonetic. Thus, it seems clear that
"yun", "xin" and "ren" were all near homophones in Old Chinese.

(*) 儿 (**) 允 (***) 信 (****) 仁 (*****) 千 (******) 身

Now, according to the Shuowen, "ren" (*) was earlier written "qian" (**); in the Yu-
pian (***), however, this same obsolete graph is treated as ancestral to "yi" (****),
an equation reiterated by **Guo Zhongshu** in his **Hanjian** (*****): "(**) is equivalent to
'yi' (****) as attested in the Shangshu". This evidence, taken at face value, means
that both "ren" and "yi" were at one time written with the same graph, implying a
rather close phonetic similarity.

(*) 仁 (**) 尼 (***) 玉篇 (****) 夷 (*****) 郭忠恕,汗簡

The name of the legendary archer Yi Yi written (*) in the Chuci, Tian Wen (:Elegies
of Chu, Celestial Questions) is found written (**) in the Shanhaijing, Haineixi Jing,
and the Shuowen description "the Yi (tribes' customs are) humane (ren (***))" (s.v.
jiang (****)) could be taken as an indication that "yi" and "ren" were used inter-

changeably. On the basis of these pieces of evidence, it seems reasonable to claim
that the "yun" of Yun Ge is a phonetic alternate of the "yi" of Bo Yi.

(*) 夷羿 (**) 仁羿 (***) 仁 (****) 羌

In this connection it should be noted that the second graph in the expressions "Dong-
yi" (*) and "Huaiyi" (**) appears as "shi" (***) in the bronzes and oracle bones and
that Zheng Xuan's commentary to the Zhouli, Tian Guan, Lingren (:Ice-Keeper) notes
that "'yi' (****) is pronounced as and means 'shi' (***)." From this we may infer
that (*****) mentioned above as the archaic writing for both "yi" and "ren", is in
fact a semanto-phonetic compound with (******) as its phonetic element. Hence, (*****)
can, by the same token, be understood as phonetic in "ren" (*******) and the syllable
so written can be understood as a human being with the shape (***) (i.e. (********))
or, in the words of Duan Yucai's commentary, "the contour of a man with crooked back
and face turned downwards", i.e. a hunchback.

(*) 東夷 (**) 淮夷 (***) 尸 (****) 夷 (*****) 屈 (******) 二

(*******) 仁 (********) 几

3. On the cloud and rain-like iconographic elements associated with dragon figures in
the decorative patterns of Yin and Zhou bronze vessels, see Hayashi Minao: Inshū seidōki ni arawareru ryū ni tsuite, in: Inshū seidōki bunka no kenkyū.
4. The preceeding investigation has attempted to clarify the meaning of the rhyming
binom "xuanyuan" as "the long curved thrill of a chariot". It would seem then that
the first syllable of this compound, "xuan", conveys the sense "curved".
In the Zhouli, Chun Guan, Xiao Xu (*) (:Spring Offices, Minor Functionaries) we read:
"(He) sets the positions of the instruments racks (yuexian (**)); the king (uses)
'palace racks', while the feudal lords (use) xuan (***) racks."

(*) 春官小胥 (**) 樂縣 (***) 軒

Zheng Xuan's commentary on this passage distinguishes between the "palace" racks
which are disposal in the four cardinal directions (i.e. in the open forecourt of a
ceremonial hall (*)) and the "xuan" racks which exist in sets of three, one of the directions left open. Zheng, in fact, specifically desribcs the "xuan" racks as "curved
in shape". "That is why," he continues, "the Chunqiu (i.e. Zuo) zhuan (year Cheng 2)
states, 'Zhongshu Yuxi ... requested curved (**) (instrument) racks and (permission
to gird his horse in) fancy bellybands when he appeared in court.' Curved instrument
racks and fancy bellybands are the formal norms (li (***)) of the feudal lords."

(*) 堂 (**) 曲 (***) 禮

This is no doubt why Kongzi (*) made the following comment on Wei's acquiescence to
Zhongshu's presumptuous request: "... Of all things, (status) implements and titles
(of rank) should not be transferred, even temporarily, to others (of incommensurate
status)." As explained by Zheng Xuan, the instrument racks of the feudal lords were
placed on only three sides (viz. north, east and west) of the forecourts to the main
chamber of an ancestral shrine or of an inner apartment or archery halls; thus, the
ensemble formed a shape similar to (**), the archaic graphic form of (***). Thus, we
find "xuanxian" (****) sometimes referred to as "quxian" (*****) as in the Zuozhuan
passage cited above, demonstrating that "xuan" itself is a synonym of "qu" (:curved).

(*) 孔子 (**) 凵 (***) 曲 (****) 軒縣 (*****) 曲縣

- Baobuzi 抱朴子 (:Book of the Master Who Embraces Simplicity)
- Cefu yuangui 册府元龜 (:Archives of the Primal Tortoise)
- Chen Pan 陳槃 :'Chunqiu dashibiao lieguo juexing ji cunmie biao' zhanyi 春秋大事表列國爵姓及存滅表譔異 (:Emendation to 'Table of Ranked States, their Titles and Surnames, and Periods of Activities' (Contained in) the Table of Main Events of the Spring and Autumn Period), Taibei 1969
- Chuci 楚辭 (:Elegies of Chu)
- Chunqiu fanlu 春秋繁露 (:String of Dew-Pearls on the Spring and Autumn Annals)
- Dadaili 大戴禮 (:Norms Compiled by the Elder Dai)
- Duan Yucai 段玉裁 : Shuowen jiezi zhu 說文解字注 (:Commentary on Shuowen)
- Erya 爾雅 (:Approaching the (Linguistic) Standard)
- Fengsu tongyi 風俗通義 (:Popular Traditions and Customs)
- Fu Sinian 傅斯年 :Fu Mengzhen xiansheng ji 傅孟真先生集 (:Collected Works of Prof. Fu Mengzhen (Sinian)), Taibei 1952
- Gongyang, Guliang zhuan 公羊,穀梁傳 (:The Commentaries of Gongyang and Guliang)
- Gu Qiyuan 顧起元 : Shuo lüe 說略 (:Gists of Explanations)
- Guo Moruo 郭沫若 1: Jiagu wenzi yanjiu 甲骨文字研究 (:Studies on Oracle Bone Graphs), Beijing 1952
- ... 2: Jinwen yushi 金文余釋 (:Additional Explanations of Bronze Inscriptions), in: Jinwen congkao 金文叢考 (:Collected Interpretations of Bronze Inscriptions), Beijing 1954
- ... 3: Yin Zhou qingtongqi mingwen yanjiu 殷周青銅器銘文研究 (:Studies on the Yin and Zhou Bronze Inscriptions), Beijing 1954
- ... 4: Zhongguo shi gao dituji 中國史禍地圖集 (:A Draft Atlas of Chinese History), Shanghai 1979
- Guoyu 國語 (:Accounts of the States)
- Guo Zhongshu 郭忠恕 : Hanjian 汗簡 (:(Dictionary of Graphs Written on)

Fire-Dried Bamboo Strips)

- Hanfeizi 韓非子 (:The Book of Master Hanfei)
- Hanshi waizhuan 韓詩外傳 (:Exoteric Commentary on the Han School Text of the Book of Songs)
- Hanshu 漢書 (:History of the Former Han)
- Hayashi Minao 林巳奈夫 1: Inshū jidai no zuzō kigō 殷周時代の圖象記號 (:The Iconographic Emblems of the Yin and Zhou Period), TŌHŌGAKUHŌ, No.39 (1968)
- ... 2: Inshū seidōki bunka no kenkyū 殷周時代器文化の研究 (:Studies on the Bronze Vessel Culture of the Shang and Zhou), TŌHŌGAKUHŌ, No.23 (1953)
- Huainanzi 淮南子 (:Book of the Prince of Huainan)
- Ishida Eiichirō 石田英一郎 : Kappa komahiki kō 河童駒引考 (:A Consideration (of the Traditions Concerning) Japanese Water Spirits and Horses), Tokyo 1947
- Jinshu 晉書 (:History of the Jin)
- Kaizuka Shigeki 貝塚茂樹 1: Chūgoku kodai shigaku no hattan 中國古代史學の發展 (:The Development of Historiography in Ancient China), Tokyo 1967
- ... 2: Kinbun ni arawareru Kazoku hyōshiki 金文に現われる夏族標式 (:Xia Clan Emblems Appearing on Bronze Vessels), TŌHŌGAKUHŌ, No.36 (1964)
- Katō Jōken 加藤常賢 1: Chūgoku kodai bunka no kenkyū 中國古代文化の研究 (:Studies in the Culture of Ancient China), Tokyo 1980
- ... 2: Kanji no kigen 漢字の起原 (:The Origins of Chinese Graphs), Tokyo 1971
- ... 3: Kanji no hakkutsu 漢字の發掘 (:Excavations into Chinese Paleography), Tokyo 1971
- ... 4: Shōkō, Kōyō Eisei kō 少皋皋陶嬴姓考 (:A Study on Shao Gao, Gao Tao and the Clan Name Ying), NIHON GAKUSHIIN KIYŌ, No.15-2 (1957), (reprinted in Chūgoku kodai bunka no kenkyū)
- Liji 禮記 (:Record of Norms)
- Lu Deming 陸德明 : Jingdian shiwen 經典釋文 (:Explications of the Canonical Texts)
- Lunheng 論衡 (:Discourses Weighed in the Balance)
- Lüshi chunqiu 呂氏春秋 (:Master Lü's Spring and Autumn Annals)
- Mengzi 孟子 (:The Book of Mencius)

- Mitarai Masaru 御手洗勝 : Kodai chūgoku no kamigami 古代中國の神々 (:The Deities of Early China - Studies in Archaic Legends), Tokyo, forthcoming
- Mozi 墨子 :(The Book of Master Mo)
- Mu tianzi zhuan 穆天子傳 (:Account of Emperor Mu)
- Qianfulun 潛夫論 (:Discourses of a Recluse)
- Shandong daxue lishixi kaogu jiaoyanshi 山東大學歷史系考古教研室 : Dawenkou wenhua taolun wenji 大汶口文化討論文集 (:Proceedings of Discussion on the Dawenkou Culture)
- Shangshu 尚書 (:The Book of Documents)
- Shanhaijing 山海經 (:Classic of the Mountains and Seas)
- Shiben 世本 (:Origins of the Generations)
- Shiji 史記 (:Records of the Historian)
- Shijing 詩經 (:The Book of Songs)
- Liu Xi 劉熙 : Shiming 釋名 (:Explanation of Terms)
- Shuowen jiezi 説文解字 (:Explanations of Simplex Graphs and Analyses of Compound Characters)
- Sima Biao 司馬彪 : Xu Hanshu 續漢書 (:Continuation of the 'History of the Han')
- Sun Haibo 孫海波 : Guwen shengxi 古文聲系 (:Phonetic System in Paleographs), Beiping 1934
- Taiping yulan 太平御覽 (:Imperial Perusal of (the Reign of) 'Extensive Peace')
- Tang Lan 唐蘭 : Tianrangge jiaguwencun kao shi 天壤閣甲骨文存考釋 (:Notes on the Decipherment of the Bone Remains in the Tianrang Loft), Beiping 1939
- Wang Niansun 王念孫 : 'Guangya' shuzheng 廣雅疏證 (:Epexegesis and (Textual) Attestation of (Glosses in) the 'Guangya')
- Wang Yinglin 王應麟 : Tongjian dili tongshi 通鑑地理通釋 (:Comprehensive Geographical Annotations to the 'Comprehensive Mirror')
- Wang Yun 王筠 : 'Shuowen Shili' buzheng 説文釋例補正 (:Revisions to the 'Examples Elucidating Shuowen')
- Wen Yiduo 聞一多 1 : Gudian xinyi 古典新義 (:New Explications of Ancient

Canons), Beijing 1954

● ... 2: Wen Yiduo quanji 聞一多全集 (:Complete Works of Wen Yiduo), Tokyo 1947

● Wu Lingyun 吳凌雲 : Wu shi yizhu 吳氏遺著 (:Posthumous Writings of Master Wu)

● Xu Zhongshu 徐仲舒 : Chengong siqi kaoshi 陳公四器考釋 (:Decipher-ment and Explanation of (the Inscriptions on) Four Vessels of the Duke of Chen), GUO-LI ZHONGYANG YANJIUYUAN LISHI YUYAN YANJIUSUO JIKAN, 3.4

● Yanshi jiaxun 顏氏家訓 (:Family Instructions of the House of Yan)

● Yang Kuan 楊寬 : Zhongguo shanggushi daolun 中國上古史導論 (:Pro-legomenon to the Ancient History of China), Beijing 1941

● Yijing 易經 (:Classic of Changes)

● Zhang Jianbao 張建葆 : Shuowen shengxun kao 説文聲訓考 (:An Inquiry into the Shuowen's Sound Glosses), Taibei 1974

● Zhanguoce 戰國策 (:Intrigues of the Warring States)

● Zhao Yi 趙翼 : Gaiyu congkao 陔餘叢考 (:Considerations Gathered in Lei-sure while Caring for My Aged Parents)

● Zhu Junsheng 朱駿聲 : Shuowen tongxun dingsheng 説文通訓定聲 (:Com-prehensive Glosses and Established Phonetic (Values) for Shuowen (Graphs))

● Zhuangzi 莊子 (:The Book of Master Zhuang)

● Zuozhuan 左傳 (:The Zuo Commentary)

QUOTED LITERATURE/OTHERS:

● Chang Kwang-chi: Shang Civilization, New Haven 1981
● A. Forke: Lun Hêng, New York 1962 (reprint)
● J. E. Harrison: Mythology, New York and Burlinggame 1963
● D. C. Lau (trans.): Mencius, Harmondsworth 1970
● E. L. Shaughnessy: 'New' Evidence on the Zhou Conquest, EARLY CHINA 6 (1980-81), pp.57-79

THAI CUSTOMS AND SOCIAL VALUES IN THE RAMAKIEN

●

BY SRISURANG POOLTHUPYA

The official or canonical culture and mythology of a nation are fashioned primarily from its own heroes, preoccupations and plots; they may incorporate foreign elements, including even episodes and symbols. Sometimes, however, a foreign epic, story or book of revelation becomes part of a national heritage, providing popular images, values and norms. When one does, it is usually transformed by assimilating values, symbols and customs of the society adopting it. This was the case with the Thai national epic Ramakien which was derived from the Indian Ramayana and rewritten in the 18th century by King Rama I (1782-1809). The author here contrasts the fundamental values and norms of the Thai Ramakien with those of the Indian Ramayana as well as with the ancient and contemporary values and customs of Thai culture. Therefore this study about the "nationalization" of a foreign epic as the Ramakien may serve as an introduction to Thai culture. The writer explains certain contradictions within the set of cultural norms and between those norms and the actual behaviour. Traditional values and customs of the Ramakien, she considers to be an important part of the national heritage and even more as "eternal" and universal, a basis for national pride. Obviously, the tale of Rama and Sita is still an important part of Thai national mythology and in dealing with it one deals with a living mythology. The writer points out, however, that Thai society is now at a cross-road where its traditional values and way of life, which are highly esteemed by her, are challenged by those of Western materialistic industrial civilization. During the 18th and 19th centuries there was a strong revival of Thai native cultural traditions due to the increased contact with the West. This same phenomenon can also be seen in the history of other Asian nations during this period. Today, however, the reaction to Western influences is producing much stronger transformations which are seriously threatening the traditional values of Thai society - their future seems uncertain.

The Ramakien is a Thai literary work based on the Ramayana
from India. There are many versions of it but only the one by
King Rama I (1782-1809) tells the complete story, and through
it the social values, norms and customs (many still in practice) of the Thai people find their way into the epos. With new
thoughts and feelings, and new gestures the ancient sacred ac-
tors of Indian myth embody the essence of the Thai way of life.

The Thai easily accepts authority. He has always revered the
king and still does. He has traditionally respected elders and
preceptors and respects them today only a little, if any, less
so. The Thai loves formality and stylization. Any guest may expect a lavish feast. Special occasions merit solemn ceremonies
of symbolic and magic significance. Not only is the consecration
of a new ruler rich in ritual but so is its annual commemor-
ation. A cremation without the mourners' expressing their forgiveness of the deceased and asking for his forgiveness would be incomplete. The Thai expects to discover rather than to make his
place in the universe. For him, cosmic forces determine the
course of every human life, and he may consult astrologers for
hints or explanations of those which determine his. Such is the
stuff of the Thai world of the Ramakien.

Social values and concepts prevalent in the Ramakien and in
Thai society are: justice, gratitude, integrity, fidelity, the belief in the Law of Karma and the recognition of the transitoriness of all things. The epos, however, stresses the importance
of justice above other values. The belief in the Law of Karma
and the recognition of the transitoriness of all things are regarded as values by a Buddhist society such as that of Thailand. These values give Thai society a uniqueness its members
are proud of. Since the Ramakien reflects the Thai ideal way of
life, it is considered a national literary work of immeasurable
value.

The Thai people are very fond of good stories, especially from
far-away lands, and some foreign stories often retold in Thai
have gradually become part of Thai literature. Such, for
example, are **Sam Kok**, retelling the Chinese **Romance of the
Three Kingdoms** and **Inao** which recounts the adventures of a
legendary Javanese hero, Radin Inu, Prince of Kuripan.

One, the Ramakien seems to hold a special place among Thai literary works based on foreign stories because among other reasons, its form of poetic drama enables it to be performed, or
read or listened to. The performances of **Nang** (1) and **Khon** (2)
make use of the story of Ramakien exclusively. Khon, in particular, has been a popular entertainment right into the present
century, although in the last decades it is not being performed
as often now as it was. Another reason for the importance of
the Ramakien is that its content has universal appeal. Although
it is not, as in India, considered religious literature, the Rama-

kien upholds high ideals of manhood and womanhood, relates her-
oic deeds and describes moving human emotions. The Thais are
particularly attracted by it because some of their social values
and customs expressed therein resemble the original Indian version while others added to it transform this foreign literary
work into an important piece of national literature.

Since there are many versions of the Ramakien and the Ramayana, comments and references must be confined to particular
versions, of which the Ramakien of King Rama I (3) and the
Valmiki's version of the Ramayana seem to be the best choices.
The King Rama I's Ramakien unlike other versions, tells the
complete story and among its models Valmiki's Ramayana is best
known and considered in India to be the original complete version.

It should be noted that the Ramakien is based on various versions told by Indian Brahmans who came to Thailand, rather
than on any written text of the Ramayana. According to **King
Rama VI**, it stemmed from three main sources – the **Sanskrit version** of the Ramayana from **Bengal**, **Vishnu Purana**, and **Hanuman Nataka** (Rama VI, p. 207). Others have pointed out that
the story of the Ramakien often bears a likeness to **Kamban's
Ramavataram** from South India (Singaravelu, pp. 137-185), and
Sathirakoses notes that when the Ramakien does not follow the
Ramayana of Valmiki, it often resembles either the Tamil version from South India or that from Bengal (Sathirakoses, 1972,
p. 237). However, arresting and engrossing these similarities
and dissimilarities, and the examination of them, is not my purpose. My intent is simply to indicate Thai customs and social
values found in the Ramakien in order to a better understanding of the Thai way of life and thus show how a foreign story
could become part of the literary heritage of Thailand.

1. THAI CUSTOMS IN THE RAMAKIEN (4)

Because of the limited scope of this paper, only some important
customs are mentioned here. They are the following:

1. Deep Reverence for the King (5)

Traditional Thai custom demands a show of deep reverence for
the king. The Ramakien reflects upon the custom of reverence
for the king in the figure of Rama.

Rama in the Ramkien, unlike his counterpart in the Ramayana,
often stresses that he is a god, and sometimes he even reveals
his four-armed divine form. However, if only for dramatic pur-

pose, he also experiences joys and sorrows as well as certain human failings.

It should be noted that the idea of regarding Rama as a god cannot be found in the Valmiki version of the Ramayana. In the Ramayana, Rama is regarded as a man, for only as a man can he kill **Ravana:** "... but thinking man to be of no account, he (Ravana) did not ask to be made invulnerable in regard to him; therefore, none but man can destroy him." (Shastri, vol.I, p.39) The reason for the divergence in the Ramakien must have been the wish to show Rama as a divine king, such being the status of the Thai king who is consecrated in the **Rajabhisek ceremony** conducted by Brahmans. The idea of comparing Thai kings to Rama continues into the twentieth century when King **Maha Vajiravudh** (1910-1925) posthumously bestowed the name of Rama upon the Thai kings of the **Chakri** dynasty, beginning with Rama I (Prabat Somdet Praputayodfa Chulalok) who founded the dynasty. King Vajiravudh himself became Rama VI, and this tradition is still carried on. The present King **Bhumibol** is King Rama IX. The meaning behind this title is meant to show the king not only as divine but also as righteous, following the benevolent path of Rama.

At present, the ideas of democracy and scientific knowledge stand in the way of the traditional monarchic concepts. The Thai people in general maintain a deep reverence for the king and the royal family, yet in the rural areas one still finds people who revere the king as a divine person.

2. Respect for Elders and Preceptors (6)

The Thais have great respect for their parents, elder relatives and preceptors or teachers; the latter group also includes holy men like sages and monks. These concepts and customs are common both for the Thais and Indians who have a somewhat similar concept of society. A society that values knowledge and experience handed down as traditions always respects elders and preceptors possessing a higher degree of knowledge and experience. Out of respect comes obedience.

In the Ramakien, we see that King **Dasaratha** obeys the holy men's wishes while Rama and his brothers obey the holy men and King Dasaratha. The younger brothers in turn obey **Rama** and his wife **Sita**. The same applies to the **Varana monkey circle. Sugriva** respects and obeys his elder brother **Bali** (Vali) and **Hanuman** respects both Bali and Sugriva who are his uncles. **Angat** obeys Sugriva and Hanuman, for Angat is Bali's son.

In **Lanka, Kumbhakarna** obeys his elder brother **Dasakantha** (Ravana) and goes to war against Rama according to his brother's command although he well knows that Dasakantha is wrong in abducting Sita. Kumbhakarna is renowned for his righteousness.(7)

It is tragic that his obedience to his brother's wish leads to his downfall.

However, there are some exceptions to the rule. **Brot** (Bharata) criticizes his mother severely for causing his father to die of grief and his elder brother Rama to go into exile (II, 345-437). Dasakantha's behaviour towards his elder brother **Kuperan** who inherits the **Pushpaka** (Flying Chariot) from his father is different indeed. While Rama refuses the proffered throne because his father gave it to Brot, Dasakantha uses force to seize the Pushpaka (I, 246-247) that his father gave to his elder brother. Towards the end of the story, Dasakantha again disobeys his grandfather, **Malivaraj**, who has ordered him to return Sita (VII, 130).

Brot's case is to show that justice is even more important than respect for elders, whereas Dasakantha's case, on the other hand, means to demonstrate his evil character.

There is another example worth mentioning. Hanuman shows disrespect to **Rishi Narada** by trying to outwit him. The reason for his conduct is to find out how powerful Rishi Narada is. First, Hanuman uses his power, expanding his body until it becomes too big for the shelter, whereupon the rishi widens the shelter by his magic power. Hanuman once again makes his body outgrow the shelter. The rishi grows angry and teaches him a lesson calling forth the rain that leaves him freezing cold. When Hanuman reveals his real self and asks for pardon, Narada invites him to warm himself by the fire. Hanuman then goes to sleep. Narada wants to teach him another lesson and turns his walking stick into a leech which none but Narada himself could take off. He puts it in the pond where Hanuman will wash and drink after waking up. As soon as he touches the water, the leech will stick on Hanuman's chin. He has to beg Narada to help him. The rishi takes off the leech which turns into his walking stick. Hanuman then recognizes Narada's power, prostrates himself before the rishi to pay his respect and asks his forgiveness (IV, 16-23). This incident is not found in the Ramayana. It may have been included in the Ramakien for comic relief and possibly as a warning to youngsters against being too high-spirited, as never to belittle their elders.

Even today, respect for elders and preceptors is maintained, though it is neither as strictly nor as widely observed as before. These changes seem to be caused by the Western influence that places ability and efficiency above seniority. The notions of equality and freedom of choice also challenge the importance of respect and obedience.

Although the respect noted is shown in the Ramayana as well the Thai custom need not have been imported from India. Such social structures and concepts are common in many Asiatic cultures and have been a characteristic of Thai society since the days of King **Ramkhamhaeng** of **Sukhodya**. In his 13th century inscription he shows his due respect for his parents and brother (Silpakorn, 1957, p.1).

3. Giving Lavish Feasts to Welcome Guests

It is a custom of the Thais to give guests a warm welcome usually in the form of lavish feasts. In the Ramakien, we are confronted with many feasts, particularly in Lanka. When Ravana asks his friends and relatives to fight Rama for him, he offers sumptious feasts and entertainments to celebrate their arrival.

When **Sahasateja** and **Mulabalam** come to help Ravana in battle they are welcomed with splendid festivities. The food is of course, Thai style, although the choice of meat is somewhat unusual, e.g. curried elephant and fried buffalo meat-balls, perhaps, to suit the .taste of these ogres. Also, there are appetizers and a wealth of alcoholic beverages (VI, 188).

Beautiful girls serve them and attend to their needs: some fan them, some pour out the beverages, some sing and play music, and some dance (VI, 186-187).

Even to this day, guests are entertained in the same way, both in the country and in town. Vast sums of money are expended on official and private feasts. As a Thai saying has it: "It is an old Thai custom to welcome those who arrive at one's house." Though the proverb does not call for extravagances, the Thais rather prefer to go hungry for some time than give a poor meal to visitors. A peasant may kill his cow and fowls to feast the government officials who pay him a visit, because to offer just enough food to satisfy those guests would not be considered a feast. There ought to be abundant left-overs to be thrown away and even having only the bare necessities can scarcely curb this type of traditional lavishness.

Giving lavish feasts is not only a Thai custom, but also very important to the whole of South-East Asia. Sociologists interpret this custom as means of preventing accumulation of wealth in the hands of private persons. The waste of food in feasting was by that way an important institution for preserving social harmony. The difference to India is clear: The Ramayana never describes feasts of the same splendour like the Ramakien.

4. Solemn Ceremonies to Celebrate Special Occasions

The celebration of special occasions such as childbirth or marriage requires solemn ceremonies. The typical ceremony calls for the use of **Baisri**, a kind of storeyed container made of banana leaves and decorated with flowers; the more tiers, the more solemn the occasion. For example, the Baisri for a prince has more tiers than that for a commoner. The Baisri usually contains steamed rice and hard-boiled eggs. There might be other food along with the Baisri such as a young coconut, a bunch of bananas, meat and desserts. After the eating, candles are lit and passed from left to right around the circle of participants three or seven times. Each participant moves the candles towards the subject of celebration and waves the smoke that way. This gesture is called **Wien Tien.** The Baisri and Wien Tien ceremonies must be quite ancient for they used to form part of the **Khwan** ceremony (Baisri Su Khwan). As it was stated, "the ancient belief in Khwan, or a vital force in any being, was common among the Thai race before it was divided into Thais, Laotians, Assamese etc". (Khanithanand, p.1) The Khwan ceremony also required threads to be tied around the wrists of the subject of celebration. The ceremonies described in the Ramakien show Brahmanical influence and therefore manifest minor differences. The basic rituals, however, are the same as in the Khwan ceremony.

In the Ramakien, the ceremony celebrating the birth of the four sons of Dasaratha serves as a good example. Both Baisri and Wien Tien are mentioned though the threads are not. Brahmans took part in the ceremony, chanting the Vedic verses and anointing the children (II, 60-64). The same kind of ceremony is described for the celebration of the marriage between Rama and Sita, except for the addition of water poured from a conch onto Rama's and Sita's hands (II, 185). The present Thai marriage maintains this latter part and usually omits the Wien Tien ceremony.

The celebration of Rama's sons near the end of the story once again presents the Khwan ceremony followed by the traditional entertainments of **Khon,** puppet shows, **Lakorn** (8), various dances, wrestling, tight-rope walkers, acrobats, **Mon-Rum** (9), etc. (XI, 38-39).

On the whole, joyous occasions among the Thais require Baisri, candles, and water poured from a white conch. Elders, Brahmans or monks will bless the subjects of celebration. Thus the ceremonies described in the Ramakien reflect the Thai customs of celebrations which are somewhat different from those shown in the Ramayana.

5. The Coronation Ceremony

Towards its end, the Ramakien relates the consecration of Rama as a god-king (VIII, 258, 263-266). The sequence is reminiscent of the Coronation Ceremony as performed in Thailand. It is presumed that these rituals came from India, possibly via the **Khmer Kingdom.**

The Coronation Ceremony is more Brahmanical than Buddhist. The use of white-tiered umbrellas (**chatra**), water from five sacred rivers and the blowing of conches, for example, are Brahmanical; Brahmans conduct the ceremony. Yet the Baisri and Wien Tien ceremonies are performed side by side with Brahmanical ones.

During his coronation, Rama bathes in the water from the five sacred rivers.(10) Brahmans pour over him sacred water from a conch and read Vedic verses. Then Rama seats himself on the throne under the white-tiered umbrella and is presented with the regalia, whereupon the Baisri and Wien Tien ceremonies begin. There were entertainments for the people to celebrate this solemn and joyful occasion. The celestials came to dance upon the occasion. Hence only **children** were left to watch the **earthly performances** of Khon, Lakorn, Mon-rum, Chinese opera, wrestling and folk-dance, while the **adults** preferred watching the **celestial performances** (VIII, 269).

Although the Coronation Ceremony is performed only when a new king ascends the throne, a similar ceremony called **Chatramangala** is performed each year to celebrate the king's coronation day. The Baisri and Wien Tien ceremonies again form a part of this courtly celebration in which royalties and high-ranking officials participate for the welfare of the king.

6. The Custom of Cremating the Dead

The Buddhist Thais cremate their dead. Funeral rites in the Ramakien are very similar to traditional funerals in Thailand. The casket, or a big urn for a dead royalty or high nobility, would be placed on the **Meru** – a symbolic mountain – which is set up for cremation purpose.(11) There used to be theatrical performances such as Khon, Mang, dances and so on. Then, the fire is lit for the actual cremation. Afterwards, a stupa may be built to retain the ashes of the dead. Nowadays, however, theatrical performances and the building of stupa are rare.

In the Ramakien, the funeral of King Dasaratha conforms to the traditional Thai funeral. The Meru or a high platform to represent Mount Meru, the abode of the gods, is built. The urn containing Dasaratha's body is conveyed to the Meru in a procession. Members of his family come to mourn. Theatrical performances are staged for seven days and nights. Then, the actual cremation is carried out (II, 350-351). Queen Kaiyadesi and her son Brot are not allowed to light the fire, since Dasaratha prohibited this before he died.

According to Thai custom, relatives and friends bring incense sticks, candles and paper flowers and call Dok Mai Chand to light the fire. During this last rite, the living will ask the deceased's forgiveness as well as forgive him any wrongs done during his lifetime. To ban a certain person from one's funeral

104

RAMNAVAMI NUMBER

BHAVAN'S
JOURNAL

VOL. XI   NO. IV
APRIL 11, 1965

30
PAISE

Figures from the Indian Ramayana

means that the banned is beyond forgiveness. On the other hand, refusing to attend a certain person's funeral means that one cannot forgive the deceased.

It is interesting to note that in the Ramakien, when Rama presides over a funeral, he lights the fire from afar, as the king nowadays does. For example, Rama puts lights to **Bali**'s funeral pyre with his arrow (III, 274). At present, the king lights the ignition line from his dais. The fire will run along the ignition line to where the casket stands, a spectacle similar to the flying arrow. In Thai, this light fire ceremony is called **Chud Fak Kae**. Apparently, this was a common practice in some areas in the old days, but at present, only the king performs it.

7. The Custom of Consulting Astrologers

At critical moments of their lives, the Thais consult astrologers for guidance. They will ask an astrologer to fix an auspicious date and time for a marriage, a long journey, or entering battle. They will consult them about the future. Indeed they will also consult them about the future of a new-born child.

In the Ramakien, too, Rama and Ravana consult astrologers. **Bibhek**, Ravana's brother, is an astrologer; banished by Ravana from Lanka he joins Rama. The character of Bibhek is quite distinct from that of **Bibishna** in the Ramayana. For example, Bibhek is a coward while Bibishna is a brave warrior. Bibhek is an astrologer who can foretell the future accurately whereas Bibishna, although quite sagacious, is not an astrologer.

Bibhek in the Ramakien is a celestial being who came to be born a helper to Rama. **Ishvara** has given him special power to know the past and future (I, 96). As Rama consults him before battles, he usually wins or avoids major disasters.

Even today, the custom of consulting astrologers about auspicious times or future plans still prevails among a considerable number of Thais who like to be on the safe side. However, scientific knowledge and the pace of modern life compelling people to seize every opportunity before it passes by tend to discourage this custom.

Examples of Thai customs can be found throughout the Ramakien; Thais reading it can feel that it is a story about their own society. King Rama I seemed to have nationalized the Ramayana; therefore, the Thais not only feel that the Ramakien is a Thai classical work but are very proud of it.

2.

Social values here mean those values a society seems to uphold or find important for its maintenance. Some social values that appear in the Ramakien may be found in the present Thai society or are at least considered ideals worth pursuing such as the following:

1. Justice

A sense of justice or fair play is stressed throughout the Ramakien. It should be considered that the Ramakien in its details differs greatly from the Ramayana: Ravana was **Nondok** in his former life. Nondok was a giant whose duty was to wash the feet of the celestials who came to visit **Ishvara**. The celestials teased him, patting him on his head or pulling his hair until he was bald.(12) Enraged by these maltreatments, he asked Ishvara to give him a diamond finger which would doom anyone at whom it is pointed.(13) The prayer granted, Nondok went about killing numerous celestials. Subsequently **Narayana** was called upon to destroy him. The god, arriving under the guise of a beautiful celestial maiden, enticed Nondok to imitate her dancing movements. Nondok inadvertently pointed his diamond finger at himself while dancing. Before he died, he protested the fight to have been unfair as Narayana had four hands while he had only two. Narayana, out of a sense of justice or fair play, gave Nondok another chance to be born as powerful Ravana with twenty hands while Narayana would be born as Rama, a mere man with two hands. Even then, Narayana was sure to destroy Nondok in his new life (I, 86). Thus the fight between Rama and Ravana, the main theme of the Ramakien, is full of meaning for the popular beliefs about reincarnation; Rama was righteous while Ravana was evil. Those who joined the side of righteousness were rewarded in the end while those who were on the evil side perished; for justice is considered the highest virtue in the Ramakien, even more important than gratitude. When the two virtues are in conflict, justice should come first, because it is felt that a society cannot maintain itself without justice.

Although Thai custom demands that one reveres one's mother above all, the Ramakien like the Ramayana introduces the character of **Brot** (Bharata) who criticizes his mother severely for her misdeed. A Thai son should never utter reproachful words to his mother, yet Brot not only criticizes his mother but even draws his sword to kill her. If **Satrud** (Satrughna) had not held him back and if he had not thought it impious to kill his own mother, Brot would have slain **Kaiyakesi** (Kaikeyi) because he considers it unjust to succeed to his father's throne before his elder brother Rama (II, 347-348). Instead of being grateful to his mother for acquiring the throne for him, he is angry with her and tries to restore Rama to it.

Rama justly refuses to accept the throne offered him by Brot since this would oppose his father's wish. His father, **Dasaratha**, had wanted him to go into exile for fourteen years, and he feels compelled to go. By doing so, he is not only being just but also honouring his father.

"Father's words are like letters carved into stone. They cannot be wiped off. I shall keep his word even at the cost of my life." (III, 26)

The conflict between justice and other virtues occurs quite often in the Ramakien. It can be observed that those who regard justice as the highest virtue triumph, while those who regard another virtue as more important, perish. Such conflict is not stressed in the Ramayana.

If we study **Kumbhakarna** and **Bibhek** (Bibishna), Ravana's brothers, we can see that each of them makes a different choice. Kumbhakarna sides with his brother Ravana because he thinks it most important to obey his elder brother and serve him even in an unjust cause. Kumbhakarna realizes that his brother is wrong in abducting Sita and asks him to return her to Rama; however, when Ravana ignores his advice and prefers to fight Rama, Kumbhakarna complies with his brother's decision. Unlike the Ramayana, the Ramakien shows Kumbhakarna to be well- -known for his piety and his devotion to **dharma**. It is his tragedy to have valued brotherly obligation more than justice (V, 101). Eventually he is slain by Rama.

Bibhek, on the other hand, chooses justice at the expense of brotherly obligation. Ravana, Kumbhakarna and **Indrajit** look down upon Bibhek as a traitor to his brothers and his clan, but Bibhek believes that justice must be upheld at all cost. He advises his brother to return Sita to Rama whereupon he is expelled by him from Lanka. Bibhek's first thought is to ask some relatives to hide him, but realizes that all will be under Ravana's power, so he decides to go to Rama who is Narayana incarnate (IV, 129). He serves Rama against his own brothers, nephews and kinsmen because they fight for an unjust cause.

When Bibhek's own daughter, **Benyakai**, disguised as Sita's corpse, comes floating down the river to deceive Rama at the bidding of Ravana (14), Bibhek finds her guilty of an unpardonable crime. Thus he tells Rama, who consults him about a suitable punishment, to give her death sentence. Fortunately she is pardoned by Rama for the sake of her honest father.(IV,199-200)

Another example of justice is the episode of the judgement of **Malivaraj**, Ravana's uncle, whose character bears a certain likeness to that of **Malyavan**'s from the Ramayana, he advises Ravana to make peace with Rama; Ravana refuses to follow his advice and Malyavan courteously wishes for Ravana's victory (Shastri, III, pp. 85-88). Malivaraj's role in the Ramakien is amplified. Ravana invites him to hear his accusations against Rama, hoping to persuade Malivaraj to condemn his enemy to destruction by the power of his utterance, because whatever Malivaraj utters will come true. Yet he is also famed for his sense of justice. Instead of listening only to Ravana's side of the case, Malivaraj summons both adversaries along with the celestials for the hearing before pronouncing judgement. Finally Ravana is found guilty, and ordered to return Sita to her husband. When he refuses, Malivaraj condemns him to die of Rama's hand (VII, 131).

All these examples stress that justice is more important than the obligations of kinship or other virtues such as reverence for one's mother. Yet the Ramakien by no means suggests that other virtues are of little importance. On the contrary, the main theme as well as the minor episodes point out important social values that should be upheld. Even in **Kumbhakarna**'s case, other virtues that he possesses are sufficient to admit him to heaven after his death (V, 189).

It is noteworthy, however, that the value of justice is not generally upheld in Thai society when it comes into conflict with one particular social value, namely "the love for friends and relations" since it seems that nepotism plays an important role in that society. The Thais who have read the Ramakien or seen it performed will prefer the character of Kumbhakarna to that of Bibhek: The former sided with his kin while the latter sided with the enemy of his kin. Bibhek's righteousness makes him a tedious figure rather than a popular one.

As it seems, the composer of the Ramakien tried in vain to instil the ideal of justice into Thai society. Up to now Thai sociologists, who are realistic possibly to the point of cynicism, do not mention the sense of justice as a Thai social value. However, protecting friends and relatives who are in the wrong is often considered harmful and recently the Thais are called to change this social habit (Suwanpradesh, p. 15). This means that justice is an ideal after all, a value that the Thais try to attain but usually fall short of when a relative or a friend is involved.

2. Gratitude

The Ramakien seems to place the value of gratitude almost as high as justice. From the beginning, Rama shows his gratitude towards his father by helping him to keep his word. **Dasaratha** promises **Brot**'s mother to grant her any wish. When she asks for the throne to be given to Brot and for Rama to be sent into exile for fourteen years, Dasaratha is reluctant. Rama then willingly goes into exile so that his father may keep his promise. He sends a message to Brot's mother saying, "Not only am I willing to remain in exile for fourteen years, but to part with my life for his sake so that the gods may praise me for my gratitude towards my father" (II, 279).

Although gratitude is much extolled in the Ramakien, it must be shown towards a righteous person. **Hanuman**, for example, is grateful to Rama but ungrateful to Ravana. In the Ramakien, Hanuman serves Ravana in order to obtain his heart which is kept in a casket (to render Ravana invulnerable). In the course of his brief service, Ravana lavishes honour and wealth on Hanuman much more generously than Rama ever did. Yet Hanuman does not feel obliged to be grateful to Ravana, for in his opinion Ravana deserves to die:

*"You are not a man of integrity. You are full of evils. You do not practise the **dasadharma** (ten virtues) of a king. So you must face calamities." (VIII, 34)*

Ingratitude is condemned in the Ramakien except where it is justified, as in Hanuman's case. The episode of **Darabi** (Dundubhi) well illustrates this point since its details differ from the Valmiki version of the Ramayana. The word Darabi has come to be a Thai epithet for ingratitude. First this buffalo kills his father to prove himself mightier. Then he challenges the celestials, the Ocean God and even **Shiva** to fight him. They refuse, but Shiva tells him to challenge **Bali**, and he does. In their fight Bali is at first unable to defeat Darabi and realizes that some deity must have given him strength. So he asks which deity has given him power. The ungrateful Darabi boasts that none has, that he is powerful in his own right and for his boasting is abandoned to be killed by Bali (II, 232-234).

As these examples show, the social value of gratitude is esteemed while ingratitude is condemned in the Ramakien. In real life the Thais, perhaps, rank gratitude slightly lower down.(15)

3. Integrity

Integrity, especially when it is a question of the keeping of one's word, receives much attention in the Ramakien. Rama and his younger brothers are, of course, integrity incarnate. Rama keeps his father's word as well as his own. He returns to the capital **Ayudhya** after exactly fourteen years, moreover he dispatches Hanuman and the hunter **Khukhanda** to announce his punctual arrival for the sake of **Brot** and **Satrud** who have given their words too, and are resolved to throw themselves into the fire in case Rama should not return as he had promised (VIII, 224).

The episode of **Bali** and **Dara** (Tara) is another example for the importance of keeping one's word.(16) **Ishvara** asks Bali to take Dara in a closed vessel to give to **Sugriva** as a reward. **Narayana**, however, reminds Ishvara of the danger of entrusting a beautiful girl like Dara to a man and Bali then pledges that if he should keep Dara for himself instead of giving her to Sugriva, he will submit to be killed with Narayana's divine arrow (I, 144). However, opening the vessel to see Dara, Bali falls in love with her and her beauty makes him forget his pledge. Narayana, reincarnated as Rama, shoots Bali with an arrow and reminds him of his word, yet still offers him the chance to live, bearing a minor scar inflicted by the arrow. Bali chooses to die according to his pledge rather than live with the scar which would be too shameful (III, 264-265).

Thus, according to the Ramakien, a man of integrity must always keep his word or, like Bali, pay for the broken promise. The Ramakien gives more importance to such values than the Ramayana, and sociologists confirm that integrity is regarded by the Thais as a very important virtue. (18)

4. Fidelity

Fidelity, especially in a woman, is stressed throughout both in the Ramakien and the Ramayana. Sita is the embodiment of fidelity. She is loyal to Rama, her husband, ready to suffer or die for his sake. When she learns that Rama has been sent into exile for fourteen years, she immediately decides to accompany him. In spite of the remonstrances of Rama and her mother-in--law who care for her comfort and well-being and try to persuade her to wait for Rama in the capital, Sita is determined to go into exile with him, considering it her duty to serve her husband:

"Although I shall face hardships in the forest, I am willing to suffer in order to be near my lord. If he is unwell, I can look after him faithfully. If I should die, I would not regret it, for my devotion would be known in ten directions." (II, 291)

Sita's fidelity towards Rama is proved beyond doubt when she is abducted by Ravana and kept in his royal garden in Lanka. Ravana courts her trying to persuade her to become his wife, but Sita spurns all his sweet words and promises of wealth. Disappointed Ravana vents his anger on the ogres who guard Sita. Those in turn vent their anger on Sita, threatening to tear her up if she will not yield to Ravana's pleas. In her dejection and despair, Sita decides to commit suicide (IV, 43). Fortunately, Hanuman arrives in time to save her. He then offers to take her back to Rama on the palm of his hand. Sita, however, refuses his offer for the following reason:

*"The fact that **Dasakantha** (Ravana) abducted me has already cast a doubt on my reputation. If you were to carry me back,*

my reputation would suffer even more in the ten directions."
(IV, 50)

So Sita waits for Rama to fight and kill Ravana. Only then does she leave Lanka to be reunited with Rama. Hanuman is deeply impressed by her good judgement and fidelity which she holds dearer than life (IV, 50-51). Sita's fidelity is stressed both throughout the Ramakien and the Ramayana.

Sita's way of thinking parallels that of Rama who is convinced of her integrity. When Ravana, disguised as a rishi, comes to induce Rama not to fight his enemy for the sake of tainted Sita, Rama replies that his wife is the goddess **Lakshmi** and thus unable to be tainted though she were fallen in the world-terminating water and fire (IV, 162).

After the death of Ravana, Sita proves her purity by the fire ordeal. She addresses all the deities declaring:

*"If I have bestowed my love on Dasakantha or any man other than Rama even in my thoughts, if I am unfaithful to Rama or have done anything improper, may the fire devour me and let me suffer in hell for a hundred thousand **kalpas** (18): But if I remain faithful, may the deities make me comfortable while I step into the fire. May my feet be cool at every step." (VIII, 104)*

Through the power of her truthfulness, lotuses grow beneath her feet to keep the fire away from her. Both gods and men are convinced of her fidelity and praise her truthfulness (VIII, 105).

It may be interesting to note that Thailand is a man's world. While women's fidelity is extolled, men's fidelity is not required. An unfaithful woman is condemned. A woman should not have more than one husband, yet a man can have many wives. Rama, having only Sita as his wife, is an exception among popular heroes. A Thai hero, whether in fiction or in real life, usually has many wives or many amorous affairs. Hanuman in the Ramakien is a typical Thai hero. Unlike the original in the Ramayana, Hanuman has many paramours in the course of his adventures.

In one Thai literary work of the 19th century called **Khun Chang Khun Phan** (:The story of Khun Chang and Khun Phan) the heroine due to unusual circumstances simultaneously has two husbands. When the king asks her to choose one, she is in a quandary because she is grateful to both. So the king, on the grounds that a woman who can love two men at the same time is unworthy condemns her to death. So, obviously, according to standard opinions women can be, and should be, faithful only to one man. In Thai society, faithful women are compared to Sita while unfaithful women are compared to Wantong.

5. The Belief in the Law of Karma

Values mentioned earlier can be found in any society. The strong belief in the Law of **Karma**, however, is regarded as a social value and is prevalent only in Buddhist societies, such as that of Thailand. Hindus also believe in the Law of Karma; however, the meaning of Karma in Hinduism differs from that in Buddhism as can be seen in the Hindu notion that different **varnas** follow different dharma. For example, if a **Shudra** practises **Vaishya**'s dharma, he will not gain any merit, while a Vaishya will. For **Manu** says: "(A Shudra who is) pure, the servant of his betters, gentle in speech, and free from pride, and always seeks a refuge with brahmins, attains (in his next life) a higher caste." (Radhakrishnan, p.168) Hindu Karma is tied up with varna's law. So the same action may not produce the same result if the performer does not belong to the same varna. In Buddhism, however, the Law of Karma is the same for everybody; anyone's action will produce the same result.

In the Ramakien, one repeatedly finds the belief in the Law of Karma. For example, when Rama has to go into exile for fourteen years, his mother is inconsolable. She says:

"Perhaps in our previous lives we two took a young animal away from its mother. This misdeed causes father to make us part from each other!" (II, 273)

When Rama pities Sita who insists on accompanying him into the forest to suffer hardship, he believes that she must have done a bad deed in the past, so she has to suffer the consequences by going into exile with him (II, 288-289). The belief in Karma makes people resign themselves to their misfortune without blaming others for the cause of their sufferings. It helps them to prevent unending retaliations. For example, Rama could blame Brot's mother and take revenge on her, but his belief in the Law of Karma restrains him.

Unfortunately, evil beings like Ravana do not seem to take into consideration the Law of Karma. For instance, when his grand--father Malivaraj orders him to return Sita to her lawful husband Rama, Ravana refuses for the following reasons:

"So many kinsmen and friends of mine were killed by Rama. Even if I returned Sita to him, my dead relatives could never return to life. Since I am considered the flower of manhood, I shall fight unto death and not return Sita." (VII, 130)

Ravana here applies the law of retaliation in kind, eye-for-eye, tooth-for-tooth. Since Rama cannot restore his friends and relatives to life, he refuses to return Sita. If he would consider the fact that they perished in consequence of Karma, Ravana might have been able to obey Malivaraj's judgement by returning Sita. At the moment of dying, however, Ravana comes to realize the Law of Karma. He says to Bibhek:

"I myself am evil, so I must die. I have caused the world many miseries." (VIII, 69)

Although Rama has led a wicked life, he dies nobly because he finally recognizes the Law of Karma.

The belief in the Law of Karma generates compassion. As no being can escape this law, one must have compassion for those who suffer from the result of their Karma and help them in whatever way one may. Above all, one must never abandon them as deserving their misfortune, but try to console them.

Even nowadays, the Thais still believe in the Law of Karma. A research survey, however, has shown that among the younger ones, fewer people believe in the effect of Karma: 67,5% of the teenagers, 81,1% of those between 30 and 39 years, and 96,7% of those over sixty years believe in the inevitable effect of one's own Karma. Education apparently plays a role since the less educated have a firmer belief in Karma than do the better educated (Master degrees and upwards). Those who accept their misfortunes as the result of their past Karma are principally the less educated (76,4%) and those with low incomes (74,8%). (See Komin, pp.250-258)

It seems that the more educated Thais have begun to feel that this highly esteemed concept is responsible for backwardness since it tends to make people inactive. They feel that people who believe in Karma will not struggle for a better life, but their feeling reflects a misunderstanding of the belief and its influence on the people. Those who believe in the Law of Karma need not be inactive. In fact they may do anything that is in their power and beneficial.

In the Ramakien, Rama does nothing to retain his throne. Yet he tries hard to fight unrighteous Ravana who abducted Sita. This evil person, together with his evil kinsmen and friends, must be destroyed for the world's sake. Belief in Karma causes men to resign themselves only to the inevitable. This resignation will make men calm and their peace of mind may promote creative forces within them. If they are angry, discontented, and trying to fight the inevitable, they will eventually become exhausted, their minds clouded with anger and devoid of creativity.

It seems deplorable that nowadays many Thais misunderstand this belief and ultimately reject it choosing now to put all blame on the government rather than on Karma. As a result, many problems they may be able to solve for themselves are now left unsolved because changes are expected from the government. As Ravana blames Bibhek for his beloved son **Indrajit's** death (VI, 129) although he himself is the real cause, some people would blame anything or anybody except themselves. These passive or negative attitudes, in fact, have nothing to do with the genuine concept of the Law of Karma.

6. The Recognition of the Transitoriness of All Things

This Buddhist concept regarded as a social value is hard to practise at times. It is difficult to accept this truth, even though the chant for the dead, which forms part of the mourning ceremony, repeats this concept time and again. People enjoy wealth, honour and happiness and cling to them, often recognizing the transitoriness of all things only when it is too late.

The Ramakien illustrates how transitory all things are. Rama on the eve of his would-be coronation is full of pride and happiness. The following day he must leave the throne and wealth and go into exile. Sita has to leave her luxurious life in the palace to accompany her husband into the forest. Yet she is happy until she is abducted by Ravana. She suffers so badly in Lanka that she decides to commit suicide (IV, 43). When Hanuman prevents her from doing so and gives her news of Rama, Sita rejoices at the news which gives her hope to go on living.

On Ravana's side, the great king of Lanka also suffers many humiliations and misfortunes. For all his wealth and power, he is unable to defeat Rama. He loses his beloved son Indrajit and other relatives and friends, and in the end, he forfeits his life. When his chief queens, **Mondo** (Mandodari) and **Aggi** are full of grief, Bibhek consoles them with the following words:

"Anyone who is born must die. Not only the King of Lanka who was almighty and invincible, but even **Ishvara** cannot escape death. Even the great **Brahma** who is the progenitor of all creatures will finally face the time of destruction. The Earth, the Four Oceans, **Mount Sumeru** and the Seven Mountains that surrounded it will be destroyed when the time comes. It is the ordinary course of the Three Worlds. Do recognize the transitoriness of all things! Do not grieve so much! Use your wisdom to abate your sorrow!" (VIII, 81-82)

Hanuman realizes the meaninglessness of pomp and wealth that have never enhanced his real self. He behaves like a monkey even when he is a ruler, causing his retinue to laugh at him. Ashamed and humiliated, Hanuman restores the city to Rama and becomes a yogi in the forest (VIII, 344-345).

The message in the final verse stresses this social value: "Whoever listens to it should not be deluded but should recognize the transitory nature of all things." (XI, 307) If one remains in delusion and clings to transitory things, mistaking them for something permanent and valuable, one will never attain peace and Nirvana but suffer endlessly. The final message of the Ramakien is to remind the reader and listener that the ups and downs of life: happiness and sorrow, wealth and poverty, honour and humiliation, victory and defeat, success and failure will never last. Those who are able to accept this important concept, regarded as a social value essential for self-perfection, can smile at both their fortunes and misfortunes. Thailand is sometimes named the "Land of Smiles"; this is chiefly due to the common recognition in Thai society of the transitoriness of all things. This recognition renders the Thais happy and free from care, with a ready smile on their lips. One can only hope that Western materialism will not come to replace this Thai social value so beneficial to the soul.

In the research survey mentioned earlier, personal ambition still ranks lowest among twenty-three instrumental values in any group of the Thais (Komin, p.78). As it seems, the belief in the transitoriness of all things may possibly suppress one's ambition. Why work hard for a transitory target, one may ask oneself. In any case we must keep in mind that the Thais' dislike of hard work may also have a lot to do with their lack of ambition. This negative attitude to personal ambition may be also related to the agricultural nature of the society (Wichienchareon, pp.157-158).

3. CONCLUSION

Thai customs and social values represented in the Ramakien make this work a valuable piece of national literature most relevant to Thai society. Of course, some customs such as lavish feasts are not commendable. Yet it should be noted that it was ogres or Ravana who practised this custom. This is a hint of bad taste and wastefulness in relating these welcoming feasts. Therefore an intelligent reader and listener will take the hint and practise this custom in moderation.

The conflict between a sense of justice and the obligation towards relatives and friends in Thai society often results in the suppression of the sense of justice. Yet where justice triumphs the people appreciate it the more because of its infrequency. Both the government and the individuals are struggling hard against nepotism, so that this social value is upheld at least in theory if not in practice.

The two Buddhist social values: the belief in the Law of Karma and the recognition of the transitoriness of all things, are very important for the Thais. They constitute a basis for the Thai identity, as a society sincerely peace-loving and striving for peace at every effort. They render the Thais compassionate; for example, the Thais welcome the refugees from the neighbouring countries as those who have suffered sufficiently through their Karma. Occasionally, the common sense of self-preservation causes the Thais to behave harshly towards the refugees. Yet compassion usually carries the day.

The recognition of the transitoriness of all things confers serenity on the Thais. This serenity can even be seen in images of the Buddha created in Thailand. Yet materialism from the West, a craving for material goods and a superiority over others, are threatening to destroy this traditional Thai tranquility. Today, some Thais have grown quite materialistic, ignoring the Buddhist social values.

Although the Ramakien contains a wealth of Thai customs and values, its ancient theme causes some people to assume that it is no longer relevant for our modern age. In truth, the Ramakien is ageless. It is an invaluable piece of Thai literature which contains eternal truth and is rich in national heritage. ●

NOTES:

1. Nang literally means "leather". It is called this name because the characters of the play are cut of leather in such a way that their shadows are distinctly seen on the white-cloth screen lit up by torches. When ones speaks of Nang, one usually means "Nang Yai". The word Yai means "big", for the leather characters are about five times bigger than those of Nang Talung, a kind of popular entertainment in southern Thailand. Nang used to be quite popular in central Thailand. Perhaps, it came into existence before Khon. However, Khon characters are played by real persons and are therefore more interesting than Nang. Eventually people tended to prefer Khon to Nang which is becoming obsolete and is now rarely performed.
2. Khon is greatly influenced by Nang, for some dance movements and the delivery of dialogues are similar. Originally, Khon was performed only at the royal court, but later it also became a popular entertainment. The chief characteristics of Khon are the following: The ogres and monkeys wear masks while the humans and divinities do not. All characters show their emotions by gestures, never by facial expression. Those who do not wear masks keep their faces calm and expressionless. No character except jesters speak with their own voice. There are speakers and singers to give the characters speech or verbal expression.
3. (King) Rama I: Ramakien, 11 vols., Bangkok (Guru Sabha Press) 1964. Further references to the Ramakien will give the volume and page number only.
4. Accepted social values eventually may turn into customs. What is here considered customs may be called social values by some Thai sociologists.
5. Supatra Suparp calls it "love for the king" and regards it as a social value among the Thais (Suparp, p.3).
6. Supatra Suparp, op.cit., p.6, calls it "respect for seniority" and regards it as a social value.
7. Note the different characterization of Kumbhakarna in the Ramakien. He is not a vicious character as portrayed in Valmiki's version.
8. Lakorn means a drama. Two kinds of early drama are Lakorn Nai and Lakorn Nok. La-

korn Nai is a dance drama in which characters are performed by females. It is usually performed in the palace. Lakorn Nok can be performed by both males and females outside the palace.

9. Mon-Rum is a kind of dance.

10. It was from the four seas and five hundred rivers in the Ramayana (see Shastri, op.cit., vol.III, p.368).

11. Nowadays the Meru is a permanent structure. It must have a tiered roof topped with a spire, being the symbol of Mount Meru where Heaven is situated.

12. According to opinions and beliefs common in South-East and East Asia, touching one's head is considered as a very serious offence, it also may heavily injure one's spirit located in the head, it may cause an illness or even the death. Only the closest relatives (the parents and wife) may touch one's head.

13. The pointing at someone is considered an impolite or offensive gesture in many Asiatic cultures, therefore it is in Thailand of a symbolic value.

14. This episode is not found in the Valmiki's version.

15. According to Suntaree Komin, gratitude ranks fourth among instrumental values (Komin, p.79).

16. This episode is not found in the Valmiki's version.

17. Suntaree Komin finds that integrity ranks second among instrumental values (Komin, p.79).

18. One kalpa is 4,3'20 million years (Basham, p.320).

BIBLIOGRAPHY:

● A. L. **Basham**: The Wonder that was India, New York (Grove Press) 1959

● (Prince) **Bidyalabhbridhiyakara**: Chumnum Pranibondh (:Collected Works), Bangkok (Prachan Press) 1974

● Wiliwan **Khanithanand**: Khwan Kong Tai: Cheung Bhasasastra (:Khwan of the Tais: From the Linguistic Point of View), paper presented at the Symposium of Philosophy and Religion at Thammasat University, 8-9 May 1980

● Suntaree **Komin** and Snit **Smuckarn**: Kaniyom Lae Rabob Kaniyom Thai (:Thai Value Systems: a Differential Measurement Instrument), Bangkok (NIDA) 1979

● Srisurang **Poolthupya** and Sumalaya **Bankloy**: Research on the Origins and Behaviours of the Characters in the Ramakien Compared with those in the Ramayana, Bangkok 1980

● (King) **Rama I**: Ramakien, 11 vols., Bangkok (Gurusabha Press) 1964

● (King) **Rama V**: Prarajabidhi Sibsong Duan (:The Royal Ceremonies for the Twelve Months of the Year), Bangkok (Klang Vidya Press) 1971

● (King) **Rama VI**: Bor Kerd Ramakien (:The Origin of the Ramakien), Bangkok (Silpabannakarn Press) 1970

● Sarvepalli **Radhakrishnan** and Ch. A. **Moore**: A Source Book in Indian Philosophy, Princeton (Princeton University Press) 1967

● Praya Anumanrajadhon **Sathirakoses**: Vardhana Dharma and Prabeni Tang Tang Khong Thai (:Culture and Traditions of Thailand), Bangkok (Klang Vidya Press) 1973

● ...: Upakorn Ramakien, Bangkok (Bannakarn Press) 1972

● Makhan Lal. **Sen** (tr.): The Ramayana of Valmiki, 2nd. rev. ed., New Delhi (Munshiram Manoharlal) 1978

● Hari Prasad. **Shastri** (tr.): The Ramayana of Valmiki, 3 vols., London (Shanti Sadan) 1962

● Krom **Silpakorn**: Khun Chang Khun Phan, 2 vols., Bangkok (Klang Vidya Press) 1963

● ...: Prabeni Karn Tum Khwan Lae Karn Len Hunkrabok (:The Traditions of Khwan Ceremony and Marionette Show), Bangkok (Thai Watana Panit) 1977

● ...: Prajum Silacharuk Bhag Tee Nung (:Collection of Stone Inscriptions, Part I), Bangkok (Prachan Press) 1957

● S. **Singaravelu:** A Comparative Study of the Sanskrit, Tamil, Thai and Malay Versions of the Story of Rama with the Special Reference to the Process of Acculturation in the Southeast Asian Versions, THE JOURNAL OF THE SIAM SOCIETY, vol.LVI, Part II (July 1968), pp.137-185

● Supatra **Suparp:** Sangom Lae Watanadham Thai (:Thai Society and Culture), Bangkok (Thai Watana Panit) 1975

● Termsak **Suwanpradesh:** Sangom Lae Watanadham Thai (:Thai Society and Culture), Bisnu-lok (Widyalaikru Pibulsongram) 1978

● Adul **Wichienchareon:** Values in Thai Society, THAMMASAT UNIVERSITY JOURNAL, Vol.II, No.1 (June-October 1972), pp.138-164

Figures from the Thai Ramakien

119

Hypothesis
▽
Discussion

Burying the Scholars Alive:
On the Origin
of a Confucian Martyrs' Legend
●

ULRICH NEININGER

1. The alleged misdeeds of **Qin Shihuang** (I), climaxing in his order to bury four hundred and sixty Confucian scholars alive, made material for an often recalled story during two milleniums. In Imperial times the Chinese elite celebrated this burial as an example of their equals fighting against tyranny without the least fear of death, and in modern times no other tale has filled the Anti-Confucian-Campaigners with such delight as that of Qin Shihuang interring the Confucianists deep under the earth.

Among the emperors of China the First Emperor (Qin Shihuang) remained the most famous throughout history. His reputation is founded on his despotism. Yet his actual significance is based on his unification policy: After he had conquered the Six States, he established in 221 B.C. his rule over the whole realm, and introduced under the guidance of his legalist advisers an administrative system, which formed the background of Imperial government till 1911. In the course of the unification he standardized the law, the coinage, the script and weights and measures. All carriages had to have gauges of the same size, and a net of roads and channels were constructed to accelerate communication between the capital Xianyang and the provinces. Within a decade Qin Shihuang converted a factioned feudal society into a centralized bureaucracy.

Qin Shihuang believed that his policy was preparing the world for the eternal rule of his dynasty, but it survived him by only three years. Instead of being remembered as the unifier of the Chinese empire he became despised as an incompetent tyrant. Written in the time of Han, the reports on his rule mention his great reforms only in passing. A detailed description of his unification policy does not exist. The reason for this silence is that the Confucianists found the story of Qin Shihuang too useful to allow an objective assessment; they considered his and his dynasty's fate as perfectly suited to admonish future em-

(I) 秦始皇

perors. Consequently the positive sides of his rule were concealed, whereas the negative aspects were excessively emphasized.

Beginning with the time of the Han Emperor **Wu** (I) (140-86 B.C.) the Confucianists, not content with merely biased judgements, gradually invented additional tales about Qin Shihuang. Among those legends the one on the martyrdom of the scholars, entwined with the authentic story about the burning of the books not in the emperors's favour, became most famous so that finally in the Chinese tradition the reign of Qin Shihuang was reduced to the formula: **Burning the books and burying the Confucian scholars alive (fenshu kengru (II)).**

During two milleniums of Confucian rule the First Emperor remained the fiend who had emerged to destroy the vessels of truth, namely the books and the scholars. As long as the Confucian bureaucracy was firmly established only some excentrics of **Li Zhi**'s (III) (1527-1602) stamp dared to doubt the official judgement on the "Tiger of Qin" (cf. Li Zhi, Cangshu, 2:13 et seq).

Only when in our century the image of the past changed with the collapse of the empire, modern historiographers stressed the lasting merits Qin Shihuang deserved for China's unity. The negative aspects of his rule receded proportionately. Thus the losses occasioned by the burning of the books were given less weight, when historians referred to the destruction of the imperial library by rebels as the chief cause for the big gaps in the pre-Han literary tradition. Yet up to the present the emperor remains in Chinese and Western accounts incriminated with the murder of the Confucianists.

2. Soon after the downfall of the Qin dynasty a number of pamphlets were written, centering around the following question:

"For more than thirty generations the Qin provided the Son of Heaven until the Zhou took over. For more than thirty generations the Zhou provided the Son of Heaven until the Qin took over. But the Qin provided the Son of Heaven for only two generations until they perished. Since human dispositions are not so different from each other, how is it then that the rulers of the Three Dynasties possessed the Way for a long time, whereas the Qin, remaining without the Way, were quickly ruined?" (Jia Yi, Xinshu, Baofu, 5:3b)

The answers produced by scholars in reply to this query were dictated less by the intention of elucidating the history of the

(I) 武   (II) 焚書阬儒   (III) 李贄

122

vanquished Qin empire than for the purpose of warning the early Han monarchs against the dangers of unbridled despotism. For the scholars, who were at the mercy of an absolute ruler, it was, quite literally, vital to convince that autocrat of the pernicious results which ensue from violence. Their message to the emperor said in short: If you take our life, Heaven will take the life of your dynasty.

Lu Jia (I) was the first scholar at the Imperial court to base an essay on this admonition. Some time after the establishment of the Han dynasty (206 B.C.), he engaged its founder **Liu Ji** (II) in a discussion on the fortune of the ruling houses, arguing: Qin Shihuang's insistence on **punishment (xing (III))** and **law (fa (IV))** at the cost of **benevolence (ren (V))** and **righteousness (yi (VI))** caused the destruction of Qin. Liu Ji, unsettled by his adviser's words, finally ordered a written report on the reasons why Qin lost their empire. Lu Jia responded with a work in twelve sections, the **Xinyu (VII)** (:New Discourses), and presented it to the throne section by section amidst the loud cheers of the Imperial retinue. (cf. Shiji, 97:2699)

In the Xinyu the author assumed the task of inducing his emperor to imitate the conduct of a Confucian sage. This was certainly no easy task, for nobody knew better than Lu Jia that Liu Ji had subdued his enemies through slyness, disloyalty and ferocity. Lu had accompanied the conqueror during his military campaigns, serving him as rhetorician on difficult diplomatic missions. Thus he participated in the negotiations to obtain the release of Liu's father after the old man had been taken prisoner by his son's rival **Xiang Yu (VIII)**. When Xiang Yu threatened to boil the father alive in order to force the surrender of the son, Liu Ji displayed his will power, although scarcely the filial piety required of a Confucian sage, by requesting a bowl of soup made from the resulting juices! (cf. Shiji, 7:328). Such behaviour, as well as his overwhelming pride in the recklessness of his actions, obviously disqualified Liu Ji from ever becoming a Confucian sage. One day the new emperor asked his retinue to tell him frankly what they thought of his rise to power. He wanted them to explain why he and not Xiang Yu had acquired dominance over the world. Two of his generals replied:

"Your Majesty is rude and treats people with contempt, while Xiang Yu was benevolent and kind. But when you send a man to attack a city or to conquer a territory, you grant him what he has subjugated, sharing your gains with the whole world." (Shiji, 8:381)

(I) 陸賈　(II) 劉季　(III) 刑　(IV) 法　(V) 仁
(VI) 義　(VII) 新語　(VIII) 項羽

123

Xiang Yu, according to the generals, had, on the contrary, claimed all spoils for himself and was jealous of able followers. Therefore Liu Ji won and Xiang Yu lost. The emperor agreed and completed this appraisal of his ascension to the throne with a lecture on the importance of making use of clever men. This whole incident demonstrates the attitude of a thief: A good gang-leader must share the spoils honestly with his accomplices. In this way he attracts the most wily scoundrels and his gang will outdo that of any rival.

Although Lu Jia claimed the Mandate of Heaven for his emperor, he did not cling to the traditional point of view, that Heaven singled out the wise and virtuous to found a dynasty. He maintained that to conquer the world one cannot be a sage, yet the emperor must become a sage to legitimatize himself. Accordingly, the failure of Qin was not due to an illegitimate ruler's conquering the world, but rather to Qing Shihuang's unwillingness to modify his behaviour once the empire had been established.

The Xinyu describes benevolence and righteousness as the ruler's guidelines:

"Benevolence is the guidepost, righteousness is the learning of the sage. Who studies them will be enlightened, who loses them will be blinded, who turns away from them will be lost." (Xinyu, 1:3)

First the heroes of Chinese history and mythology are called in to provide unquestionable evidence that only a kindhearted ruler can secure a lasting reign; Yao, Shun, Yu, King Wen, the Duke of Zhou and Duke Tai are all exemplary paragons of virtue. Then the villains who brought their dynasties to ruin are paraded before the reader: Count Zhi (I), who relied on awfulness (wei (II)) and trusted in force (li (III)) and who was destroyed by an alliance of enemy states; Li of Jin (IV), Zhuang of Qi (V) and Ling of Chu (VI) who once ruled over great states, yet who "by insisting on their superior strength, lost their states. They intensified punishments and through this destroyed themselves. That serves as a warning from the past and an example for the future!" (Xinyu, 8:14) Of course Jie (VII), the last Xia ruler, and Zhou (VIII), the last Shang ruler, also figured among the villains. But the focal point of the warnings is an accusation against Qin Shihuang. The Xinyu enumerates his crimes: He took delight in punishment and retaliation and introduced the torture of stretching on the wheel. His armies terrorized the entire realm. Being proud and extravagant, he built high terraces and extensive palaces. (cf. Xinyu, 4:6f)

(I) 知伯   (II) 威   (III) 力   (IV) 厲   (V) 莊

(VI) 靈   (VII) 桀   (VIII) 紂

It is characteristic that the Xinyu summarizes its reproaches under the heading **Wuwei** (I) (:Non-action). The crimes of Qin Shihuang appear as result of his activism: Instead of harmonizing the realm just by his imperial charisma, he interfered with his administration and exhausted the state by his magnified demands. Lu Jia remarks to that:

"The more activities that were displayed, the deeper the world lapsed into chaos. The more laws that were promulgated, the wider crime spread. The more troops and horses that were mobilized, the higher the number of enemies." (Xinyu, 4:7)

This artful attempt to fight tyranny by prescribing a passive role to the ruler refers to a chapter in the **Lunyu** (:Analects), wherein Confucius praises the mythical emperor Shun. Shun, says Confucius, governed without acting (cf. Legge, vol.I, p.295). Thus Lu Jia contrasts the harmonizing inactivity of Shun with the unseeming industry by which Qin Shihuang led his dynasty to the abyss.

Although Lu Jia visibly endeavours to illustrate his warnings with a most gloomy picture of the First Emperor, he does not refer to the outrages which in later times became synonymous with Qin tyranny; His treatises never mention the story of the notorious burial nor the burning of the books. The Xinyu has not been handed down to us in the best condition and we have to consider the possibility that it once contained reports on the two events in passages which have been lost long ago. Although (or maybe because) the Xinyu is considered the earliest Confucian text written in Han times, the literati did not deal with it very carefully. For them Lu Jia was not such an important author as he had neither the authority of a pre-Qin writer, nor was he, in view of his open declaration for eclecticism, an accepted founder of Han Confucianism. Thus his works fell into oblivion. Yet after centuries of negligence a certain Li Tingwu (II) collected all fragments of the Xinyu he could secure and published in A.D.1502 a reconstruction of the text, said to be nearly complete. On this reconstruction all current editions of the Xinyu are based.

The thesis that the Xinyu contained no references to burnt books and buried scholars can also be upheld even if we doubt the reliability of its modern editions. For the following reasons: When some decades after the death of Lu Jia the formula "fenshu kengru" came into circulation, the Confucianists would surely have welcomed the slightest evidence referring to these crimes. As Lu Jia was an eye-witness of the Qin reign any utterances by him concerning the important issue would have been taken up and cited in many other writings. Thus his evidence would have been preserved irrespective of the original source's

(I) 無為　(II) 李廷梧

condition.

An event like the murdering of four hundred and sixty Confucian scholars was monstrous enough to be surely mentioned in a treatise dealing with the despotism of the First Emperor. That the Xinyu contains no comment on this atrocity proves the whole story as a later invention. Lu Jia's silence on the burning of the books, however, does not defeat later reports on this measure. As a man who seized every opportunity to cite from the **Shujing** (:Book of Documents) and the **Shijing** (:Book of Songs) he felt irritated on the destruction of such texts. On the other hand he certainly appreciated the emperor's attitude; afraid of diverging political opinions, Qin Shihuang had tried to standardize the mind of his people as he had previously standardized weights and measures. This idea to destroy anything not in accordance with one's teaching was well known to the Confucianists. Long before Qin Shihuang proceeded to action, Mencius shrilly denounced his opponents for deluding the people, and called for the suppression of "heretical doctrines" (xieshuo (I)) (cf. Legge, vol.2, p.283). That some decades after the composition of the Xinyu the burnt books nevertheless became an important issue is connected with the emergence of the New Text School. We will revert to this point.

3. The need for a benevolent and righteous monarch became more urgent than ever after the death of Liu Ji in 195 B.C., when his widow, the Empress Dowager **Lü** (II), usurped rule over the country. Fifteen years of most wicked despotism followed. During this period the Empress Dowager sought to consolidate the power of the Lü clan and to repel the Liu clan. Many officials who stood in the wrong camp were executed. The conflict ended with the natural demise of the Empress Dowager and the systematic extermination of her relatives. It was with great expectations that the scholars hailed the ascent to the throne of Liu Ji's fourth son as Emperor **Wen** (III) (180 B.C.); for the first time the united China now had a monarch not incriminated by a long record of atrocities.

The scholars celebrated the new emperor as the long awaited sage. To support this theory **Jia Yi** (IV) sought confirmation in the cycle of five hundred years already mentioned in the book **Mengzi** (:Mencius) (cf. Legge, vol.2, pp.232, 501 et seq). During the decline of the Zhou dynasty people had started to speculate that every five hundred years a true king arises. When Qin Shihuang united the realm under his rule, he was believed to have been the predicted sage, coming with great delay. Jia Yi remarks in a memorial to Emperor Wen:

(I) 邪說　(II) 呂　(III) 文　(IV) 賈誼

A 19th century Chinese painting showing the scene of "burning the books and burying the Confucian scholars alive" (:fenshu kengru)

"I have heard that five hundred years passed between the foundation of the Xia dynasty by Yu and the foundation of the Shang dynasty by Tang. From Tang's reign to the rise of King Wu of Zhou it took more than five hundred years. Hence there is a natural law that every five hundred years a sage king makes his appearance. After the reign of King Wu five hundred years passed and no sage king arose. How strange Qin Shihuang seemed to be the long awaited one, but in the end was not. Expectations for a sage king were unfulfilled until the world rallied around Your Majesty." (Xinshu, Shuoning, 1:9b)

"Qin Shihuang seemed to be the long expected sage." For the Confucianists of later times this statement must have sounded absurd. For us it is evidence that the First Emperor was not even by his enemies considered the personified evil from birth. At the time of Jia Yi (201-169 B.C.) the older generation could still remember the rule of Qin. As long as the eye-witnesses were still alive there was no chance that the pseudo-sage could become a figure to whom imaginary deeds were attributed, and thus Jia Yi's evaluation of Qin Shihuang is biased but free from flight of fancy. According to Jia Yi the First Emperor had failed the time of probation imposed by Heaven. He investigated the reason for that and summarized his findings in **Guo Qin** (I) (:The Transgressions of Qin), a treatise which became famous as a primer on despotism.

The recipient of Jia Yi's treatise was again Emperor Wen. Boisterous jubilation over the sage ruler of Han could not obscure the fact that the celebrated emperor was a dedicated follower of Legalism. In order to sound a warning as Lu Jia before him, Jia Yi describes the fall of the Qin dynasty. He describes the rise of Qin Shihuang, his victory over the huge armies mobilized by the Vertical Alliance, and his daring campaign deep into barbarian lands. He also recalls the unique strategic position of the capital "within the Pass", which was protected by strong garrisons. Qin seemed to be forever invincible. But then a band of ragged conscripts with weapons improvised from hoes and sticks shook the empire, and the powerful dynasty collapsed. This disaster, according to Jia Yi, was caused by the Qin emperor's refusal to abjure their practices of punishment and **deceit** (**zha** (II)). Jia Yi repeats the familiar reproaches on the multiplication of laws, the intensification of punishments, and the increase in taxes and of soccage. Yet he also adds a story not to be found in earlier sources: the burning of the books. (cf. Xinshu, Guo Qin, 1:4a) He tells that Qin Shihuang decreed the destruction of all writings propagated by the Hundred Schools of Philosophy in order to make the people ignorant.

Although Jia Yi in his collected works, known as the **Xinshu** (III) (:New Writings), repeatedly draws up attention to the

(I) 過 秦   (II) 詐   (III) 新 書

crimes of Qin, he nowhere refers to any Confucian martyrs. In lieu of that, he discusses the role of the scholars at the Qin court. Obviously, he felt obliged to justify the attitude of these people and to explain the absence of any resistance from them. After all, for centuries the upright official who risked his life to **admonish** (jian (I)) the ruler and to save the dynasty, already ranked among Chinese paradigms. Thus **Bigan** (II), minister of the last Shang king, became worshipped as a hero because of his intrepid remonstrating. It is said that, even when threatened with death, he refused to escape from the court of his monstrous ruler. Advised to go into hiding he answered: "The man who is a minister has no choice than to fight till death." (Shiji, 3:108) Driven by this conviction he intensified his remonstrances till one day the king ordered his body to be cut into two pieces. Such heroism was unknown at the Qin court. Jia Yi tries to explain why:

"In those days there were really thoughtful and accomplished scholars (shi (III)). However, they did not dare to be faithful unto death and to oppose transgressions, because Qin constantly multiplied the restrictions in order to avoid that things taboo be mentioned. Had a sincere address been delivered, the speaker would have been killed before the words had taken shape in his mouth." (Xinshu, Guo Qin, 1:7a)

This explanation must be considered an admittance of common failure which contrasted the sublime values propagated by the Confucianists. There were scholars at the Qin court who opposed the tyrant in secrecy, among them many Confucianists, but no man like Bigan stood up and articulated his grievances.

4. Seventy years after his death Qin Shihuang was assigned an additional role. Thus far he was only a bugbear who warned the Han emperors against harsh government and unreasonable activism. When the Han Emperor Wu established Confucianism as a bureaucratic monopoly, in order to supply the realm with officials, a need developed for a cohesive myth welding together the diverging elements which accumulated under the roof of this favoured school. Thus Qin Shihuang became the fiend who had emerged to destroy the Way guarded by the Confucianists.

In the first decades of Han rule, the influential among the Confucianists adhered to a syncretism consisting of thoughts derived from the most differing currents within the Hundred Schools. Each of them seems to have selected those doctrines which were useful to promote his own career. At best they had a familiarity with the Classics (jing) and a knowledge of the old rites in common. Lu Jia writes from the viewpoint of this

---

(I) 諫　(II) 比干　(III) 士

129

eclectic Confucianism:

"Books must not only be circulated by the school of Zhongni (Confucius) as medicines need not in every case be prescribed by (the famous physician) Bian Que. Everything that agrees with this school is good and may be taken as a model. Thus by adjusting to the epoch, the course of events can be influenced." (Xinyu, 2:5)

Eclecticism was the Confucian answer to modernization. The aspirations of the literati to the sinecures of the new empire were difficult to reconcile with their enthusiasm for antiquity. Yet they were sagacious enough to realize that this Golden Age of antiquity was an unfit example for governing a centralized state. They also understood that their traditional ideas were by no means helpful in solving the political problems faced by the Han dynasty. On the contrary, the Han dynasty judged by orthodox Confucian doctrines lacked any legitimate right to rule. Moreover, orthodox doctrines supported the restitution of feudal structures. These two existential problems collided with imperial interest.

Not all Confucianists approved of eclecticism. An embittered orthodox minority observed their fellow scholars borrowing freely from the teachings of alien schools to fit to the changing social conditions. Even during the reign of Liu Ji, when the first group of Confucianists entered the Imperial services, orthodox voices made themselves heard. They complained that those literati currently seeking public office did not follow the Way of the Ancients. In turn, the court scholars ridiculed the orthodoxy as **"vulgar Confucianists (biru (I))** who do not comprehend that times are changing" (Shiji, 99:2722 et seq). Things got worse, from an orthodox point of view, when after the death of the anti-Confucian-minded Empress Dowager Dou (135 B.C.), her grandson Emperor Wu appointed several hundred Confucian scholars to his administration. Among them was **Gongsun Hong** (II), a former pig-breeder, who advanced to the highest offices as an expert in interpreting the **Chunqiu** (:Spring and Autumn Annals). Incited by reports of such fabulous career possibilities, all office-seekers flocked together under the roof of the Confucian school and started to study the **Six Classics** (Liu Jing). Sima Qian remarks sarcastically upon the onset unleashed by the story of Gongsun Hong's rise: "Henceforth the scholars (xueshi (III)) throughout the empire followed the trend" (Shiji, 121:3118). The distinct esprit de corps which had knitted together the Confucianists during the epoch of the Warring States became ever weaker as more and more of them reached office.

In two movements called the New Text and the Old Text School the Confucianists tried to overcome this dispersal. The **New Text** (**jinwen** (IV)) **scholars** united the hitherto incoherent eclectic

(I) 鄙 儒   (II) 公 孫 弘   (III) 學 士   (IV) 今 文

ideas into a system of learning. They argued that because of the losses due to the burning of the books the Confucian teachings needed to be completely restructured. They were referring to an "oral tradition" (koushuo (I)) and "secret words" (weiyan (II)) said to be traceable to Confucius. This artifice helped them to declare their syncretistic work as the legacy of the great sage. Above all the "secret words" were instrumental in forming the New Text version of Confucianism: The scholars developed with extensive commentaries and subcommentaries to the Chunqiu a timely political theory. At the same time they created an immense cohesive power with a doctrine, which the community of literati attributed to saving the tradition through the perils of Qin rule, when the books went up in flames. Additional cohesiveness was then derived from the feeling of a closed group initiated in secret words. As soon as the first New Texts were published, **Dong Zhongshu** (III) submitted a memorial to Emperor Wu, which urged him to declare those writings for imperial dogma and to cut off the competing teachings propagated by the Hundred Schools (cf. Hanshu, 56:2523).

The New Text scholars soon realized that the process of textual "reconstruction" which they had launched, resulted not only in cohesive powers. The creative licence yielded by a system of learning based on "oral tradition" and "secret words" meant a permanent danger to the consistency of their doctrine. As long as the literati used their inventiveness in conflict only with the emperor or non-Confucian cliques it proved very advantageous to them. But as soon as they had a political quarrel among themselves and each party referred to arguments from the New Texts, the "oral tradition" became destructive to Confucian solidarity and weakened the position of the literati against their adversaries.

In the **Old Text School** (**guwenjia** (IV)) the orthodoxy tried to purify the doctrine from its many foreign elements. Thus they excluded "oral tradition". Nevertheless the tale of the burning of the books fulfilled an important function in the genesis of this school. **Kong Anguo** (V) (ca.165-ca.74 B.C.), an eleventh generation descendant of Confucius, created the legend of Qin Shihuang killing the literati and entwined it with the strange story of the rediscovery of Confucian manuscripts thought to have been lost. In his foreword to the Old Text edition of the Shujing he mentions the martyrdom of the literati for the first time:

"When Qin Shihuang destroyed the ancient records, burnt the books and killed the Confucianists (fenshu kengru), the scholars fled the terror and dispersed in all direc-

(I) 口 說   (II) 微 言   (III) 董 仲 舒   (IV) 古 文 家
(V) 孔 安 國

tions. My ancestors then hid their books in the walls of our house ... (In the middle of the second century B.C.) Gong, the king of Lu, showed enthusiasm for restoring monuments. Pulling down the old residence of Confucius in order to enlarge some hall, he suddenly heard bells ringing and the sound of flutes and harps. He stopped and did not dare to go on with his work. In the wall he discovered the Old Text books hidden by my ancestors: the Yu, Shang and Zhou parts of the Shujing including a commentary, the Lunyu (:Analects) and the Xiaojing (:Book of Piety), all written in tadpole characters." (Shangshu zhengyi xu, 1:3a/b)

The creation of the martyrs' legend and its propagation through the formula "fenshu kengru" thus is connected with the beginnings of the Old Text School. Kong Anguo, by "proving" the existence of a continuous line of written tradition tracing back to his great ancestor shows that neither the destruction of books nor the persecution of scholars could interrupt the Way.

5. Kong Anguo had an influence on the author of the **Shiji** (:Records of the Historian) **Sima Qian** (145-ca.90 B.C.), who wrote the earliest biography of Qin Shihuang. Thus Sima asked Kong for help with his research on the Old Text version of the Shujing (cf. Hanshu, 88:3607). We can be sure that the two scholars on this occasion discussed the assertions which Kong Anguo had written in his preface to this work. Nevertheless Sima Qian adopted his mentor's legend only in part: He reports that Qin Shihuang in the 35th year of his reign (212 B.C.) became annoyed at the **magicians (fangshi (I))** in his service, who in search of a way to immortality had wasted a fortune without producing the elixir they had promised to him. But only when the two magicians who had pocketed most of the money fled the court did the emperor become aware that he had been taken in. Finally intelligence of certain rumours said to be spread by the magicians to confuse the people, gave rise to an investigation. Sima Qian tells us about the subsequent events in detail:

"The masters (zhusheng (II)) incriminated each other. Thereupon the emperor himself singled out four hundred and sixty of them who had violated his prohibitions, and ordered them to be killed in Xianyang. He made these executions known throughout the empire as a warning for all future generations and banished a great number of suspects to the border region. The eldest son of Qin Shihuang, Fusu, remonstrated him, saying: 'The empire is newly established and the Blackheads of distant regions have not yet united with us. All those masters recite and imitate Confucius (Zhusheng jie tong fa Kongzi (III)) and now as you have bound them with your severe laws, I am afraid the realm will not remain at peace. Will you please consider the matter.' Angered by this, Qin Shihuang sent Fusu to the north to supervise Meng Tian in the commandery of Shang." (Shiji, 6:258)

(I) 方 士　(II) 諸 生　(III) 諸 生 皆 誦 法 孔 子

Sima Qian's description of the events leading to the death of the "masters" is only concerned with the magicians. The masters here no doubt were magicians. Except the strange remark, ascribed to Fusu, that all the masters distinguished themselves through Confucian virtues no word suggests any connexion between this affair and the Confucian school. Certainly Sima Qian was aware that the contempt of the literati for the magicians was as big as the ignorance of the Confucian teaching. So why did he create such confusion by labelling the magicians as followers of Confucius?

The things took approximately the following course: In early Han times there circulated an authentic story about some magicians at the Qin court who had died in pursuance of their risky vocation. Scholars like Lu Jia and Jia Yi might have known this story but naturally they were not disposed to look at the elimination of such troublemakers as a misdeed which is to be added to the list of Qin crimes. When Kong Anguo heard of the affair he used it for his own end by turning the dead magicians into Confucian martyrs. Now Sima Qian was in a quandary: As a historian, aspiring for a factual, though not fully objective picture of Qin Shihuang, and, as a member of the bureaucracy, he felt obliged to support the legend created by his mentor Kong Anguo. Thus he just told the whole story according to his knowledge, yet added this half sentence in Fusu's remonstration, which imputed Confucian inclinations to the magicians. Although Sima Qian in his work never mentions any **ru** (:literatus, Confucian scholar) involved in this gruesome affair, his descriptions were sufficient for all later historians concerned with the Qin reign to consider him the chief witness of the Confucian martyrdom.

On the execution of the masters Sima Qian only reports that they have been **killed (keng (I))**. He uses the word "keng" several times in his writings and from the context we learn that it has to be translated "to kill" and never "to bury alive". Originally standing for "pit, moat", "keng" took the meaning of "to trap and kill" and is frequently used by Sima Qian in describing troops who annihilate an enemy army.

From the times of Kong Anguo and Sima Qian it took more than a century for another scholar to embroider the legend by adding a description of how the martyrs met their death. **Wei Hong** (II), gentleman consultant (yilang (III)) at the court of Emperor **Guangwu** (IV) (A.D.25-57) and notable expert on the Old Texts, traced out, obviously stimulated by the connotations of the word "keng", the following story:

"At the time of the burning of the books Qin was very distressed that the world still

(I) 阬   (II) 衛宏   (III) 議郎   (IV) 光武

did not follow the laws which had been reformed by him. Now when the masters (zhu-sheng), approximately seven hundred men, came to apply for positions as palace gentle-men (lang) he gave orders to secretly plant in winter time a pumpkin in a sunny place in the valley afoot of mountain Li. As the pumpkin grew bigger he told the **erudites** (**boshi** (I)) and masters to discuss what it is. All uttered different opinions and so he ordered them to go down and look at it. Yet before the arrival of the masters and the **worthy Confucian scholars** (**xianru** (II)) a hidden mechanism had been constructed and as they incriminated each other and did not reach an agreement this mechanism was released which filled the valley with earth, squeezing them all to death. It ended noiselessly." (Wei Hong, quoted in Yan Shigu's commentary to the Hanshu, Hanshu, 88: 3592)

From now on "keng" took the meaning "to bury alive". Wei Hong's attempt to adjust the content of the legend to the for-mula "fenshu kengru" proved not so convincing.

To Wei Hong it seemed first of all important to depict the vic-tims of Qin Shihuang as real Confucianists. Sima Qian's author-ity, however, rendered such an intention extremely difficult, as he had shown that the masters were mere magicians. Wei Hong dispensed with the attempt of imputing Confucian propensities to the masters, as Sima Qian had done. He instead tried to have the **boshi** and **xianru** involved and opposed them to the masters; the role of the Confucianists in this story was not very impres-sive, though. The fact that they appeared quarrelsome in-stead of behaving like heroes could not stop the veneration for the "martyrs". Wei Hong's tale closes the creation of our legend. From now on it experienced only minor changes and ad-ditions.

Some decades after the publication of Wei Hong's writings, the great sceptic **Wang Chong** (A.D.27-ca.100) in his **Lunheng** (:Dis-courses Weighed in the Balance) discussed the errors of his con-temporaries and tried to uncover some wide-spread Confucian teachings as legends. In this connexion he also got down to the imaginative assertions concerning the life of Qin Shihuang.

Wang Chong did not aspire to a vindication of Qin Shihuang's honour. Adhering to the theory of non-action as taught by the Huang-Lao-School, he shared the Confucianists' distaste for the busy emperor. Nevertheless, driven by his "hatred of the hollow and preposterous" (Lunheng, 20:413) he criticized those stories about the rule of Qin, which he considered as "Confucian exag-gerations". Thus he rejected the opinion that Confucius once had written down a prophecy foretelling the usurpation of the em-pire by Qin Shihuang: "I regard this all as empty talk ... The plain image of Confucius has been magnified in order to dissemi-nate prodigies, and certain people in later times fabricated rec-ords to furnish the evidence they needed." (Lunheng, 26:519)

(I) 博士　　(II) 賢儒

Although Wang Chong in general conceived the process which leads to the establishment of legends as "facts", he took it for granted that Qin Shihuang had Confucian scholars buried alive. By now this thriller was so deeply rooted in the Chinese presentation of history that even a sceptic of Wang Chong's rate did not find anything wrong with its tradition. In his discussion of the "fenshu kengru" formula he stated that the literati in question had fallen victim to evil rumours which had been created by the masters. While Wei Hong only had hinted at the different opinions which had been uttered by the Confucianists and the masters, Wang Chong maintained unmistakably:

"The Confucian scholars were buried alive due to the weird talk of the masters. Thus four hundred and sixty seven men perished." (Lunheng, 7:164)

The role of the masters in the affair was now completely inverted. Whereas in Sima Qian's report their model was still Confucius, they now appear as enemies and slanderers of the literati.

Wang Chong confirms and "clarifies" the proceedings which led to the burial. Nevertheless he remains loyal to his sceptical attitude: He attaches to his "clarifying" interpretation a fundamental criticism of the cohesive myth. He refuses to accept the assertion that the Confucianists sacrificed their life in defense of their teaching. Thus he remarks:

"It is said that the buried Confucian scholars were all people who had hidden the Five Classics and other writings, and that the burning of those books and the murdering of those men stopped the circulation of the Songs and the Documents. Now the destruction of the Shijing and the Shujing and the burying alive of the Confucianists (kengsha rushi (I)) are indisputable. But the assertion that those men were killed in order to wipe out the Songs and the Documents is dishonest and an exaggeration." (Lunheng, 7:163)

These objections of a sceptical outsider did no damage to the legend. The martyrdom of the Confucian scholars in Xianyang remained a famous "historical incident" even in our days.   ●

QUOTED LITERATURE/CHINESE:

● Ban Gu 班固 : Hanshu 漢書 (:History of the Han Dynasty), Beijing 1975 (Zhonghua shuju edition)

● Jia Yi 賈誼 : Xinshu 新書 (:New Writings), Taibei 1975 (Shijie shuju edition)

● Li Zhi 李贄 : Cangshu 藏書 (:The Concealed Writings), Beijing 1959 (Zhong-

---

(I) 坑殺儒士

hua shuju edition)

- Lu Jia 陸賈 : Xinyu 新語 (:New Discourses), Taibei 1975 (Shijie shuju edition)
- Shangshu zhengyi, shisanjing zhushu 尚書正義，十三經注疏(:Correct Meaning of the Shangshu, Thirteen Classics with Commentaries), Taibei 1973 (Shijie shuju edition)
- Sima Qian 司馬遷 : Shiji 史記 (:Records of the Historian), Beijing 1972 (Zhonghua shuju edition)
- Wang Chong 王充 : Lunheng 論衡 (:Discourses Weighed in the Balance), Taibei 1962 (Shijie shuju edition)

QUOTED LITERATURE/OTHERS:

- J. Legge 1: The Chinese Classics, vol.I, Confucian Analects, The Great Learning, The Doctrine of the Mean, London 1865 (reprint Taibei 1972)
- ... 2: The Chinese Classics, vol.II, The Works of Mencius, London 1865 (reprint Taibei 1972)

Qin Shihuang, the First Emperor,
as shown in the Sancai tuhui

Field Reports
·
Sources
·
Information

Cognitive Play:
Some Minor Rituals
among Hong Kong Cantonese (1)

Among the Cantonese Chinese in Hong Kong, there are certain minor but not uncommon expressive activities or rituals in broad sense which often embarrass laymen and puzzle specialists. Laymen lump them all as superstition and apologically accept them as signs of backwardness. Specialists on the other hand find it difficult to put them into any of the categories they are familiar with - religion, magic, sorcery, etc. (2). My hypothesis is that whatever they may be classified as, they all have a basic form which I will call **"cognitive play"**. A cognitive play is a deliberate display of symbols, which may be words or objects, by the individual himself or his agent in order to adjust or readjust his life through analogy and metaphorism. In the following, I will describe two examples of such rituals to illustrate this point.

The first example is a ritual generally known as **da xiaoren** (ta siu-yan (I)) (3) or "Beating the Small Person" practiced by the Cantonese in Hong Kong. **Da** (ta (II)) means to beat and **xiaoren** (siu-yan (III)) means small person. **Xiaoren** or small person is the opposite of **guiren** (kwai-yan (IV)) or the honourable person. Both are defined in terms of the ego's self interests. Thus, those who are harmful to the ego are "small persons" while those who are helpful to the ego are "honourable persons". This binary opposition is universal among the folk Chinese. In more general terms, **xiaoren** refers to harmful elements while **guiren** refers to beneficial ones. The main objective of the ritual is to chase away the former while attract the latter for the sole interests of the ritual's recipient who may or may not be the performer of the ritual.

In comparison with other Hong Kong Chinese rituals, **da xiaoren** is relatively simple. Still, one has to bring food, various **"fu"** (fu (V)) or "credentials", paper cut figures including that of **xiaoren** as well as of **guiren** and mock paper money and gold or silver bullion (thick squares of rough paper bent into bowl

---

(I) 打小人   (II) 打   (III) 小人   (IV) 貴人

(V) 符

138

"Small person" paper wrapping beaten with a rubber shoe

Feeding "White Tiger" with pork fat

shape). When the ritual begins, two candles and three sticks of
incense are lit, food is displayed, then the small person paper
figure wrapped in the "small person paper" is fiercefully
beaten with a shoe or pierced into pieces with a sword while a
chant is being sung. Then paper "credentials" are rolled and
waved over the recipient's body before they are burnt together
with mock paper money and other paper goods. Finally two
small pieces of plano-convex shaped wood which are known as
"bei" (pui (I)) or "cup", are thrown to the ground to find out
whether the ritual is a successful one.

A person may hold this ritual himself, or for three or four
Hong Kong dollars which is about sixty or eighty cents in the
US currency, have a professional performer to perform for him.
There are also individual variations in the performances. For
one thing, the "small person" paper wrapping can be either
beaten with a shoe or pierced with a short sword. What is left
after beating or piercing may be just left on the ground or
burnt. In a still fancier way, they may be put on a small
paper-folded boat and burnt together.

Cross-road is a favorate place to hold the ritual. It may also
be held at a White Tiger altar. Images of the White Tiger are
usually made of stone and found under altars to the major
gods. Such altars only exist in small temples where the profes-
sionals who are usually men known as **nan'm lao** (nan-mo loa
(II)) or the chanting fellow may perform the ritual at a small
fee (about five to ten Hong Kong dollars). A special place for
the ritual is the Lover's Stone Park in the mid-level area on
Hong Kong Island. On the sixth, sixteenth and twenty-sixth
days of each lunar month, many "Beating the Small Person" rituals are held right below the Lover's Stone, a pointed stone
formation which becomes a popular fetish.

The chants used in the ritual vary in length according to the
different persons who sing them. I have collected nineteen such
chants, eight of them clearly involve supernaturals whose names
are loudly announced in the chanting. All the rest do not mention any supernatural beings. The following is an example of
the latter:

> *So and so is now beating the small person,*
> *The small persons on streets,*
> *The small persons on roads,*
> *Male small persons,*
> *Female small persons,*
> *Foreign small persons,*
> *Beat the small persons and invite the honourable persons.*

(I)杯   (II)喃嘸佬

140

> *The honourable persons are invited with their honourable*
> *horses.*
>
> *(The recipient) gets what he wants,*
> *Good luck all year round,*
> *Thousand things are to his satisfaction.*

As you can see, this type of chants only states the recipient's wishes. No help from the supernatural is sought. In fact they are basically the same as the blessing speeches often said by Chinese at weddings or other happy occasions.

Food displayed in the "Beating the Small Person" ritual also suggests strong symbolic and cognitive significance. The standard food displayed here includes: peanuts, walnut, candy, pork fat, sesame seeds and pears. They are selected because their names bear special symbolic meanings, not because they are good for consumption. Thus, the Chinese name for peanuts is **huasheng** (fa-sang (I)), and **sheng** (sang (II)) also means growth and prospects. The name for walnut is **hetao** (hop-to (III)), one character (IV) of the **he** (hop) sound means union and harmony, the right blessing for a troubled marriage or breaking family. Candy is something sweet which symbolizes good things in life. While these symbolize positive things the rest have negative meanings. Pork fat is used to seal the mouth of the White Tiger, a mythological animal classified together with small persons as harmful and vicious elements. Sesame seeds which are scattered by the performer in the ritual are used to disperse the small persons and other bad elements. The Chinese name for "pear" is **li** (lei (V)) which has the same pronunciation as another character (VI) meaning to keep away. Therefore, display of pears would symbolically keep away the small persons from the recipient of the ritual. Clearly all these kinds of food are not offered to either the good or bad elements to consume, but to be displayed for their symbolic functions. To be sure, at the performer's special request, other kinds of food for consumption may be offered.

The symbolic meanings of the paper goods burnt are even more obvious. Among them, the most important one is **bai jie ling fu** (Pak Kai Ling Fu (VII)) or the "Reliever of a Hundred Catastrophies" which is an "all-purpose" credential for disaster-preventing and luck-soliciting. Though there is mock paper money burnt, the images of the honourable person and his horse being also burnt, these can also be interpreted as symbolic display rather than as offering.

(I) 花生   (II) 生   (III) 核桃   (IV) 合   (V) 梨

(VI) 离隹   (VII) 百 解 靈 符

141

As we can see from the above description more than half of the "Beating the Small Persons" ritual does not solicit supernatural help. Through a set of symbolic actions such as displaying the food the names of which are phonetically or metaphorically associated with the effects desirable to him, burning paper goods and chanting, the performer hopes to re-order "his world". He is in fact an idealist in the very crude sense.

The second case is probably more illustrative of the concept of cognitive play. Cantonese love all the numbers whose pronunciations come close to the words with lucky connotations. Thus **san** (sam (I), three), **ba** (pat (II), eight) and **jiu** (kau (III), nine) are the most popular numbers since their pronunciations are similar to the words which mean growth, prosperity and adequacy respectively. It would give one great satisfaction, if some of his possessions bear these numbers and do not include any number which suggests unpleasant prospect such as the four, **si** (sei (IV)), which is pronounced the same way as the word for death, **si** (sei (V)). One kind of object which attracts a lot of people to compete for is the car licence plate which bears those good numbers. Hong Kong car licence has one to four numbers after two English letters. A desirable licence plate may have one to four same good numbers listed together such as 3388 or 8888. It may also have several different numbers listed in a way which can be read as a sentence with blessing connotations such as:

> **yi** *(yat 一)* **ba** *(pat 八)* **yi** *(yat 一)* **ba** *(pat 八)*
> one   eight   one   eight
> *When read in Cantonese, it sounds like*
> **sut fat sut fat** 實發實發

which means truly prosperous truly prosperous.

> **yi** *(yat 一)* **liu** *(luk 六)* **ba** *(pat 八)*
> one   six   eight
> *When read in Cantonese, it sounds like*
> **yat lo fat** 一路發

which means to prosper all the way.

> **yi** *(yat 一)* **san** *(sam 三)* **jiu** *(kau 九)*
> one   three   nine
> *When read in Cantonese, it sounds like*
> **yat sang kau** 一生夠

which means being adequate for the whole life.

(I) 三   (II) 八   (III) 九   (IV) 四   (V) 死

All these lucky figures do not produce any magic power. They are not regarded as sacred nor offered to any supernaturals. Hong Kong Cantonese pay high price for them and display them for no other reasons than adding more lucky elements into their lives. The principle here is that luck attracts more luck, and symbolic luck would eventually bring in real luck. Wishes are fulfilled not through the application of any mystic or supernatural force but rather through the cognitive relationship between the symbolic and the real world. For the same token, undesirable elements in the real world can also be driven away by symbolic actions. While the cult of the lucky licence plate number manifests only the positive principle, the "Beating the Small Person" ritual shows both the positive and the negative ones.

True, some performances of minor rituals clearly involve supernaturals. In regard to the "Beating the Small Person" ritual, as mentioned before, eight chants I have collected do solicit supernaturals. For example, one chant begins like this:

Gods and buddhas in the heaven, please all come!
I first invite you the Earth God,
Then I invite you the God of Old Stone
I beg Buddisatva Kwannon to be here
I also invite the God of Cow

Some performances of the "Beating the Small Person" ritual even have a specific "small person" as the target. His or her name, address and other information available such as the time and date of his birth, names of other members of his family are all written on a piece of paper which will be wrapped together with the small person paper figure to receive fierce beating. This practice is indeed close to black magic, though it was only intended to stop the target small person from making further troubles rather than to hurt him.

The key point here is, however, even in the performances of the "Beating the Small Person" ritual which clearly solicit supernaturals or have strong magic flavor, that the display of symbolic items as described above is still the main part of the ritual. Furthermore supernaturals are solicited mainly for their presence instead of for their power. This is why some chants make a long list of dieties. The calling of these dieties' names, has the same function of displaying the symbolic items. In short, in some minor rituals practiced by the Hong Kong Cantonese, "cognitive play" seems to be the elementary form. ●

NOTES:

1. This paper was originally read at The Symposium on Current Anthropological Studies of Hong Kong which was part of the 78th Annual Meeting of the American Anthropologi-

cal Association held November 27 — December 1, 1979 in Cincinnati. The author would like to thank the Chinese University of Hong Kong for financial support, and its Social Research Centre for logistical assistance to the research involved.

2. Topley calls some of such rituals "occasional rites" which by her definition are "in fact individual. People act singly, or with the aid of a companion or sometimes a ritual expert, to change circumstances in their lives." (Topley, p.99)

3. Throughout the paper, every Chinese term is given both the Mandarin and the Cantonese pronunciations (in a bracket) at its first appearance. Only the Mandarin pronunciation is used after the first appearance.

QUOTED LITERATURE:

● M. Topley: Chinese Occasional Rites in Hong Kong, in: Some Traditional Chinese Ideas and Conceptions in Hong Kong Social Life Today, Weekend Symposium, October 1966, The Hong Kong Branch of The Royal Asiatic Society

●

Paper "credentials" rolled together with mock paper money ready to be burnt

144

How I Came to Doubt Antiquity

GU JIEGANG (I)

Translated and Annotated by Ursula Richter

Gu Jiegang, one of the most eminent Chinese scholars of our century initiated in the 1920s a basic revision of the popular image of China. The Chinese traditionally considered their country and the state as the embodiment of the "proper moral order" and of the highest moral virtues. They believed that the state, preserving CIVILIZATION, was created by great sage-rulers of early antiquity. Gu Jiegang's attempts to prove that these creators were merely mythological personages, and scientific analysis of the canonical books met fierce opposition. Here one may find an interesting explanation of how he started to raise doubts about the traditional image of the Chinese past and a description of the various difficulties he met. It is a good example of how a national mythology is defended and why it is difficult for a historian to promote historical truth.

The following passages were selected from Gu's preface to the 1982 Shanghai reprint of the **Gushibian** (II) (:Critical Discussions of Ancient History), first published in seven volumes between 1926 and 1941 under the general editorship of Gu Jiegang. This gigantic work comprises 350 entries by more than 100 authors, many of whom were leading intellectuals of the "New Culture Movement" (cf. note 13 below). For Gu's preface to vol.I (1926), cf. Arthur W. Hummel: The Autobiography of a Chinese Historian. Being the Preface to A Symposium on Ancient Chinese History (Ku shih pien), Leyden 1931. The present text, which Gu wrote in 1979 and early 1980 before he passed away in December of that year, was extracted with a view to his exposition of the origins and growth of his scepticism towards ancient myths and documents, and is here translated with bracketed specifications, and annotated. The translator's acknowledgment is due to Gu Jiegang's erstwhile assistant, Professor **Wang Xuhua** of the Chinese Academy of Social Sciences, Beijing, for reading and criticizing the draft manuscript of this translation; he also generously supplied the Chinese characters.

***

After having graduated from Beijing University (**Beida**) (III) in 1920, I was appointed assistant librarian by Deputy Chancellor **Jiang Menglin** (IV) (1886-1964)... In November of that year, **Hu Shi** (V) (1891-1962) wrote me a letter, inquiring why **Yao Jiheng** (VI) (1647-1715?) was not listed in my **Qingdai zhushu kao** (VII) (:Treatise on **Qing** Writings).(1) Hu added that Yao's **Jiujing**

(I) 顧頡剛　(II) 古史辨　(III) 北京大學(北大)
(IV) 蔣夢麟　(V) 胡適　(VI) 姚際恆
(VII) 清代著述考

tonglun (I) (:General Survey of the Nine Classics) (2) revealed
his valour for which he merited particular emphasis; whereupon
I told Hu Shi all I knew about Yao Jiheng.

In fact, I had long since paid attention to Yao, finding his
scholarly notions far ahead of traditional views. He had had
the courage to take a critical stand against his (intellectual)
predecessors. Not only did he venture to attack **Zhu Xi** (II)
(1130-1200), the Grand Master of **Song** scholarship, but even
criticized the scholarly authority of the Eastern **Han, Zheng
Xuan** (III) (127-200); not only did he dare to doubt the **zhuan**
(IV) and **zhu** (V) (:Commentaries and Annotations to the Classics), but even the Classics themselves. Consequently, given the
extreme conservatism prevailing among Qing scholars, he fell
into discredit. His works, although most correctly and conscien-
tiously written, were suppressed by his contemporaries, nor did
his family dare to have them printed, so that not much time
went by before they were scattered and lost.

(In order to explain) why I had paid such special attention to
a man like Yao Jiheng, I must refer to my youth. When I was
fourteen,... (laid up with illness for more than two months),
while confined to my bed, I read **Han Wei congshu** (VI) (:Anthol-
ogy of Han and Wei Writings) compiled by Wang Mo (VII). Subsequently I was happily deluded to believe that now I had
studied all books from Han, Wei and Six Dynasties times, understanding the political and intellectual atmosphere of those periods. Some time later, I chanced to browse through Yao Jiheng's
Gujin weishu kao (VIII) (:Treatise on Spurious Books, Ancient
and Contemporary) in which he comes to the conclusion that
eight or nine out of ten such books (as contained in Wang's
anthology) were spurious. This struck my mind like a thunder-
bolt. Only then did I realize that not all the books I had read
were genuine products of the writing brushes of Han, Wei and
Six Dynasties scholars, but had, indeed, to a fair amount been
falsified by Song or even Ming writers. This is how I came to
notice Yao Jiheng. To my dismay, however, I found that all
that remained of his oeuvre was the slim volume of Gujin weishu kao... While copying it, I came to understand that he had
also written (the following): **Yizhuan tonglun** (IX) (:Survey of
the Commentaries to the Book of Changes) in six juan (:sec-
tions); **Guwen Shangshu tonglun** (X) (:Survey of the Old-Text
Version of the Book of Documents) in ten juan; and **Zhouli tonglun** (XI) (:Survey of the Rites of Zhou) in ten juan. Yet, I was
unable to trace any of these.

(I) 九經通論　　(II) 朱熹　(III) 鄭玄　(IV) 傳　(V) 注
(VI) 漢魏叢書　(VII) 王謨　(VIII) 古今僞書考
(IX) 易傳通論　(X) 古文尚書通論　　(XI) 周禮通論

In 1920, working as a postgraduate at the library of my Alma Mater, I chanced upon a complete table of contents of (Yao's) Jiujing tonglun in a Qianlong (1736-95) issue of **Zhejiang tong-zhi** (I) (:Zhejiang Province Gazetteer). This chronicle contained a chapter, **Jingji men** (II) (:Classical Documents), compiled by **Hang Shijun** (III) (1696-1773) who lived about a hundred years later than Yao Jiheng when that great yet unpublished work had (obviously) still existed. Hang writes:

"The 170 juan of the Jiujing tonglun were written by Yao Jiheng - Li Fang (IV) - from Renhe (V). 135 juan deal with genuine works, another 28 with falsifications."

Hang fails to account for seven juan, and I do not know what this means. His account reflects the general arrangement of Yao's book. He divides the Nine Classics in two major categories, viz. the **biewei** (VI), i.e. falsifications done by others (than the alleged authors) or later (than traditionally maintained); and the **cunzhen** (VII), i.e. preserved genuine texts. Rated among the biewei, and meticulously identified as **"weishu"** (VIII) (:spurious books) were the **Yizhuan** or "Ten Wings" to the Book of Changes; the **Guwen hangshu**, i.e. the version already identified by Qing scholars from **Yan Ruoju** (IX) (1636-1704) down to **Ding Yan** (X) (1794-1875) as "Spurious Old-Text Book of Documents";... and the entire Zhouli. How great and valiant an authorial endeavour! But the Yao family dared not publish the book, nor was it included in the (Qing official bibliography of the Qianlong period) **Siku quanshu** (XI)... If one assumes one juan to comprise 10,000 characters, one arrives at a total of about 1,7 million characters - yet such a colossal work was to perish!

After having searched for it wherever I went, I was at least able to borrow from Beida Professor **Wu Yu** (XII) the chapter **Shijing tonglun** (XIII) (:Survey of the Book of Odes) which had somehow survived. While the Book of Odes itself was classified as cunzhen, the interpretations of Mao (Heng) (XIV), Zheng Xuan, and Zhu Xi were put to doubt. I punctuated this chapter and had it printed. Later, **Qian Xuantong** (XV) (1887-1937) told me that (another chapter) **Liji tonglun** (XVI) (:Survey of the Book of Rites), comprising 400,000 characters, was embodied in

(I) 浙江通志　　　(II) 經籍門　　　(III) 杭世駿

(IV) 立方　　(V) 仁和　　(VI) 別偽　　　(VII) 存真

(VIII) 偽書　　(IX) 閻若璩　　(X) 丁晏

(XI) 四庫全書　　(XII) 吳虞　　(XIII) 詩經通論

(XIV) 毛(亨)　　(XV) 錢玄同　　(XVI) 禮記通論

Xu liji jishuo (I) (:Collected Essays on the Book of Rites) edited
by the aforementioned Hang Shijun; I asked permission to make
a copy. More than ten years had passed when, at the home of
the bibliophile (Shanghai) Furen-University (II) Professor **Lun
Ming** (III), I discovered (yet another chapter,) **Chunqiu tonglun** (IV) (:Survey of the Spring and Autumn Annals) which I
once again borrowed and copied, although but a fraction of
five ce (V). (Finally,) in 1935, I visited the Hangzhou home of
one **Cui** (VI) who was an eminent bibliophile... (In his huge library) I discovered Yao Jiheng's **Yili tonglun** (VII) (:Survey of
the Yili) (3); this, too, I borrowed and asked somebody to
make a copy of it. One year later, Beida Professor **Ma Yuzao**
(VIII) borrowed the copies of the Chunqiu- and Yili-chapters.
(Because of the anti-Japanese propaganda activities)..., the
Japanese military leaders had long since kept their eyes on me;
after the "July Seventh Incident" (in 1937) (4) I had no choice
but to escape (from Beijing) in a flurry, leaving me no time to
request the return (of those two copies). Upon my return to Beijing (after the Japanese surrender in 1945), Professor Ma had
already died. I went to call on his family, learning that all
his books had been donated to Beida. For more than twenty
years, I kept searching Beida library, asking the head librarian and his staff for help - to no avail. As to the original
kept in the Cui household, it was taken by Japanese forces during the occupation of Hangzhou. Henceforth, the only authentic
copy of the Yili tonglun will have to be looked for in Japan.

Until today, I have been able to recover merely those four chapters; it is to be feared that the other five are not even preserved in fragments...

While still at home, at the age of about twelve or thirteen, I
once came across a copy of **Guochao xianzheng shilüe** (IX) (:Bib-
liographical Notes on Outstanding Personalities of Our Times) by
Li Yuandu (X) (1821-87).(5) The "Statesmen" section was incomplete, but those on "Scholars" and "Writers" were preserved in
toto. It were these, of course, that most suited my taste... In
the entry on **Cui Dongbi (Cui Shu)** (XI), the following works by
him were listed: **Bu shanggu kaoxin lu** (XII) (:Additional
Notes on the Credibility of High Antiquity); **Tang Yu kaoxin lu**
(XIII) (:On the Credibility of Yao and Shun) (6); **Xia kaoxin**

(I) 續禮記集說　　(II) 輔仁大學　　(III) 倫明

(IV) 春秋通論　　(V) 册　　(VI) 崔

(VII) 儀禮通論　　(VIII) 馬裕藻

(IX) 國朝先正事畧　(X) 李元度　(XI) 崔東壁(崔述)

(XII) 補上古考信錄　　(XIII) 唐虞考信錄

lu (I) (:On the Credibility of the Xia); **Shang kaoxin lu (II)** (:On the Credibility of the Shang); **Fenghao kaoxin lu (III)** (:On the Credibility of the Legends Concerning Wenwang (IV) and Wuwang (V) (7)); and **Zhusi kaoxin lu (VI)** (:On the Credibility of the (Alleged Transmission of the Teaching in the)State of Lu (8)). In these three works he meticulously expounds the history preceding the Western Zhou as well as the life of Confucius himself, proving many entries in the zhuan and ji (VII) (:notes) (on the Classics) to be spurious. This was, after all, something to delight me! However, since it was so rare, I had to wait until after my graduation before I could set eyes upon this magnificent work.

The plain truth that one has to distinguish between the **jing** (VIII) (:the Classics per se) and the **zhuan** and **ji** was something I had already grasped in my childhood by reading **Liujing zhengming (IX)** (:The Correct Terms Concerning the Six Classics) by **Gong Zizhen (X)** (1792–1841). Classical scholars of his day generally dealt with the Thirteen Classics, but he disagreed, maintaining, "Before Confucius was born, there had existed the Six Classics ... One must not arbitrarily add to these." How, then, did the "Six" expand to "Thirteen"? The explanation is probably that during the Han and later, scholars followed the principle, **zhongshi zenghua (XI)** (:following a model, enhancing its glory), subsequently declaring the zhuan, ji and even the zhu Classics. At first glance, it may seem as if they had had nothing in mind but expanding classical scholarship, but in truth they met the obligations of their times by distorting and falsifying coherence and meaning (of the Classics). In mid-Qing times when classical scholarship reached its prime, attempts were made to expound the matter, trying to establish the nature of the additions as well as analysing their time (of origin). Gong, however, was a man of letters, and although he seriously attempted to "determine the Six Classics", in the end he lacked time for research – in which he differed from Cui Shu who devoted a lifetime to classical scholarship...

In his **Shiji (XII)** (:Records of the Historian) in the beginning of the chapter **Bo Yi liezhuan (XIII)** (:Biography of Bo Yi) (9), **Sima Qian (XIV)** (ca.145–90 B.C.) says, "Scholars have extensive knowledge, since they put their trust in the Six Arts." (10) Indeed, the attitude of **kao er hou xin (XV)** (:investigate first, and only then trust) is a serious obligation for all of us who

(I) 夏考信錄　　(II) 商考信錄　　(III) 豐鎬考信錄

(IV) 文王　(V) 武王　(VI) 洙泗考信錄　　(VII) 記 (VIII) 經

(IX) 六經正名　　(X) 龔自珍　　(XI) 踵事增華

(XII) 史記　(XIII) 伯夷列傳　　(XIV) 司馬遷 (XV) 考而後信

149

have devoted their lives to research of historical source material. Sima Qian, however, although advocating the principle, did not follow it unconditionally in his own writings. When we open the Shiji, we are met with a wealth of ancient myths and legends that do not agree with historical fact. Such passages have already been disclosed by **Liang Yusheng** (I) (1745-1819) in his **Shiji zhiyi** (II) (:Doubts about the Shiji) (11). Cui Shu and Liang Yusheng were contemporaries, but owing to the difficult traffic conditions of their day, they were not acquainted, nor did they ever consult each other. Thus Cui Shu, while applying Sima Qian's principle of relying on the Six Arts, merely trusted in the traditions handed down in the Classics, refuting only such legends and myths as held by the "Hundred Schools" (12).

During the May Fourth Movement (of 1919) (13), almost everybody took a sceptical stand against antiquity and strove for a critical reception of it. Then, I frequently discussed with Hu Shi, Qian Xuantong, and others the problem of how to identify ancient writings as spurious or genuine. We gained the assistance of a book-seller who procured a fragmentary copy of **Cui Dongbi yishu** (III) (:Works Left by Cui Shu) (compiled after Cui's death by his sponsor, Chen Lihe (IV)). Somewhat later, with the help of some colleagues from **Yanjing** University (V), I discovered at Yanjing library a copy of Cui Shu's **Zhifeiji** (VI) (:Inventory of Clarified Errors). Later again we formed a travelling company and went to (Cui's home) Daming (VII) in order to collect further material. Unexpectedly, one Yang (VIII) family from Guangping district (IX) sent us another four volumes (of the writings of Cui's brother). In this way, we were able to know yet a little more about him.

With Yao Jiheng and Cui Shu, more and more problems concerning ancient history and documents had risen and caused us to doubt them. At first, we adopted Cui Shu's stand, accepting the Classics, (merely) turning to such material as he had accumulated by his studies of the zhuan and ji. We then proceeded, like Yao Jiheng, to investigate the credibility of the Classics themselves...

Yet another person who inspired my scepticism towards ancient history was **Zheng Qiao** (X) (1104-62). When I entered Beida in 1912, that university employed a number of highly competent scholars under whose guidance I began to do research. I studied literary criticism by reading works such as **Wenxin diaolong** (XI)

(I) 梁玉繩　(II) 史記志疑　(III) 崔東壁遺書
(IV) 陳履和 (V) 燕京大學　(VI) 知非集　(VII) 大名
(VIII) 楊　(IX) 廣平縣　(X) 鄭樵　(XI) 文心雕龍

(:The Literary Mind and the Carving of Dragons) by **Liu Xie** (I) (early 6th century); historical criticism by reading **Shitong** (II) (:General History) by **Liu Zhiji** (III) (661-721); and combined literary and historical criticism by reading **Wenshi tongyi** (IV) (:General Principles of Literature and History) by **Zhang Xuecheng** (V) (1738-1801). After having read these books, I decided for myself to use the path of criticism which is why, from then on, I went in search of books written in the same spirit. Thus, I finally came across (the works of) Zheng Qiao...

He found much to say against the academic writings of ancient times. In his **Shi bianwang** (VI) (:Absurdities in the Book of Odes), for example, he refutes the views of all five commentators, viz. Qi (VII), Lu (VIII), Han (IX), Mao (X), and Zheng (XI). Still, his book was to share the fate of Yao Jiheng ('s work): It is lost. I managed to assemble it from quotations in other books and found his views much to the point... He says, "The Book of Odes and the Book of Documents are trustworthy (sources), yet one must not believe every single character in them to be genuine." ...Zheng Qiao opened my eyes to the dubious aspects of the Book of Odes. On the one hand I studied his ideas, while on the other I inquired into the Odes, following him in that I abandoned the interpretations of those five (commentators) traditionally held (to the present day by conservative scholars). By and by, I began to establish the correct meaning of the Odes for myself. As a result, I wrote a few articles, the first of which were **Zheng Qiao zhuan** (XII) (:Biography of Zheng) and **Zheng Qiao zhushu kao** (XIII) (:Treatise on the Works of Zheng). They were published (in 1923) in the quarterly of the (newly established) Sinological Research Institute of Beida, **Guoxue jikan** (XIV) (subtitled in English, "A Journal of Sinological Studies"), nos.1 and 2. Relying on historical statements, I maintained that the Odes, having originally comprised 3,000 entries, were curtailed by Confucius to a mere 300 (as contained in the present version of the book). However, after having read **Shibenyi** (XV) (:Elucidation of the Odes) by **Ouyang Xiu** (XVI) (1017-72), I was doubtful again, since he states that Confucius did in fact nothing of the kind. (Be this as it may) the Book of Odes represents a collection of ancient popular music, **yuege** (XVII) (:songs and instrumental music), but is not (as held by conservative scholars) a collection of pious **tuge** (XVIII) (:hymns of the disciples (of Confucius)). Such hymn-books did indeed exist in great numbers, but they were soon

---

(I) 劉勰 (II) 史通 (III) 劉知幾 (IV) 文史通義

(V) 章學誠 (VI) 詩辨妄 (VII) 齊 (VIII) 魯 (IX) 韓 (X) 毛

(XI) 鄭 (XII) 鄭樵傳 (XIII) 鄭樵著述考 (XIV) 國學季刊

(XV) 詩本義 (XVI) 歐陽修 (XVII) 樂歌 (XVIII) 徒歌

lost. As regards yuege collections, they contained both text and notation of popular songs and were therefore most scrupulously preserved by the musicians. Desirous of establishing the true character of the Odes, we ought to take into consideration the working conditions of musicians in those days (when the book was compiled)...

Thus, it was Zheng, Yao, and Cui who enticed me into academic work... Thanks be to them, my courage grew considerably, and I soon dared to smash to pieces the idols revered in the Classics. As far as antiquity is concerned, the opinions I brought forward in the **Gushibian** were based on Zheng, Yao, and Cui; as regards the present time, I received the instruction and assistance of **Hu Shi** and **Qian Xuantong**.

Qian had been a student of **Zhang Taiyan** (I) (1869-1936) in Japan. Zhang also dared to criticize the (prescriptive) figures and texts of antiquity. His courage, however, could not stand comparison with those three great scholars... Zhang, being an Old-Text scholar, revealed in his treatment of problems connected with ancient history the views of the Old-Text school. As for Qian, he later came under the influence of **Cui Shi** (II) (1852-1924) who, as a New-Text scholar, was strongly opposed to the views of Zhang Taiyan. The... New- and Old-Text schools originated from the Han.(14) In subsequent centuries the New-Text school broke up into numerous subaltern groups some of which continued... to exist into modern times. I had wondered at this from my youth, failing to comprehend it. Although the Old-Text school was established later than the New-Text school, it had (by the end of the Eastern Han) become generally accepted. However, its renditions of the Classics were far from authentic, having been manipulated or invented during the Han, Wei, and Six Dynasties by scholars who inserted their own ideology. On the other hand, the New-Text scholars gradually deviated from their Confucian views, submitting to influences of magicians and soothsayers as well as absorbing the **Yin Yang** (III) and **"Five Elements" theories** (15). Thus, both the New-Text and Old-Text schools had their strong and weak points.

Qian Xuantong, having experienced the impact (of both), could no longer accept (either of the two) without reservations. He often told me that, when it came to the re-organization of ancient texts, neither (school) observed the principle of **shishi qiushi** (IV) (:to search for truth in the facts) but rather maintained erroneous, subjective views... Later (in May, 1930), enlightened by Qian's words, I wrote my long essay, **Wude zhongshi shuo xia de zhengzhi he lishi** (V) (:Politics and Historiography un-

---

(I) 章太炎 (II) 崔適 (III) 陰陽 (IV) 實事求是

(V) 五德終始說下的政治和歷史

der (the Influence of) the Five-Elements Theory) (16)...

(As an assistant librarian at Beida in 1920)..., the writings I profited by most of all were those of **Luo Zhenyu** (I) (1866-1940) and **Wang Guowei** (II) (1877-1927).(17) Their veraciousness and objectivity, their copious material as well as their comprehensive and precise argumentation once more widened my field of vision considerably. I understood that a reconstruction of genuine ancient history could only be successful if one proceeded from the real objects (of antiquity) ... while I had one-sidedly confined my previous studies to the destruction of the spurious system of ancient historiography ...

In the past,everybody seemed to know that I had been in close contact with and influenced by Hu Shi, while it was obviously unknown how deeply I revered Wang Guowei and how great an intellectual influence he exercised over me. One should never stop short at outward appearances. There were, of course, instances when I disàgreed with him as well. In my opinion he lacked courage to uncover certain fabrications accounting for the fact that so-called genuine history still contains spurious elements. As an example, let me take his Yin Zhou zhidu lun (III) (:On Shang and Zhou Institutions). This essay is based on the Dixixing (IV) (:Clan-Names of the Imperial Houses)which is lost, while parts of it are preserved in the different benji (V) (:Records of Generation) of the Shiji as well as in the Dadai liji (VI) (18). In his essay Wang maintains:

"The abdication of the throne by Yao (VII) in favour of Shun (VIII) was due to the merits of Shun and Yu (IX) (19); however, both Yao and Shun were descended from Zhuan Xu (X) (20), thus possessing (natural) eligibility for state rulership on the ground of their (noble) birth. (Again), Tang (XI) and Wu (XII) (21), due to their virtues, gained (the thrones of) the Xia and Shang; however, they were descended from Di Gu (XIII) (22), (likewise) possessing eligibility for state rulership on the grounds of their birth."

This account (by Wang Guowei) rests entirely on spurious history fabricated during Qin and Han times. It is such fabrications, after all, that supported the claims entered in those days by the **wang** (XIV) (:princes) of the various states for direct descent from the **Di** (XV) (:Holy Emperor of lore), since they

---

(I) 羅振玉　　(II) 王國維　(III) 殷周制度論

(IV) 帝繫姓　(V) 本紀　(VI) 大戴禮記　(VII) 堯

(VIII) 舜　(IX) 禹　(X) 顓頊　(XI) 湯　(XII) 武

(XIII) 帝嚳　(XIV) 王　(XV) 帝

wished it to be believed of themselves that they possessed quali-
fications of state rulership (other than their princely titles).
This shows how Wang was still spellbound by conservative doctrines, unable to unmask them. Still, in my view he remained
the most comprehensive and creative (scholar) of them all...

After my grandmother had passed away, I spent the summer of
1922 on leave of absence from Beida. Through Hu Shi's interven-
tion I received a position with the Shanghai Commercial Press
compiling text-books (for grammar-schools)... Since I had very
few acquaintances in Shanghai, I was at leisure on Sundays,
using the time for investigations of ancient history and source
material. I would note down my results and discuss them with
like-minded friends, the most important of whom I had found
Qian Xuantong, a man of upright character who would never
fail to speak his mind. Yet he had one shortcoming – apart from
giving lectures (at Beida), he used to spend his entire day
visiting and talking to his friends, while at night at his dormi-
tory he would read letters and peruse bibliographical material
...until well after midnight, when it would soon be time for
classes again. Consequently, ...unanswered letters by his friends
would pile up for half a year or were never dealt with. When I
was still in Beijing, he used to be one of my regular visitors,
giving me invaluable advice. After I had gone to Shanghai, however, we lost contact.

In 1922, I wrote him a number of long letters, never receiving
an answer. A year went by, when in February, 1923, he did
write me after all... I was quite delighted and spent a whole
Sunday answering his letter, telling him about the problems I
had pondered over during the past six months, as well as sug-
gesting possible solutions. As for his reply, I waited once more
...in vain.

It was in those days that Hu Shi happened to come to Shanghai
... At Beijing, he edited two periodicals, the weekly **Nuli zhou-
bao** (I) (:"The Endeavour") where he published his political
views, and the monthly supplement **Dushu zazhi** (II) (:Scholars'
Miscellanea). While in Shanghai, he was able to commission some
of his (Beijing) friends of similar political leanings (to carry
on publishing articles in "The Endeavour")... As to scholarly
essays, he could not find a substitute (in Beijing), offering this
task to me. I had then just passed thirty, and courageously accepted, thinking, "Professor Qian never answered my letter...Is
this not an excellent occasion to urge him on a little?" Thereupon, I shortened my letter by its first part concerning the
Book of Odes, and published the second, dealing with ancient
history, in Dushu zazhi, no.9 (April, 1923).(23)

(I) 努力周報   (II) 讀書雜志

154

Who would have expected that the publication of this fraction of a letter under the caption, **Yu Qian Xuantong xiansheng lun gushi shu** (I) (:Correspondence with Professor Qian on Ancient History) would land as a nuclear bomb in Chinese historiography! Even I myself had not anticipated such militant success of my vague attempt. All over the country, everybody who had ever studied some ancient books felt concern with the problems (raised). After all, drummed into the heads of the Chinese from time immemorial had been the stereotype, "Ever since **Pangu** (II) (24) created Heaven and Earth, in the course of the (reigns of) the Three Rulers or Five Holy Emperors, down to the present day" – while now, all of a sudden, they were told that there had never existed a (man like) Pangu, nor had there been any Three Rulers and Five Holy Emperors. They were bound to be excited. Most of them condemned me, while some agreed. The most conservative among them claimed that I must be possessed by a demon to dare raze a sacred temple to the ground by one stroke of my fist...

On the one hand I compiled historical classroom material for Chinese grammar-schools..., on the other I continued vigorously to publish articles in Dushu zazhi wherein I subverted the myths and legends of ancient history. Would these two activities not come into conflict? It was indeed inevitable that they did. I once discussed this predicament with the Chief Editor of the Department of Historical Geography (of the Commercial Press) **Zhu Jingnong** (III) (1887-1951), who told me, "The present government is not likely to bother about such matters yet. If you try and write in a somewhat indirect way, it will be quite all right." I followed his advice, left Pangu downright unmentioned and dealt with the Three Rulers and Five Holy Emperors merely in broad outline, adding the word "so-called" in order to make the reader aware of their fictive character. Regarding text-books published by the Commercial Press, this method already had its history. Early in this century the Press commissioned Xia Zeng-you (IV) (1863-1924) to compile a history book for grammar--schools. He yielded three volumes in which he introduced Chinese history up to the Tang. In the first volume he includes a comparative study of the legend of the Deluge as contained in Genesis and the Epistles of Paul in the Bible, and the legend Yu the Great as controller of the floods. He calls the era of the Three Rulers and Five Holy Emperors the "doubtful age", designating only the time after Zhou Wuwang's victory over the Shang as the "age of culture" in order to express that only at this time (eleventh century B.C.) did China enter the civilized world. If one compares his text-books with mine, the latter appear by no means more radical than the former. But he lived

(I) 與錢玄同先生論古史書   (II) 盤古

(III) 朱經農   (IV) 夏曾佑

in a different time when the imperialist powers were about to slice China up and divide her among themselves. Who, in such times (of external danger), would worry about...ancient history! My own time, however, was marked by (internal) strife between the North and the South. Everybody yearned for reunification (of the divided nation), and the Northern Expedition (1926-27) by the Guomindang (I) (25) was seen as a success... Dai Jitao (II) (1891-1949) (26), quoting (a complaint by a Shandong parliamentarian about the author's "irreverence"), wrote in an article:

"If China is to unite depends solely on the firm belief of the people to have been descended from a common ancestor. If, in a time like this, one claims that the Three Rulers and Five Holy Emperors never existed, one undermines the desire of the entire people for unification. This is simply outrageous!..."

He used such vehement language that the authorities of the Commercial Press, upon learning of this at Shanghai, got quite agitated. The managing director... hurried to talk to **Wu Zhihui** (III) (1864-1953) (27), the "Grand Old Man" of the Guomindang, in order to find a solution, since the Parliament had indeed imposed an extremely severe fine (on the text-book in question), ... which the Press could not afford to pay. (Therefore, Wu) was asked to put in a good word with the government to remit the penalty and merely suppress distribution. Thus, I nearly ruined the Commercial Press by my representation of ancient history...

In 1940, **Chen Lifu** (IV) (*1900) (28) once played a practical joke on me. Since this episode pertains to my academic work and I have been frequently reminded of it, I might as well relate it (at last). In my "Correspondence with Professor Qian" (mentioned above), I quoted the Shuowen (V) (29) as follows:

*"Yu = **chong** (VI) (:animal) (30) derived from **rou** (VII), i.e. a pictorial description;"*
and
"rou = hoof of an animal trodding the ground."

Whence I concluded that Yu the Great had originated from a mythical beast of antiquity. Such phenomena are quite common in totemistic societies and therefore not at all surprising. Now, Chen Lifu in his public speeches would repeatedly drop the remark:

"Has not Gu Jiegang defined Prince Yu the Great as a reptile?"

(I) 國民黨   (II) 戴季陶   (III) 吳稚暉

(IV) 陳立夫   (V) 説文   (VI) 蟲   (VII) 爪

by which he never failed to have the laugh on his side. Well, opinions are not the same when all is said and done. Later, in 1940, when I lived in Chengdu (Sichuan province) (31), it so happened that Vice-Minister of Education **Gu Yuxiu** (I) paid me a visit. After some small-talk,... he touched upon the question whether it might still be possible to determine the birthday of Yu the Great. I said:

*"Yu is (certainly) a legendary figure. It is rather doubtful that he ever existed at all - how can one establish his birthday? Interestingly enough, however, there existed a custom among the **Qiang** (II) people... in Western Sichuan to celebrate the sixth day of the sixth (lunar) month as Yu's birthday. It was a cheerful occasion, with sacrifices and contests, as one can learn from the ancient chronicles of the area."*

Not long after, he parted. I certainly never dreamed of his true intentions! Some time later I heard that the Guomindang government had declared the Double-Sixth the "Day of the Civil Engineer". On this day the papers published a supplement with a speech made by Chen Lifu, wherein he states:

"The controlling of the floods by Yu the Great was the first outstanding achievement in our country's history of civil engineering. Now that Professor Gu Jiegang has determined the Double-Sixth as Yu's birthday, we declare this day the 'Festival of Civil Engineering'."

Only then did I understand why Gu Yuxiu had inquired about this matter during his visit. Of course, Yu's birthday being on the Double-Sixth rests on Qiang lore; besides, it is mentioned in the **Wuyue chunqiu** (III) (:Annals of the (Ancient) States of Wu and Yue) (32) and also occurs in the poems of Su Dongpo (IV) (33), while the gazetteers of the Qiang people contain copious indications (thereof). Thus, one really does not need to quote my name as a reference. Later, **Miao Fenglin** (V), then Professor at Nanjing Central University, wrote an article in which he blamed me for my inconsistency, holding against me that on the one hand I had denied the existence of a man like Yu, while now I came to the fore determining his birthday – this, he found, was really a bit too fickle! One can see that Chen Lifu deliberately used the pretext of his article in order to make a fool of me and give me a bad name as an investigator of ancient history.(34)　●

(I) 顧毓琇　　(II) 羌　　(III) 吳越春秋

(IV) 蘇東坡　　(V) 繆鳳林

NOTES:

1. Compiled by Gu Jiegang in 1916, comprising not only bibliographical material on Qing books but also bibliographical notes on the respective authors.
The names of the Chinese dynasties are assumed to be too generally known to render them in characters or specify their duration or chronology.

2. The "Four Books" and "Five Classics", i.e. the Analects of Confucius, the Great Learning, the Doctrine of the Mean, and the Mencius; the Books of Changes, Documents, Odes, Rites, and the Spring and Autumn Annals.

3. The Yili, together with Zhouli and Liji, forms the present Book of Rites.

4. The date marks the formal beginning of the anti-Japanese war.

5. First printed in 1866, containing 500 biographies of Qing scholars, writers, and statesmen.

6. Tang = Yao; Yu = Shun. Legendary rulers of antiquity. The legend that Yao, although not related to Shun yielded the throne to him because he considered him more virtuous than himself (the "abdiction myth") played a key role in the Confucian notion of meritoriousness as a criterion for civil service assignement.

7. Wenwang, legendary founder of the Zhou, whose capital was Feng; Wuwang, his son, whose rule allegedly began in 1122 B.C. and whose capital was Hao.

8. The ancient state of Lu, home of Confucius, where he is said to have taught his disciples, is conventionally represented by its two main rivers, Zhu and Si.

9. An official, son of a prince, who allegedly lived in the Shang period and serves as a model of modesty and loyalty.

10. The original meaning of the term, Six Arts, had been, ritual, music (and ritual dance), archery, charioteering, writing, and mathematics. During the Han, however, the term became a synonym for the Six Classics, i.e. the Five Classics (cf. note 2) with the addition of the lost Classic of Music. Sima Qian applies it in the latter sense.

11. First published, in 36 juan, in 1787.

12. The numerous philosophical schools of pre-Qin times.

13. The date marks political events; the reformist intellectual "New Culture Movement" affiliated with May Fourth began in 1915 or thereabouts and lasted well into the 1920ies. Its general aim was to re-organize Chinese cultural heritage and to uncover and remove orthodox Confucian preconceptions.

14. These two schools of Confucian scholarship were concerned with restoration of the Classics that had allegedly perished in the Qin fire, i.e. the burning of the books (particularly the Confucian canon) by the Legalist-minded First Emperor in 213 B.C.

15. Ancient Chinese concepts of cosmological order and balance, later used to justify the seizure of power by an ursurper or a new dynasty.

16. Cf. Gushibian, vol.V (1935), pp.404-617.

17. Eminent scholars who, among other important research, did archaeological studies on oracle bones from the Shang. Both were Qing loyalists after the founding of the Republic in 1912.

18. "Rites of the Greater Dai", to be distinguished from those of the "Lesser Dai" which form part of the canonical Book of Rites.

19. Yu the Great, the "controller of the floods" who allegedly succeeded to the throne after Shun.

20. Legendary grandson of the Yellow Emperor, second of the Five Holy Emperors.

21. Tang = Shang Tang, legendary founder of the Shang dynasty; Wu = Wuwang (cf. note 7).

22. Successor to Zhuan Xu, fifth of the Five Holy Emperors.

23. Cf. Gushibian, vol.I (1926), pp.59-66.

24. Legendary founder of the universe.

25. The Nationalist Party founded by Sun Yat-sen. It ruled the Republic of China until 1949, and continues to do so on Taiwan.

26. Secretary to Sun Yat-sen; later extremely conservative politician of the Guomindang.

27. Scholar, social reformer; one of the "Four Elder Statesmen" of the Republic.

28. One of the Chen brothers who formed the extremely right-wing "CC-Clique" of the Guomindang.

29. The Han dictionary.

30. It is important for the following passage to note that the connotation of chong as "insect, reptile" is of more recent origin, while the Shuowen connotes it as a collective name for animals. Gu applied the term in this sense, merely wishing to indicate possible totemistic origins of the cult of Yu the Great.

31. During the anti-Japanese war, the Republican government as well as a number of universities and individual scholars withdrew to the Western Chinese hinterlands.

32. Compiled by Zhao Yi of the Eastern Han.

33. One of China's most famous (Song) poets (1036-1101).

34. Ironically enough, this instance of modern "myth-making" fabricated by right-wingers found devout imitators in those leftists who subjected Gu Jiegang and the "Gushibian clique" to a criticism campaign during the 1950ies, who quoted Gu's "settling of Yu's birthday" as a proof of his scholarly ineptitude. Then, Gu found it below himself to clear up the matter. The Gushibian was hushed up in Mainland China and during the Cultural Revolution became downright taboo, the more so as Gu and his colleagues abstained from applying Historical Materialism "as a spice for each and every dish" (Gu Jiegang in his preface to Gushibian, vol.IV (1933), pp.22-23). Owing to the iconoclast demolition of the Confucian myths put forward by many of its authors, the book was not much welcome in Taiwan, either. It is therefore all the more noteworthy that the Shanghai Guji chubanshe (:Publishers of Ancient Literature) undertook the 1982 reprint in a completely unaltered photostat, the only addition being Gu's new preface from which these passages were extracted. However, an entirely new vol.VIII to the Gushibian, devoted to discussions of historical geography, was drafted by Gu Jiegang, edited by Wang Xuhua, and is forthcoming in 1984.

159

The Village State in Traditional Vietnam

NGUYEN TIEN-HUU

In all social classes of the traditional Vietnamese society religious feeling expresses itself by means of a powerful, intense vi-
tality. Religiosity permeates daily life, surrounds every action,
important as well as unimportant. An intense activity shows itself everywhere: With great love and gratitude one offers a sacrifice to the Ong Troi (:"Lord Heaven") or bows down deep in
reverence before Buddha. With the same piety, however, one prays
before the statues of the departed, who in life were beggars,
toilet cleaners, criminals, those guilty of incest and licentious
behaviour, at the foot of a tree, before a rough stone, a dead
whale, the picture of a tiger or a deserted boundary post. Magi-
cal acts are mixed in with the noblest of religious rites. In
the Buddhist temples (chùa), next to Buddha and Boddhisattvas
are enthroned Daoist deities and popular spirits. As foreign major religions, Buddhism, Confucianism and Daoism were introduced into Vietnam very early. However, it would be completely
false to call Buddhism the national religion of the Vietnamese –
quite the contrary. L. Cadière: "I dare say that in the provinces of the kingdom, almost all of the Vietnamese live and die
without ever having performed in their whole life one single act
of the Buddhist religion." (Cadière 1958, p.31) In the course of
centuries, Buddhism, as well as Daoism and Confucianism, has
been completely assimilated into the native faith, an animistic
nature religion. So, in the Vietnam of today Buddhism remains
a degenerated, mixed popular religion, just as Confucianism
has almost died out since the disappearance of the old scholars,
who were strongly influenced by the Chinese. So, too, Daoism is
a combination of superstition and fortune-telling for the people.
As an additional religious syncretism, Caodaism has not yet
found its expression in the people. Therefore, only the belief
in spirits remains as the true ancestral religious form of the
Vietnamese. And although this belief contains many superstitious
elements, one finds, especially in ancestor worship and the cult
of heaven, a true, deep religious feeling. With the great mission-
ary, ethnologist and philologist Léopold Cadière, who lived among
the Vietnamese people for more than 63 years, we can say: "The
true religion of the Vietnamese is the spirit cult. This religion
has no history, because it dates from the origins of the race."
(Cadière 1958, p.6)

This belief in spirits expresses itself most clearly in the numerous village cults, in which the peasant develops his religious
life in complete freedom. While family cults and the state cult
were strongly influenced by the Confucian state morality, the

village cults - thanks to the great political-social independence from the state - remain a true expression of traditional cultural wealth.

The examination of village cults and their importance in daily life allows us to look deeper into the character of Vietnamese culture than we would be able to do by a study of the foreign major religions (Buddhism, Confucianism, Daoism, Christianity), which remain more or less alien to the masses of the people. A great deal of work has been done on these introduced religions, at the cost of understanding the ancestral faith - the major component of Vietnamese culture. This has led to a hasty, superficial judgment, namely that Vietnamese culture is only a regional form of the Chinese civilization. New archaeological research has proven "the falsity of this simplistic conception" as Prof. O. Jansé maintains: "One can assert that the Vietnamese civilization has its own originality." (Jansé, p.1645) This "own originality" of Vietnamese culture, especially in the field of religion, can evidently not be found in the societies of the cities and the court, which, in the course of thousands of years, bloomed under the influence of foreigners. It can be found rather much more in the outlying, closed-off villages. They are looked upon as independent "Village States" (làng-nước; villages--états) and count as a "fundamental element of the unity of Vietnam since the most remote times." (Ibid., p.1645)

The Vietnamese Village: a "Village State" (LÀNG NƯỚC)

From a distance, the stranger approaching a Vietnamese village sees only a thick, green bamboo fence, which surrounds the entire village area. If he wants to enter the village itself, he must go through a large gate, which, especially in North Vietnam, is often built of fired stone. Only then can he see the houses, which stand between ponds and bamboo groves. During the night the gate is always locked. The living, evergreen and untouched bamboo fence and the strong, secure gate serve not only as a protection against thieves, robbers and wild animals, they are much more a symbol of the **unity of the village and its independence from the state.**

In the last few centuries there has developed a far-reaching independence in the Vietnamese village. The village has its own political administration and its own cult, both completely independent from the state and respected by the state as customary law. Pierre Gourou writes:

"At the same time a protection against dangers from the outside, the fence is a kind of sacred boundary for the village community, the sign of its individuality and of its independence! If during a period of troubles a village has taken part in disturbances or given refuge to rebels, as the first punish-

161

ment inflicted upon it, it is forced to cut down its bamboo fence. This is a grave insult to its self-respect, a mark of degradation; the village feels itself to be in a situation as embarrassing as that of a human being who has been stripped and left naked in the middle of a crowd of clothed people." (Gourou, p.250)

From the political point of view, the Vietnamese village is a state in itself, a "village state". This is clear also in the language. Whenever as matter of the village or of village affairs, the expression "LÀNG-NƯỚC" is used; "LÀNG" means village and "NƯỚC" means state, nation, fatherland. In common speech the village problems are called "VIỆC LÀNG" and "VIỆC NƯỚC", which mean the problem of our village-nation. Administration and local justice are the duty of the council of elders. Its meeting house, the ĐÌNH, is at the same time town hall and temple of the guardian spirits of the village. All administrative, judicial, religious and cultural matters are discussed in the ĐÌNH. The council of elders bears full responsibility for the village in its dealings with the state, which considers the village as a whole, and not its inhabitants as individuals. About the village, Vũ quốc Thúc says that it is "a moral personality in the legal sense ... it conducts itself not like an administrative division, but like a kind of vassal state. Foreign observers have often remarked, and rightly, that the traditional Vietnam behaves like a federation of communes." (Vũ quốc Thúc, p.20) The only one who speaks for the community before the government authorities is the village leader, lý-trưởng.

Numerous proverbs express with pride this feeling of independence. For example: "vô vọng bất thành quan" (:"No one becomes a mandarin without a feast in the village"). This means: Only after the village feast at which the new mandarin, appointed by the king, is presented to the village dwellers can he take office. This is demanded by the custom of the village, and, in the eyes of the villagers, this tradition is superior to the imperial orders. For: "Phép vua thua lệ làng" (:"The king's law yields to village tradition").

In this respect the villagers enjoy perfect political freedom. This is maintained also by Léopold Cadière: "The Vietnamese communes are in effect true moral persons enjoying all civil rights, administering themselves just as they wish in internal affairs, where the mandarins intervene very rarely and only in case of conflicts." (Cadière, p.55) (1)

The Vietnamese are proud of this independence, just as the villagers are proud of their bamboo fence as the characteristic of their village. As Prof. Jansé remarks, "... a village-state, so typical of the Vietnamese nation and which was still to be seen recently, protected by thick hedges of cactus and bamboo, evoking the idea of the autonomy of which the villagers were so

An example of a village gate (Tho Ha village, Vietnam)

jealous." (Jansé, p.1668)

In religious life also this freedom is reflected. Each village has its own cult: that of the village guardian spirit. The guardian spirit of the village (Thân Thành-hoàng, literally: spirit of the walls and of the pits, meaning the fortress) rules only over the territory of the village. This cult is local and completely independent, not only of the state but also of the neighbouring villages. The guardian spirit of the village is chosen and named by the villagers themselves. A few, well-known spirits have received an imperial certificate (thân-sắc) from the Ministry of Religion. This imperial recognition of the guardian spirit sanctions the ceremonials of veneration and the construction of a temple in honour of the spirit. This thân-sắc represents the only religious connection between state and village.

This is, however, only a purely formal sanction. The connection between cult and government authorities is made no stronger by these means. Sometimes through this imperial certificate the local cult becomes important beyond its own region. Then people from all the neighbouring villages come together in this one place to celebrate the more important festivals – a true cultural meeting. Then even more respect and recognition are shown for the independence and authority of the guardian spirit in its own village.

The state sees, however, by means of this thân-sắc a way to get a deeper insight into village conditions. The emperors of the later Lê dynasties (towards the end of the 17th century) tried once to regulate the village cults; the imperial laws, nevertheless, had to yield to the deeply rooted local traditions in many villages. Jeanne Cuisinier reports:

"... when the certificate has been delivered, it is committed to the care of either the first notable in the village or the guardian of the ĐÌNH (sometimes to the guardian of the pagoda); the cult becomes neither more solemn nor more lively, but a local tradition enters thus into the framework of general tradition, and the custom is, by this act, linked to the state. Towards the end of the seventeenth century, the sovereigns of the later Lê dynasty saw in this linkage a means of exercising a more effective control of communal affairs; they tried to standardize the rites and even the legends, but, thanks to the autonomy of the customs a certain individuality was preserved." (Cuisinier, p.365)

The religious independence of the village is strengthened even more by means of the taboo of the "period of closure" (bế-tỏa thôn-xóm). During the commemorative ceremonies of the guardian spirit, when the commemorative rite (HÈM) is practiced, the village is closed to strangers, cut off from the rest of the world. The village gate is locked; the independence of the village can-

164

not be better symbolized. (Le van Hao, p.33)

This custom corresponds to the "pali-time" (period of time when the village is closed) during the Tiwah Festival (festival of the dead) among the Ngadju of southern Borneo (Stöhr, Zoetmulder, p.32), and the "kiêng-time" of the NHANG in the mountainous area of North Vietnam during the festival honouring the village guardian spirits (phi) (Abadie, p.91). As the village is an entity within the state, so also does it form a unit in religious life. The Sino-Vietnamese word for village is "xã". The word "xã" (I) is made up of two class symbols: the symbol for saint or godly one (II), and the symbol for ground or place (III). Therefore, (the village) means literally: the place sealed with the sign of the saint, or, in other words, the place that is divinely protected (by the guardian spirit). According to the etymology of the word, the village is **primarily a religious community**. (Phan thi Dac, p.25) The destiny of all those who live in the village is tightly bound up with the cult of the village guardian spirit. If the spirit is not content, then the whole village is punished:

"Toét mắt là tại hướng dình
cả làng toét mắt chứ chi mình em đâu."

"Because of the wrong orientation of our ĐÌNH
now I have an eye inflammation.
But I am not the only one affected,
everyone in the community has
an eye inflammation."

Each villager must submit himself to the old traditions. This is expressed in a proverb:

"nhập giang tuỳ khúc,
nhập thôn tuỳ tục."

"A ship
that finds itself on a river
must follow the current of the river.
A man
who lives in a community
must respect the customs of the community."

Like the government regulations, the customs of the community have their authority in law:

"làng theo lệ làng
nước theo lệ nước."

(I) 社   (II) 礻   (III) 土

165

> "The village has its own laws,
> just as the state has its own laws."

The political, social and religious ties with one's village are so strong that one knows only a little of the world outside of it, and there is very little that binds one to that outside world. A Vietnamese peasant without village ties is a man without a home.

"The village, the commune, is almost something sacred for the Vietnamese. The Vietnamese does not seem to have the idea of patriotism which we have in Europe ... But if the Vietnamese loves his large country with a rather embryonic and unconscious love, in return, he is attached to his village, to his little country, with all the fibers of his soul..." (Cadière, p.55)

Within the village now, the clan, stable in itself, represents a social and sacred entity, to whose interests the family is subordinate. To sum up, the Vietnamese "does not exist as the citizen of a nation, but rather as the member of a commune." (Vũ quốc Thúc, p.20)

This is how Vietnam appears at the beginning of the colonial period and in sources related to its more distant past. It seems that each tribe, each community lived isolated from the others. There was, perhaps, an indefinite ethnic consciousness activated during foreign aggressions and propagated by the court in the form of national cults (such as the Hung kings, the Trung sisters, etc.). But under peaceful conditions the village commune remained the most important entity for the Vietnamese population. The state identity was shared predominantly by the ruling elite.

The MUONG, the mountain tribesmen of North Vietnam, also still live in this way. The MUONG are very similar to the Vietnamese in all aspects of daily life, so that Jeanne Cuisinier, who studied the MUONG, could say: "The Muong are the backward Annamites (= Vietnamese)." (Cuisinier, p.563) "The Muong are very conscious of the responsibility of each individual in a well-defined group: the family, the village, and to a certain degree the canton; but they do not realize a responsibility and a solidarity wider than that." (Cuisinier, p.294)

The situation is just the same among the Ngadju in southern Borneo. "The world of the Ngadju is his own village," says W. Stöhr. "What lies outside of the familiar village area is sinister and evil." (Stöhr, Zoetmulder, p.29)

During the colonial period, the new Vietnamese nationalism and the state identity evolved and were popularized. One should note, however, that the classical nationalism similar to those accepted in Europe was relatively weak. On the other hand, there was a strong Communist ideological influence and it became predominant. One may relate it to this old communal tradition, but, perhaps, the weak nationalistic feeling was no less significant. Therefore, a universal social ideology constituted an important factor in the war for national liberation. ●

NOTES:

1. "In northern and central Vietnam the XA (village) has traditionally functioned as an almost autonomous social and economic unit." (Lebar et al., p.167)

QUOTED LITERATURE:

● M. Abadie: Les races du Haut-Tonkin de Phong thô à Lang son, Paris 1924
● L. Cadière: Croyances et pratiques religieuses des Vietnamiens, vol.1, Saigon 1958; vol.2, Saigon 1955; vol.3, Paris 1957
● J. Chesneaux (ed.): Tradition et révolution au Vietnam, Paris 1971
● J. Cuisinier: Les MUONG. Géographie humaine et sociologie, Paris 1946
● P. Gourou: Les paysans du delta tonkinois, Paris/La Haye 1965
● O. Jansé: Vietnam, carrefour des peuples et des civilisations, FRANCE-ASIE/ASIA, no.165, Tokyo 1961, pp.1645-1670
● Le van Hao: Ngôi Dînh và hôi mùa Viêt-nam (:The DINH and Season Festivals in Vietnam), NGHIEN CUU VIETNAM (:Vietnamese Studies), no.5 & 6, Hue 1967, pp.33-40
● F. Lebar, G. C. Hickey, J. K. Musgrave: Ethnic Groups of Mainland Southeast Asia, New Haven 1964
● Nguyen Tien-Hu 1: Vietnam, Geschichte und Kultur, with A. Eckardt, Freudenstadt 1968
● ...2: Dörfliche Kulte im traditionellen Vietnam, Munich 1970
● Phan thi Dac: Situation de la personne au Vietnam, Paris 1966
● W. Stöhr, P. Zoetmulder: Die Religionen Indonesiens, Stuttgart 1965
● Vũ quôc Thúc: L'économie communaliste du Vietnam, Hanoi 1951

An example of a "DÌNH"

The Challenged National Identity:
When Chinese Wanted to Become Westerners
THE "DEBATE ON TOTAL WESTERNIZATION" IN CHINA 1934-1935

●

PETRA KOLONKO

As an addition to the contributions on "Ethnic Identity and National Characteristics" in EAC/No.1 I would like to refer to a discussion which took place in China in the 1930s which had as its basis the proposals made by several Chinese sociologists for a total westernization of China. The themes of this debate ranged from the comparison of Eastern and Western cultures to the question of the national characteristics of China and their validity.

This debate "Quanpan xihua lunzhan" (:"debate on total westernization") is relatively unknown and documentation for it is hard to come by. In the radicalness of its demands for a complete and total acceptance of Western culture it went one step beyond the tradition of leaning towards the West begun with the May Fourth Movement of 1919.

Although the debate shows a considerable lack of clear definitions, its study reveals what kinds of elements were regarded as constituting culture in the Chinese view, some concepts probably still being valid at present. It appears surprising that such a demand for a total acceptance of a foreign culture was ever made of China. Therefore the most important points behind this proposal will be briefly discussed below.

The debate began in 1933, continued until 1935, and was published mainly in two Canton newspapers, "Guomin ribao" and "Guangzhou ribao", as well as in the magazine "Independent Critique" ("Duli pinglun"). Articles by the supporters of total westernization and several replies from their opponents were published in three collections:

1. **Lü Xuehai** (ed.): **Quanpan xihua yanlun ji** (:Collection of Essays on Total Westernization), Canton 1934
2. **Feng Enrong** (ed.): **Quanpan xihua yanlun xuji** (:Continuation of Collected Essays on Total Westernization), Canton 1935
3. **Mo Faying** (ed.): **Quanpan xihua yanlun sanji** (:Third Collection of Essays on Total Westernization), Canton 1936

Chen Xujing is considered the most active supporter of total westernization. Born in 1903, he served as Professor of Sociology and Political Science at **Lingnan** University in Canton (Cole, pp.85-91). Three of his fellow supporters – **Lu Kuanwei, Feng Enrong** and **Lü Xuehai** – also taught at the same university.

The thinking behind the proposal of these four Chinese scholars can be summarized in the following four main points:

1. Culture is a complex whole and cannot be divided. (Lü Xuehai, p.11, p.87; Feng Enrong, p.7) Each part of culture – for example politics, philosophy, economics and social institutions – stands in close relation to all the others, the changing of one part will automatically influence the others.

2. Western culture (1) is far more developed and advanced than Chinese culture (Lü Xuehai, p.12, p.81). Ancient Chinese culture is not suitable for the modern world with its different political and economic conditions.

3. Westernization is a trend which is to be seen all over the world, not only in China (Lü Xuehai, p.12). If China wishes to attain an influential position in the modern world, she must westernize.

4. Some parts of Chinese culture have already been westernized but only externally (Lü Xuehai, p.107). China's new system of government, communications and industry are westernized, but this kind of westernization is not only insufficient but dangerous, for it focuses on the materialistic achievements produced by Western culture and neglects the spiritual foundations of Western society which served as the basis for these very achievements.

The "total westernization" point of view as summarized above was criticized by conservative scholars who wanted to "restore the old" (fugupai (I)) like **Zhang Dongsun** and **Liang Shuming** and by moderate scholars who wanted to blend elements of Western culture (zhezhongpai (II), "the compromisers") like **Wu Jingchao** and **Zhang Qing**. Still, most of the opposing participants of the debate have to be classified as "compromisers" since, as Lu Kuanwei points out, even the conservatives had already accepted some westernized aspects of Chinese culture (Feng Enrong, p.168).

•

First of all, the opponents of westernization had to attack the basic assumption that culture can not be divided. Wu Jingchao, a sociologist, refused to accept this principle since no scientist had ever proved it (Wu Jingchao, p.2.). Instead he maintained that some areas of culture are independent and can change independently without affecting other areas; others are intercorre-

---

(I)復古派   (II)折衷派

169

lated and a change in one area influences one or more of the others. Therefore he came to the conclusion that it is possible to adopt desirable areas of Western culture and reject undesirable ones. "We can learn from their political thinking, but we don't have to copy the custom of lifting the hat when we meet a woman;..." (Wu Jingchao, p.3.) Finally Wu Jingchao asked Chen Xujing whether the Chinese would have to speak Western languages after a complete westernization.

Such attempts to group things together which in a Western sense cannot be categorized, like here the way of political thinking and superficial things as to lift the hat when one meets a woman, appear often in this debate and may seem strange on the first view. On the other hand attempts like that may reveal to what extent (and specific manner) "superficial" things, day to day habits, manner of dress etc. are regarded by the Chinese as important for constituting culture and identity. Terms and concepts such as culture, identity, state, nation, religion etc. are of an abstract nature, but the integral parts of what constitutes such abstract concepts differ from society to society. Therefore this debate is of interest as it provides the framework for further analysis of how the Chinese view culture and identity.

Although **Hu Shi**, who is said to be the first to have used the phrase of "total westernization" in the 1920s (2) was sympathetic towards the propagation of this principle he took a moderate position in this debate. Without literally rejecting the hypothesis of cultural indivisibility he gives a more differentiated view of culture: Every culture has certain powers of resistance. It tends to reject new influences from within as well as from without. Whether or not the new aspect of culture is incorporated into the prevailing society depends on how useful and suitable it is seen to be by the members of that society. Therefore, it is fully possible that some parts of a culture remain unchanged even as others are in the process of changing. For example, guns are more useful than bows and arrows, but there is no necessity to change one's clothing if it is suitable for the surrounding. (Hu Shi, pp.5-6) But Hu Shi also admits that there is no reliable standard for the evaluation of cultural elements (Hu Shi, p.6).

●

The supporters of total westernization were not in agreement with the idea of selecting bits and pieces of a culture. Although they admitted that there were undesirable areas in Western culture they saw a bigger danger in holding on to a dualistic division in the tradition of the 19th century's formula "zhongxue wei ti, xixue wei yong" (I) (:Chinese studies for es-

(I) 中學為體,西學為用

sence, Western studies for practical use). This "**ti-yong**"-sol-
ution which was propagated by **Zhang Zhidong** (1837-1909), a
Qing-dynasty statesman, had served as the basis for all reforms in the 19th century. By using the terms "ti" (I) (:body,
substance, essence) and its contrary "yong" (II) (:praxis, tech-
nique, application) it implied the superiority of Chinese culture
and indicated the belief that there was no need to change the
Chinese "ti"-basis and that it would be enough to add some
Western "yong"-techniques to it in order to modernize China.

"The 'compromisers' want to combine Chinese principles (dao
(III)) with Western instruments (qi (IV)), but what use have
our principles got if they have to rely on foreign instruments?"
asked Chen Xujing (Lü Xuehai, pp.6-7). To classify Western culture as materialistic and Chinese culture as spiritual is wrong
according to Chen, because materialistic achievements must have
a spirit which produced them (Lü Xuehai, p.7). And to say
that Western culture is moving (dong (V)) whereas Chinese culture is static (jing (VI)) is already admitting that Chinese culture is dead for a culture which does not develop is not alive.
Chen accuses the followers of a "ti-yong"-solution of opportun-
ism for they want the best of both worlds: " They want to be
able to have several wives and ride in a modern car;..."
(Feng Enrong, p.116). And Lü Xuehai warns the Chinese to
adapt basic principles of Western culture unless they want to
become helpless victims of imperialism. If China had westernized
during the **Tongzhi**-period (1862-1875) he writes, then Japan
would not be occupying Manchuria now. (Feng Enrong, p.66)

•

What is going to happen to Chinese culture after complete westernization? Is it not obligatory to save the ancient Chinese culture (**guyou wenhua** (VII)) and the national characteristics (**guo-
qing** (VIII)) and build a culture on a Chinese basis (**zhongguo
benwei wenhua** (IX))? It was difficult for Chen and his colleagues to find convincing answers to these questions in the
light of growing nationalism and conservatism. Like their predecessors in the May-Fourth era they had to revaluate the Chinese past to make their demands plausible. First of all there
existed different concepts of "national characteristics".

"If some people argue that geographical conditions are a national characteristic, then they must admit, that China's conditions
are not so different from other countries'", writes Chen Xujing
(Chen Xujing 1, p.7). Natural conditions alone do not justify a
different development of culture; the more advanced a culture
is, the less important are its geographical foundations. Others

(I)體 (II)用 (III)道 (IV)器 (V)动 (VI)静
(VII)固有文化 (VIII)國情 (IX)中國本位文化

171

named religion as a national characteristic and claimed that Chinese polytheism could not be changed into Christian monotheism. Lü Xuehai rejected this thesis by arguing that China had already had one hundred years experience with Christianity and although it was contradictory to Chinese faith the country had been able to adopt it (Feng Enrong, pp.59-60).

Is Chinese literature a characteristic which is to be preserved? According to Lü Xuehai there was no progress in Chinese traditional literature. Old forms were copied, old opinions reappeared in new formulations. (Lü Xuehai, p.73) China's literature was aloof from daily life, he writes, repeating the argument of the May Fourth Movement. A new kind of literature is needed. If the Chinese were to reestablish the standards of literary tradition, what use could the literary revolution be said to have had?

To those who maintained that traditional customs and institutions were national characteristics the "Westernizers" answered: Such traditional Chinese customs and institutions like footbinding and pig-tails, monarchy and the examination-system have already been abolished. Customs and institutions are the result of specific social and political thinking prevalent in the society. Consequently the bulwork of Chinese national characteristics is to be found in the thinking of its foremost philosophers Confucius and Mencius and not merely in the customs and institutions resulting there from. (Feng Enrong, p.99) As the anti-Confucian arguments of the debate were similar to those propagated in the May Fourth Movement they will not be repeated here. Feng Enrong, for example, follows Lu Xun in describing Confucian morals as the morals of men-eaters (**chiren de daode** (I)) (Feng Enrong, p.12) and Chen Xujing demands that the Chinese change from a "**Lunyu**-brain" (II) to a "Plato-brain" (Chen Xujing 2, p.8).

The supporters of total westernization did not only have to defend themselves against conservatives. Leftist scholars who took economy as the basis for a society did not agree with their demands either. "It is impossible to put the culture of developed capitalism on top of Chinese feudalism", writes Zhang Qing, one of the "leftists". According to Zhang Qing the basic difference in the development of Chinese and Western culture was that "a spinning-wheel cannot produce electricity." (Lü Xuehai, p.29) The reply was: Both the spinning-wheel and electricity are inventions of men - why did the Chinese not invent electricity? Are people who live in a "spinning-wheel culture" content with their conditions or do they merely lack the opportunity for further development? In the view of Chen and Feng the philosophical foundation of Chinese society hindered progress and technical advancement. Even when the news of science and inventions

(I) 吃人的道德   (II) 論語

came to China at the end of the Ming-dynasty it had little effect, and it was then that China missed her chance to modernize. (Lü Xuehai, p.100) The supporters of total westernization refuse to accept economics as the determining force of society. For them economics is only one part of culture.

The final question in the debate was the conservatives' and compromisers' demand to "build a culture on a Chinese basis" – a slogan which was put forward in a manifesto by ten professors in 1935. (3) The professors argued that a total neglect of traditional Chinese culture would be the end of the Chinese people. This assumption was fiercely rejected by the "westernizers" and by Hu Shi. From their definition of culture as the means and the result of a people's struggle through life they drew the conclusion that culture can change but it can not cease to exist. They stressed that culture should be developed, not preserved, and added that westernization does not just mean to copy but also to build something new (Feng Enrong, p.12). Both the supporters of total westernization and Hu Shi accused the ten professors' manifesto of propagating the old "ti-yong"-argument in a new form which can hardly disguise its origins (Hu Shi 1, pp. 3-4). Hu Shi from his more moderate point of view goes on to say: "The 'Chinese basis' is nothing else but our people." (Hu Shi 1, p.6.) In spite of all and any changes, Chinese will still be Chinese and therefore according to Hu, there is no need to fear that China's new culture will not be Chinese.

Since the debate was led from a "cultural intellectualistic approach" (Lin Yusheng, p.26) the participants were not required to offer practical methods as to how to adopt a complete culture. Their basic belief was that the Chinese "habitude of mind" was to change, therefore a modern education was one of their few practical demands. As a main obstacle to progress the supporters of total westernization saw the ambiguity of their countrymen who believed they could select the best parts of each culture without inquiring into background or consequences. Chen and his colleagues demanded a complete westernization to put an end to these half-hearted attempts at modernization. That was why they had to demand a "total and thorough westernization" knowing maybe if they demanded all, they might eventually get some 70%. Nevertheless the ideas of a total westernization did not gain many followers and its supporters as Chen Xujing claims,were "victims of their time" (Feng Enrong, p.115) for, in addition to the critique from both conservatives and compromisers, they had neither a Western surrounding which would have helped them, nor the support of Western people. In their outspoken rejection of any "ti-yong"-solutions they might still be victims of their time nowadays. ●

NOTES:

1. By "Western culture" the authors mean European culture or a culture which stands in the European tradition.
2. Hu Shi, 2, p.558, admits that he advocated the expression of total westernization.
3. Chen Xujing's answer to the manifesto is included in Feng Enrong, pp.95-103.

QUOTED LITERATURE/CHINESE:

● Chen Xujing 陳序經 (1): Jiaoyu de zhongguohua he xiandaihua 教育的中國化和現代化 (:The Sinification and Modernization of Education), DULI PINGLUN 獨立評論 (:Independent Critique), No.43, 1933, pp.6-12

● ...(2): Zai tan quanpan xihua 再談全盤西化 (:Another Discussion of Total Westernization), DULI PINGLUN, No.147, 1935, pp.4-9

● Feng Enrong 馮恩榮 : Quanpan xihua yanlun xuji 全盤西化言論續集 (:Continuation of Collected Essays on Total Westernization), Canton 1935

● Hu Shi 胡適 (1): Shi ping suowei Zhongguo benwei de wenhua jianshe 試評所謂中國本為的文化建設 (:Attempt of a Critique of the Construction of a So-called Culture on a Chinese Basis), DULI PINGLUN,No.145, 1935, pp.4-7

● ...(2): Hu Shi lunxue jinzhu 胡適論學近著 (:The Recent Academic Writings of Hu Shi), Shanghai 1935

● Lü Xuehai 呂學海 : Quanpan xihua yanlunji 全盤西化言論集 (:Collection of Essays on Total Westernization), Canton 1934

● Mo Faying 麥發穎 : Quanpan xihua yanlun sanji 全盤西化言論三集 (:Third Collection of Essays on Total Westernization), Canton 1936

● Wu Jingchao 吳景超 : Da Chen Xujing xiansheng de quanpan xihua lun 答陳序經先生的全盤西化論 (:Reply to Chen Xujing's Theory of Total Westernization), DULI PINGLUN, No.147, 1935, pp.2-4

QUOTED LITERATURE/OTHERS:

● J. H. Cole: "Total Westernization" in Kuomintang China: The Case of Ch'en Hsü-ching, MONUMENTA SERICA, No.34, 1979/80, pp.77-143

● Lin Yü-sheng: The Crisis of Chinese Consciousness - Radical Antitraditionalism in the May Fourth Era, Madison 1979

AUTHORS

CHIEN CHIAO

Chairman of the Department of Anthropology of the Chinese University of Hong Kong, studied at the Indiana and Cornell University. His writings include: "Continuation of Tradition in Navajo Society" and many articles about some aspects in the transmission of Confucian tradition. His main interests are social structure, political anthropology and expressive culture.

ADDRESS: The Chinese University of Hong Kong, Department of Anthropology, Shatin, New Territories, Hong Kong

•

KRZYSZTOF GAWLIKOWSKI
*1940

Assistant professor; studied psychology and sinology in Warsaw and Beijing; took his doctorate in political sciences (1971); habilitation in history (1977); head of the Section of History of Asia and North Africa in the Institute of History, Polish Academy of Sciences in Warsaw (1976-81). His writings include: "A New Battle against Confucius" (1976), "China's Encounter with Europe, The Military Reforms of the 19th Century" (1979), both in Polish, and a number of studies on Chinese military and political thought and national identity. Among his manuscripts awaiting publication is one on Chinese mythology. Presently he is Visiting Professor in Naples.

Present ADDRESS: Istituto Universitario Orientale, Seminario di Studi Asiatici, Piazza San Giovanni Maggiore, I-80134 Napoli, Italy

•

GU JIEGANG
1893-1980

Received both traditional tutoring and modern schooling, finished his studies at the National Peking University in 1920; Professor of Chinese history at Yenching University in the 30ies; since 1953 head of the Department of History of the Academia Sinica; best known for his famous "Gushibian" (:Critical Discussions of Ancient History), published in seven volumes between 1926 and 1941, in which he reorganized China's national heritage, freeing it from historical forgeries and myths. His biography was the subject of several studies by western scholars.

•

PETRA KOLONKO
*1955

Studied sinology, history and political sciences in Munich and Beijing. Main interests: Chinese-European relations in the 18th century, German intellectual impact on China during the early 20th century, history of German sinology.

Present ADDRESS: Blütenstr. 14, D-8000 München 40, Federal Republic of Germany

•

MITARAI MASARU
*1924

Professor of Chinese philosophy; studied at Hiroshima and Kyoto Universities. His publications include: "The Commentaries on Pao-p'u-tzu Wai-p'ien", vols.1-4, 1965-1970, and a number of studies on Chinese mythology.

ADDRESS: Hiroshima University, 1-1-89 Higashi-senda, Hiroshima-shi, Japan

ULRICH NEININGER
*1945

Studied political sciences and sinology in Munich. His major interests: state and religion in East and Central Asia, mythology and Chinese folk literature. Publications: Essays ("Das China der Europäer", "Das Prinzip der großen Zahl im tibetischen Buddhismus"), translations, contributions to reference-works.
ADDRESS: Bauerstr. 18, D-8000 München 40, Federal Republic of Germany

NGUYEN TIEN-HUU
*1939

Studied ethnology and missiology in Paris, Münster and Munich; took his doctorate in vietnamese ethnology (Munich 1969). He taught at universities of Munich, Los Angeles. He did scientific research for the German Research Association. His publications include: "Vietnam. Geschichte und Kultur" (together with A. Echardt), "Dörfliche Kulte im traditionellen Vietnam", "Zauber der vietnamesischen Küche" and numerous other books and studies in German, French and Vietnamese.
ADDRESS: Friedenstr. 29, D-8039 Puchheim, Federal Republic of Germany

SRISURANG POOLTHUPYA
*1936

Assistant professor, History Department, Faculty of Liberal Arts, Thammasat University; studied at the University of Dublin and the University of Wisconsin (Madison). Among her publications: "Collected Essays on Eastern Civilizations" (1979), "The Origins and Behaviours of the Characters in the Ramakien Compared with those in the Ramayana" (1981) and others. Main field of interest: the interrelation of history and literature.
Present ADDRESS: History Department, Faculty of Liberal Arts, Thammasat University, Bangkok 10200, Thailand

URSULA RICHTER
*1942

Studied Chinese in Taiwan and at Munich University; received M.A. in 1981, PhD in 1983 (thesis on Gu Jiegang); lives in Beijing.

ARMIN SIEVERS
*1944

Studied sinology, ethnology, political science in Berlin, Bochum and Munich. Main interests: Central and Northeast Asian history, archaeology, ritual behaviour, mythology.
Present ADDRESS: Viellenstr. 2, D-8081 Kottgeisering, Federal Republic of Germany

East Asian Civilizations
New Attempts at Understanding Traditions
•

1 ETHNIC IDENTITY and NATIONAL CHARACTERISTICS
•

Contents:

STUDIES: Two National Ways of Reasoning: Interpretation of the Cause-Effect Relationship by Chinese and Polish University Students. A Psychological Study (K.Gawlikowski,
Poland) || The Korean State and National Identity in the Ambit of the Chinese Civili-
zation According to the Thought of a Korean Sirhak: Yu Suwon (P. Santangelo, Italy)
|| Settlement and Community among the Mongolian Nomads. Remarks on the Applicability
of Terms (S. Szynkiewicz, Poland) || DISCUSSION: Mythology and History / Religion /
Local and National Identities / Stereotypes of Behaviour || Is Sinology still Confu-
cian-Minded? (W. Eberhard, USA; H. Franke, W-Germany) || Myths and History (M. Mita-
rai, Japan) || The Origins of National Identity in China (C.-A. Seyschab, W-Germany)
|| FIELD REPORTS, SOURCES, INFORMATION: The "Science and Civilisation in China" Pro-
ject (J. Needham, Britain) || The Chinese Community in Burma (Win Shein, Burma) ||
The Scientific Activities of the Vietnamese Institute of History (Van Tao, Vietnam)
1982, 208 p., illustrations

▽

VERLAG KUNST & ALLTAG - W.BAUR

Gartenstr. 1
D-8000 München 40
Federal Republic of Germany

Nguyen Tien-huu: "Bruder Eiche - Schwester Bambus" (:Brother
Oak - Sister Bamboo), Munich 1982

.................: "Tee der Welt - Welt des Tees" (:The Tea of
the World - the World of the Tea), Recipies,
Ethno-Gastronomy, Munich 1984

.................: "Der schwimmende Kuchen" (:The Floating
Cake - Eating and Sex in Vietnam), Munich
1984

.................: "Die innere Chefin" (:The Family General -
The Position of the Woman in Vietnam), Munich
1984

△

PERIPHERIE

A QUARTERLY OF RADICAL THIRD WORLD STUDIES

Important Themes so far:
- Subsistence economy, sexual division of labour and the state (Nos. 2, 3, 5/6)
- Debate on Mozambique (Nos. 3 + 5/6)
- Education: The School as a Colonizing Instrument; Education and Mobility in China (No 4)
- Debate: Beyond *Dependencia* (No 5/6)
- Culture and Imperialism/Imperialism of Culture (No 8)
- Political Culture of Afghanistan (No 9)
- National Liberation, State Power and Socialist Reconstruction (No 10/11)

Forthcoming:
Religion and religious movements
Women
Internationalisation and Crisis
Nation and Nationalism

In every issue: **Reviews, Review of Reviews,** etc.
English Summaries of main articles

Subscriptions for one year:	Individuals	Institutions
Europe	DM 28	DM 50
Elsewhere (Airmail)	US $ 18	US $ 30
	or DM 45	or DM 75

For **Subscriptions** and full details write to: LN Vertrieb, Im Mehringhof, Gneisenaustr. 2, 1000 Berlin 61, West-Berlin
Editorial Adress: c/o Institut für Soziologie, Bispinghof 5 - 6, 4400 Münster, West Germany

Literatur zum Fernen Osten

Verlag Simon&Magiera

Nymphenburger Strasse 166   D — 8000 München 19

BILDBÄNDE

Dirk Renckhoff:
JAPAN — Harmonie und Widersprüche
1983, 100 Seiten, 94 Schwarzweißphotographien,
2/3 DIN-A-3Großformat, Preis: 39,80 DM

Wilhelm Thiemann:
**CHINA — Photographische Aufzeichnungen aus den
Jahren 1929 - 1936**
1982, 100 Seiten/Großformat, 180 Photographien,
Preis: 19,80 DM

Reihe OSTWIND — Erlebnisse/Entdeckungen/Abenteuer

Gertrud Claussen (Hrsg.):
**FREMDE HEIMAT KOREA. Ein deutscher Arzt erlebt
die letzten Tage des alten Korea (1901 - 1905)**
Herbst '83, ca. 120 Seiten, ca. 40 seltene Photographien
aus den Jahren 1901 - 1905, Preis: 19,00 DM

Reihe PFLAUMENBLÜTEN — Frauenthemen

Shu Ting:
ZWISCHEN WÄNDEN. Moderne chinesische Lyrik
(aus dem Chinesischen übertragen von R. Mayer)
Herbst '83, ca. 80 Seiten (mit Photographien von D.
Renckhoff), Preis: 14,60 DM

Zhang Kangkang, Zhang Jie:
**DAS RECHT AUF LIEBE. Drei chinesische Erzählungen
zu einem wiederentdeckten Thema**
(Übersetzung und Einleitung: C. Magiera)
1982, 116 Seiten, Abbildungen, Preis: 14,60 DM

LYRIK

Hartwig Hossenfelder, Thomas Hemstege (Ill.):
AUCH DEIN SCHATTEN IST DIR NICHT TREU
Deutsche SENRYU. Gedichte in japanischer Versform
1981, 128 Seiten, 39 Tuschmalereien, Preis: 15,80 DM

KINDERBÜCHER

Hans-Martin Große-Oetringhaus:
NINI UND PAILAT
Eine spannende Geschichte aus Papua-Neuguinea von
Kindern zwischen Steinzeit und Heute
Herbst '83, ca. 90 Seiten, zweifarbig, ca. 60 Photos,
Preis: ca. 14,80 DM

Gerd Simon:
**BANYA aus Thailand schreibt Briefe an die Kinder in
Deutschland. Ein Buch zum Lesen und Vorlesen**
1980, 34 kartonierte Seiten, farbig unterlegt, zahlreiche
Zeichnungen und Photos, Preis: 9,60 DM

*Reihe POLITISCHE BILDERBÜCHER ZUM FERNEN
OSTEN*

Wolfgang Föste:
**VERKAUFTE TRÄUME — Kinderarbeit und Kinder-
prostitution in Thailand**
1982, 56 Seiten Bildband, Preis: 12,60 DM

Andreas Lentz (Photos), Albrecht Lein (Texte):
Menschen in CHOSON/Nordkorea
Herbst '83, 56 Seiten Bildband, Preis: 12,60 DM

Ulrich Geisler, Ulfert Sauer:
„Land der Morgenstille": Land im Aufbruch (Südkorea)
1982, 56 Seiten Bildband, Preis: 12,60 DM

SACHBÜCHER

Christiansen, Posborg, Wedell-Wedellsborg:
**DIE DEMOKRATISCHE BEWEGUNG IN CHINA —
Revolution im Sozialismus?**
1981, 243 Seiten, Bilddokumente, Preis: 19,40 DM

Summers, Detobel, Kößler:
**KAMPUCHEA — Ende des linken Traums oder Beginn
einer neuen Sozialismus-Debatte?**
1981, 120 Seiten, Abbildungen, Preis: 11,80 DM

Franz R. Herres:
**ASEAN — Ein Weg aus der Unterentwicklung? Grenzen
und Möglichkeiten regionaler wirtschaftlicher Zusam-
menarbeit**
1981, 144 Seiten, Abbildungen, Tabellen, Schaubilder,
Preis: 16,80 DM

Löhrke, Multhaup, Pränger:
**DIE STILLE KRAFT DES BAMBUS. Marginalisierung,
Slumbildung in der Dritten Welt und Ansätze zur Selbst-
organisation: Das Beispiel MANILA**
1981, 186 Seiten, 2/3 Din-A-3-Großformat, 500 Illu-
strationen, Preis: 29,20 DM

Hans U. Luther (Vorwort Dieter Senghaas):
**SÜDKOREA   (K)ein Modell für die Dritte Welt?
Wachstumsdiktatur und abhängige Entwicklung**
1981, 232 Seiten, Abbildungen, Preis: 19,40 DM

WISSENSCHAFT

Book Series: EAST ASIAN CIVILIZATIONS — New
Attempts at Understanding Traditions
Wolfram Eberhard, Krzysztof Gawlikowski, Carl-Albrecht
Seyschab (Editors)
No. 1: Ethnic Identity and National Characteristics
1982, 208 p., Price: 23,00 DM
No. 2: Nation and Mythology
Autumn 1983, appr. 176 p., Price: 23,00 DM

Interessenten senden wir gern regelmäßig unseren Katalog zu.

East Asian Civilizations
New Attempts at Understanding Traditions

EAC book series is published twice a year
●
Each single issue contains between 170 and 210 pages
●
Price of single copy:
23.00 DM / 9.50 US$ / 165 ÖSch

Orders for non-subscribed copies may be channelled through
your local bookstore

Subscription rates for **EAC** (4 nos.)

Ordinary Subscription:
84.00 DM / 36.00 US$ / 600 ÖSch
●
Subscription for Libraries and Institutions:
116.00 DM / 48.00 US$ / 830 ÖSch
●
Sponsorship Subscription:
165.00 DM / 70.00 US$ / 1180 ÖSch
●
Partnership Subscription
(for Partners in Countries with
Currency Convertibility Problems):
70.00 DM / 30.00 US$ / 500 ÖSch

Please forward your subscription order
●either to editors' address
●or to publishers' address

●or directly to publishers' distribution companies:

●CON●	●ÖIE/drilit●	●AVA -buch 2000-●
Westerdeich 38	Tuchlauben 8/6/16	Alte Dorfstr. 28
D-2800 Bremen	A-1010 Wien	CH-8910 Affoltern
West Germany	Austria	Switzerland